Praise for *Liking the Child You Lo*

"Bernstein guides parents down a more 'mindful' path, helping them to reduce stress and negative emotions by changing their thoughts. He also suggests ways to use 'collaborative logical consequences' instead of empty or damaging threats."
—*Publishers Weekly*

"Bernstein explains appropriate discipline, natural consequences, and 'collaborative logical consequences' within the context of the annoying things kids do to tick off their parents . . . realistic and helpful."
—*Library Journal*

"Bernstein helps you identify toxic thought patterns with lots of fun charts, and he doles out concrete help."
—*Boston Globe*

"Helps you find solutions for your toxic, negative thoughts about your difficult child and develop a healthier emotional connection with him or her."
—*Newsday*

"Bernstein offers strategies for taming the most common toxic thought patterns that stop [parents] from parenting effectively."
—*Adolescence*

"Bernstein recognizes the harsh realities of child rearing, but focuses on getting parents to recognize their own toxic thinking in dealing with the problems."
—*Chesapeake Family*

"*Liking the Child You Love* can help you recognize the symptoms and help you cope with and stomp out those negative thoughts, which could inadvertently harm our children."
—*San Francisco Book Review*

Praise for the first edition of
10 Days to a Less Defiant Child

"Dr. Bernstein has written a truly impressive book about dealing with angry, defiant children and adolescents. His astute, empathic insights about these youngsters and his practical, sensible suggestions for lessening their defiance and increasing their cooperation will be of assistance not only to parents but to teachers and mental health professionals as well. This book will serve as an invaluable resource for adults raising or working with defiant children and adolescents."
> —*Robert Brooks, PhD, Faculty, Harvard Medical School and co-author*, Raising Resilient Children

"Here's a unique, straightforward approach for resolving difficult behavior THAT MAKES SENSE! Dr. Bernstein shows the reader how to achieve what all parents and children *really* want—a quality, loving relationship."
> —*James D. Sutton, EdD, psychologist and author of* If My Kid's So Nice, Why's He Driving ME Crazy? *and* 101 Ways to Make Your Classroom Special

"This readable book helps empower parents to raise cooperative and happy children. Dr. Bernstein tells parents what to do, not just what not to do. By using calm firmness and dependable discipline, parents can break the cycle that allows (or reinforces) defiance in children. Dr. Bernstein understands families and helps parents get their children moving in the right direction."
> —*Samuel Knapp, Director of Professional Affairs, Pennsylvania Psychological Association*

"Defiance seems to be on the rise, but now parents have one more great resource to bring peace to their home and to their children's lives. In *10 Days to a Less Defiant Child*, Dr. Bernstein offers practical, straightforward advice that is solidly grounded in psychological theory and practice. Parents will find something useful on every page."
> —*Ari Tuckman, PsyD, MBA, clinical psychologist and author of* More Attention, Less Deficit

"*10 Days to a Less Defiant Child* is a must read for parents and educators alike! In short order, Dr. Bernstein has masterfully created a program that allows parents to improve family and school relationships by giving them the user friendly tools necessary to address long-term child defiance. Familial support, positive reinforcement, and a team approach that includes working with school staff are the cornerstones that make this work rise to the top. Every school psychologist and every educator who deals with defiant children should have a copy of this book in their libraries!"

 —*Ivan J. Katz, EdD, Superintendent of Schools,*
 Eldred Central School District, Eldred, New York

"What a much needed resource for parents experiencing the frustration of raising a defiant child! This book provides insights into why some children and teens reject rules and resist authority, but, more important, provides an easy-to-implement plan to manage these negative behaviors. The information on ADHD and other disorders is particularly valuable. The sooner you get started with Dr. Bernstein's plan, the sooner you will have a more peaceful home."

 —*Marie Paxson, coordinator of a support group for*
 parents of children and teens with ADHD

"Parents need to go no further; this book is THE resource book for parents of defiant and challenging children. *10 Days to a Less Defiant Child* empathizes and actively supports parents like myself—who have looked fruitlessly for help—in making changes in ourselves in order to help our children live more comfortably in the world. This book should be on the shelf of every parent, mental health professional, and educator. A unique approach that should become a classic!"

 —*Judith Roth, MSW, LISW*

"Dr. Bernstein has accomplished the difficult task of writing a practical and readable book that will be a very valuable tool for parents. It is a potpourri of good ideas for intervening with a difficult child in an enthusiastic and positive way. I highly recommend this book!"

 —*Clare B. Jones, PhD, author of* Practical Suggestions for ADHD

About the Author

Jeffrey Bernstein, PhD, is a licensed psychologist specializing in child and family therapy in the Philadelphia area. He has helped over two thousand defiant children and their families restore their relationships. A well-known relationship expert and the author of *Liking the Child You Love, 10 Days to a Less Distracted Child*, and *Why Can't You Read My Mind?*, Bernstein lives outside Philadelphia, Pennsylvania.

SECOND EDITION
Completely Revised and Updated

10 days
to a
less defiant
child

*The Breakthrough Program
for Overcoming Your Child's Difficult Behavior*

JEFFREY BERNSTEIN, PhD

Da Capo

LIFE
LONG

A Member of the Perseus Books Group

Designed by Trish Wilkinson
Set in 11 point Goudy Oldstyle STD

Cataloging-in-Publication data for this book is available from the Library of Congress.
Second Da Capo Press edition 2015
ISBN: 978-0-7382-1823-6 (paperback)
ISBN: 978-0-7382-1824-3 (ebook)

Published by Da Capo Press
A Member of the Perseus Books Group
www.dacapopress.com

Da Capo Press books are available at special discounts for bulk purchases in the United States by corporations, institutions, and other organizations. For more information, please contact the Special Markets Department at the Perseus Books Group, 2300 Chestnut Street, Suite 200, Philadelphia, PA 19103, or call (800) 810-4145, ext. 5000, or e-mail special.markets@perseusbooks.com.

10 9 8 7 6 5 4 3

To my parents, Evelyn and Lou—I am so grateful for all you've done and do for me.

To my three adult children, Alissa, Sam, and Gabrielle—You are the source of my determination to put my best foot forward. I continue to grow with you as you continue to learn with me. You are my inspiration.

To Marina—For broadening my world and inspiring me to keep learning and growing in ways I never knew were possible.

Contents

Introduction

This Is Not What I Expected Parenting to Be Like

You knew that parenting wouldn't be easy, but never in your wildest dreams did you think it would be this hard! You are probably reading this book because you feel exhausted and at your wit's end. Your child is defiant and he is driving you up a wall. He is colossally resistant to following even the simplest requests. He is moody, seriously stubborn, overly dramatic, rude, and disrespectful—not every once in a while, but quite often. He doesn't just question your authority, he actually thinks he has just as much authority as you do. Let's be clear: all parents deal with children who challenge them by occasionally being difficult. Defiant children, however, take the challenges to a whole new level. You've probably spent a lot of time trying to figure what makes your child tick. Where does this intense anger come from? What caused her short fuse and vindictive attitude and behaviors? You've probably had to watch these defiant behaviors interfere with your child's learning, school adjustment, outside interests, and relationships with others. At times you may even marvel at the extent to which your child is in denial about the situation. Does he really believe that you, his teachers, and even his friends are so unfair? I'll bet you've tried countless strategies, but still the situation isn't getting better. You're burned out and you're desperate for a solution and a normal family life.

If this sounds familiar, you've come to the right place. Over the past twenty-five years, I have been privileged to work with more than two thousand families struggling with defiant children. In that time, I have gained many important and valuable insights about how to help

defiant children and the distressed parents and families who walk on
eggshells around them. On a personal level, I have also learned a
great deal about parenting as the father of three adult children.

I applaud you for taking the initiative to read *10 Days to a Less Defiant Child*. You will find that this book is loaded with powerful strategies and techniques that will help you significantly reduce your child's
level of defiance. You will learn why defiant kids act the way they do
and why defiance is so destructive to the family, and you will discover
step by step how to reduce the defiant behavior and improve your
relationship with your child. I will give you tips and exercises to help
you evaluate your own behaviors and respond to your defiant child
in a more constructive manner. Many of my counseling clients have
accomplished these goals, and I know you can, too. Please note: my
ten-day program was originally designed for children from ages four
to eighteen. Since this book was first published, I have received feedback from readers, parents of toddlers as well as parents of adult children who also derive benefit from this ten-day program. Furthermore,
many parents of children who are "simply stubborn" without actually
being fully defiant also reported this book as being valuable for their
more general parenting concerns. For the purposes of this text, I use
the term "child" to represent this entire age group. Many examples
from my psychology private practice appear in this book. All names
and identifying information were changed to protect confidentiality.

Defiant Children Are Angry, Difficult, and Complex

Defiant children struggle in different areas of their lives in different ways, but they all share some common characteristics—they are
quick-tempered, overly dramatic, and almost constantly resistant to
doing what they are asked. The biggest problem I see with defiant
children is their unwillingness to accept the authority of adults. They
have distorted views of what is fair, and when their parents react in
a way that leaves them feeling invalidated, they become emotionally
flooded and defiant.

These children may also behave in ways that their peers think is
"weird" or "wrong." The bottom line is that relationships are challenging for defiant children. Parents often hear angry outbursts like,
"You're not fair to me," or "Why am I always the one you punish?"

While defiance tends to rear its ugly head at home more than any-where else, teachers may hear, "This class is stupid and boring," or "Your tests are unfair." Friends of defiant children may be told "You're stupid" or asked "How come you never include me?"

A crucial part of my program is learning to understand and react to your defiant child in a whole new way. I realize you have probably tried everything you can think of to improve your child's difficult and problematic behaviors. This has likely included ignoring him; issuing time-outs, reward charts, and stickers (that probably ended up in the trash); or being either too hard or too soft in the way you discipline. None of these strategies work, because defiant children lack the emotional maturity to manage their frustration and learn from their mistakes. You need to use a different approach. Once you truly understand your child and learn not to take the things she says so personally, things will get much easier.

Defiant kids are not defiant all the time, and this can be confusing for parents. Children who struggle with defiance can be very sweet and cooperative—until they explode. In many cases, the defiant child becomes difficult at what seems like the drop of a hat. But the linger-ing emotional strain parents feel from defiant children is exhausting and overwhelming. Most maddening for some parents is that often defiant children can appear very even-keeled at school, with peers, and even on sports fields. Teachers, other parents, and coaches may gush praises about how wonderful these children appear to them.

A Note of Caution

If your child has a pattern of physical aggression toward people or an-imals, destroys property, or has had problems breaking the law, then I advise you to seek out a trained mental health professional. These symptoms are more indicative of conduct disorder as opposed to a typical pattern of the more manageable defiant behavior. Kids with conduct disorder can be physically forceful and cruel, and in more extreme cases may even use weapons. They may destroy property by starting fires and flagrantly violate rules by doing things like running away and staying away overnight. The strategies in my program can be beneficial in such cases, but a child with problem behaviors such as these merits more attention than I can provide for you in this book.

Should your child also show signs of other psychological problems (such as depression or anxiety) that are more serious in nature, I also advise you to seek out a mental health professional for his treatment. In some cases where more serious emotional distress is involved, medication may be deemed appropriate in combination with counseling. In most cases, however, the strategies in this book can complement any other interventions or approaches used to accomplish success with your child.

You Are Not Alone

As a parent of or caregiver for a defiant child, you *have chosen* this book for a reason—most likely because you want to restore balance and sanity to your life. Maybe you have found yourself thinking things like the following: Isn't parenthood supposed to be about tender moments and great memories? Shouldn't all the meals I have cooked, the laundry I have folded, the clothes, toys, and activities I have paid for, the chauffeuring around town of my child and others, count for something? Why do other families seem to have it so much easier?

I understand how deeply hurt, frustrated, and confused you feel. You've been through a lot trying to figure all of this out, and you have a right to these thoughts. *But know this: you are not alone in your struggle to manage a defiant child. There are countless parents out there going through the same thing that you are, even if they appear to have a "perfect" family.*

Ten Life-Changing Days Lie Before You

This ten-day program is the beginning of good things to come for you and your child. I want to stress, though, that you must continue using the strategies and principles outlined in these chapters when the ten days are over in order to lessen or end your child's defiance for good. It will certainly take more than one day for you and your child to get used to each new step and set of rules, so you must be patient and keep moving forward. My program is broken down into ten steps, with each day presented in a chapter format. At each step you will learn powerful defiance-lowering strategies that build on one another.

I will show you how to lessen your child's defiance and channel it into healthier directions. If you follow it, my ten-day plan will work for you. Just don't give up at the first signs of resistance. You will have resistance and even some setbacks, so you need to make an effort to stay positive and focused on the big picture. Keep using the strategies in this book as part of an ongoing effort and you will get the results you're looking for.

Step Out of Your Comfort Zone

I know that what I'm asking you to do in this book may not be easy for you. Each day of my plan I call upon you to respond to your child in ways you may not be used to doing. I am asking you to give up your old thinking process and any patterns of overreacting. Even though you may feel that many of my suggestions require you to give up power and control, I can assure you that this is not the case. You will see by the time you complete this program that you have gained more control than you may have ever thought possible.

How to Get the Most from This Book

Whether or not you actually read this book in ten days, I recommend that you go through each of the ten days consecutively. It's best to read each day in the morning and then use the strategies through-out the day. You won't be able to use each and every strategy right away because I have provided a lot of them. Just keep adding new strategies on an ongoing basis after you've mastered the one(s) you're currently working on. If you choose to read this book in ten days, keep in mind that you can reread it as often as you like to further strengthen the skills you learn and try out new ones. Or, if you wish to spend a longer period of time reviewing each day and applying as many of the suggested strategies as possible before moving on to the next day, that is fine, too. Your main goal is to complete the whole program, readily apply it, and review it as needed.

Please give yourself and your child time to get used to your new approach. Sticking to the changes you make is critical. Most parents I have worked with see appreciable decreases in their child's defiant behavior within ten days. Parents often also report to me that their child is significantly less defiant after even four days! Still, I encourage you to complete this full ten-day program. You will gain the most penetrating and lasting success by learning and practicing as many skills as possible. Above all, you must remember that this is a work in progress. You've got to keep using these strategies over the long haul. These ten days are just the beginning for you. Think of it this way: the more you use my strategies the less defiant your child will be.

I recommend that you keep a log of the positive changes you see in yourself and in your child. The log does not have to be formal or elaborate. Any format that records your positive breakthroughs and successes with your child will be helpful. I wish you the best of luck on this important journey.

Introduction to the Second Edition

I wrote *10 Days to a Less Defiant Child* to help parents like you break free from those destructive, fruitless power struggles that come from having challenging and oppositional children. I am very grateful for the continued success of this book. The ongoing popularity of this ten-day program compelled me to update it to meet the needs of an emerging new generation of readers. Over the ten years since the first edition was published, children, teens, and parents are facing even more complex challenges in an even faster-paced world that is increasingly driven by the influences of the Web, new screen technologies, video games, and social media. I have combed through all of the chapters from the first edition and revised them accordingly to enhance this ten-day program to meet the needs presented by changing times for parents, caregivers, children, and teens.

This book comes amid the emotional pain and triumphs from the front lines of my counseling practice. I have developed my program based on over twenty-five years' experience as a child and family psychologist working with difficult children ranging from simply stubborn to drastically defiant! I am proud and appreciative to share that since the time the first edition was published nearly ten years ago, readers from around the world have relayed to me their success stories from using this ten-day program. They have provided some excellent feedback and have strongly affirmed that this program works! They say it gives them a quick, compassionate, and highly effective way to reduce and even eliminate power struggles and improve their relationships with their defiant children. Parents and caregivers who have read this book have discovered how to change their own behavior and have witnessed how this remarkably transforms their children to be less defiant and better behaved.

Before I share more about the changes in this edition, I want to divulge something very personal: My writing of this book was inspired not only by the children and families I have counseled but also from my own parenting struggles.

Prior to writing the first edition of *10 Days to a Less Defiant Child*, I overreacted and yelled way too often at my own kids. Ironically, even though so many children and families in my psychology practice were getting better, I was stuck in my own yelling trap—until I changed my mind-set and ways of reacting to my children. The turning point for me came when my oldest daughter, Alissa, nine years old at the time, said, "Dad, you have anger issues and you can't even manage your own kids."

I realized that Alissa was right. I learned a humbling lesson about how managing my emotions and reactions was crucial to my being able to manage those of my children. I officially changed from being overly reactive to becoming a calm, firm, and noncontrolling parent! While this did not set me on the path to being a perfect parent, I became a "yeller in recovery." This program will help you, too, become a better parent. You, too, will learn that making changes in how you manage your defiant child will help him manage his own behaviors as well.

The calm, firm, and noncontrolling approach—the heart and soul of this ten-day program—remains a major theme in this book. I have woven a coaching element into the presentation of this calm, firm, and noncontrolling approach in this second edition. Since the first edition was published, I have found that when I guide parents to consider themselves as "emotion coaches" with their defiant children, this helps them to be even calmer and to not take things so personally, as parents often do. Helpful exercises and strategies from mindfulness approaches, cognitive behavioral therapy, and dialectical behavioral therapy are newly presented with examples from real life.

The case examples from my practice provide easy-to-follow demonstrations of the latest, effective methods on how to coach yourself and your child out of perpetual conflicts using the calm, firm, and noncontrolling approach. I have added several new examples of parents and children/teens in this program to address the media and screen device-related pressures and concerns that today's parents are increasingly facing. Teens, in particular, are highly drawn to social media, which may become a forum for bullying. The pressures preteens and teens feel to be "liked," that is, popular on social media, can weigh down their self-esteem.

I have also included the latest, updated criteria for oppositional defiant disorder in the recently released diagnostic manual of the American Psychiatric Association, *DSM-5*. This second edition of *10 Days to a Less Defiant Child* will include these new descriptive criteria, where relevant, with examples throughout the book. Also presented are the new revisions to the diagnostic criteria of attention-deficit/hyperactivity disorder (ADHD). My goal, when citing diagnostic criteria and considerations about mental health conditions throughout this book, continues to be to keep this book light on psychological jargon and reader-friendly.

In this second edition each day now ends with action steps to empower readers and prepare them to advance to the next day. These action steps are designed to help readers digest and integrate the information and skills they learn as they move through the ten-day program. While all of the chapters have been updated, the ones with the most significant revisions are described below.

Day 3, Sidestepping the Yelling Trap, was retitled Coaching Yourself Around the Yelling Trap. It now addresses the impact of yelling on self-esteem in children. New strategies are included to help parents manage their impulses to yell and instead use alternative strategies. Text-message communication and "yelling" through this electronic medium are discussed. Consistent with the new title for this chapter, the concept of being your child's emotion coach is described. I have also introduced the emerging, increasingly important concept of self-compassion and will present how parents can use this as a valuable tool in managing defiant children.

Day 4, Avoiding Power Struggles, was retitled Rising Above Power Struggles to include and address those times when parents may face some unavoidable and not so easily resolved conflicts with their children. This chapter continues to describe the key component of this program: the calm, firm, and noncontrolling approach. This revised chapter, the most extensively expanded, goes further to help parents manage their children's media and screen time use. Discussion of the constantly evolving new challenges and pressures of technology and their effect on children is included.

The chapter also covers how screen devices may be restricted by parents or removed, but because children and teens use electronic media for school and in daily life, doing so can be very hard to maintain over the long term. My observations from counseling parents and children, as well as feedback from readers, provide new, effective strategies to help reduce these conflicts. I also discuss how parents can further support their children to feel emotionally safe with them. This stability is crucial for parents to explore with their children how they can manage screen-technology pressures and temptations such as online instant messaging, social media, and video games.

Day 6, Dependable Discipline, was retitled Discipline Without Desperation and largely modified to reflect and emphasize the importance of parents managing their own thoughts and feelings when trying to teach and inspire their children to be less defiant and to make better behavioral choices. I continue to find that parents struggle by confusing the concepts of punishment (presenting a negative consequence) and discipline (teaching children how to make better choices). In the heat of quarrels, it is hard for parents to give up delivering ineffective consequences even when they don't work. This chapter explains how parents of defiant children will find that rigid or harsh consequences usually make their children's behavior worse. Presented here are new ways for parents to manage their children's defiant behavior through effective discipline and also new ways to manage their own strong emotions that can get in the way. The calm, firm, and noncontrolling approach continues to be a key element in helping parents have an influential voice that penetrates the ears of children—even when they are absorbed and floating in cyberspace.

I have also expanded Day 10, Reducing Defiance for the Long Run, to include a new combined visualization and writing exercise, which provides a way to continue positive progress from the program over the long term.

Last, I have expanded the appendices as follows:

Appendix 1 provides guidance to parents for children who have mental health issues that are beyond the scope of this program. It is titled Determining If Your Child Needs Professional Help.

Appendix 2 follows up discussion from Day 4 and provides additional strategies for parents and children managing screen time usage. It is titled Further Considerations with Age-Specific Guidelines for Managing Your Child in Cyberspace.

The original appendix from the first edition is now Appendix 3, which is a guide for teachers on how to handle defiant students.

Whether you read the first edition or are new to my program through this revised book, I encourage you to go forward with a learner's heart. If you follow this program in earnest, you will be far more in control as a parent, have a better relationship with your child, and your child will be much less defiant.

DAY 1

Grasping Why Your Child Acts Defiantly

In order to help your child become less defiant, you must first understand why he is acting this way. So today you will learn about the motivations behind your child's defiant behavior. You'll also discover how your parenting behaviors can affect your child's defiance—for better or worse. Parenting is not an innate set of skills that you are born with. It's a learned set of skills—and it takes even more specialized skills to guide your defiant child to a better place.

Even more important than having strong, effective parenting skills, however, is having the right parenting mind-set. All the skills in the world will not help you if are locked into thinking that you have to "win the war" with your defiant child or teen. A healthy, balanced mind-set helps you parent smarter instead of harder. I have seen many smart parents work way too hard by fruitlessly battling with their defiant children.

You've likely been getting yourself worked up, feeling emotionally desperate and drained, and giving out ill-fated consequences that may at first seem effective but then stop working or just don't seem to work at all. As you will see, the calm, firm, and noncontrolling approach described in this book fosters the empathy and compassion crucial for successfully managing defiant children. This will help your child—and you—bypass the emotional reactivity that fuels defiant

1

behavior. Staying calm, firm, and noncontrolling in your approach is crucial to making effective all the skills you will learn.

This Is Not a Stage

There are struggles that come with any stage of childhood, adolescence, and even adulthood. But passively waiting for your child to outgrow his defiant behavior will just make the problem worse and not solve it. It's our job as parents to help our children learn appropriate behavior, not to enable poor behavior by making excuses for it. We do this by instilling solid values through role modeling, patient teaching, and leading by example. When necessary, we provide appropriate consequences to actions that, in time, will instill in the child the knowledge that he is accountable. With defiant children who tend to be more reactive and defensive, you will learn on Day 6 how to provide effective consequences to help them become more accountable. He'll understand that there is a consequence to bad behavior, whether it is cleaning up a mess he made, going on a time-out (when age appropriate), or going to bed earlier. As you will further see in Day 6, the use of consequences with defiant children requires careful consideration.

The Roots of Defiance

At school and with friends, Josh behaves like a perfectly normal ten-year-old boy. At home, however, it's a very different story. Josh pushes every limit possible. Requesting him to stop or even take a break from playing video games is like talking to a wall. He often swears at his parents and harasses his siblings. Forget about asking Josh to do things around the house—he refuses to do even the most routine chores without serious resistance toward his parents. Communication between Josh and his parents consists of a series of arguments, leaving them all exhausted, angry, and tense.

Though their marriage was solid for several years, Josh's parents have recently begun to fight with each other about their son, each blaming the other for his abrasive behavior. They are sick of hearing advice from well-meaning friends, who are sure all Josh needs is a firmer hand to "set him straight."

"Serena looks at me like she hates me," said Serena's very distressed, single mother. While she was a solid student up through sixth grade, fourteen-year-old Serena, now in eighth grade, was really giving her mother a hard time. Serena hounded her mother over and over to be taken to see her boyfriend, whom she felt was the only safe person for her to be with and escape from nasty social media comments about her being ugly. She told her mother she would make her life miserable unless her mother complied.

When Serena and her mother came to me, they shared stories of ugly arguments and they exhibited high levels of hostility toward each other. Serena's teachers also noticed a growing defiant edge to her personality. Serena had begun skipping classes and refusing to comply with schoolwork expectations from her teachers.

The stories above are typical examples of why parents bring their children to see me. A blowup occurs at home (usually just one of many such meltdowns), and the parents decide it's time to get help.

No one can say for sure what causes defiant behavior in children. It may be inherited through genes. Defiant behavior patterns may be caused by problems in brain chemistry. How a family reacts to a child's behavior and how a child is disciplined also play a big role in the development of defiant behaviors. The truth is that many children, especially when they are tired, hungry, or upset, tend to disobey, argue, and defy authority. One of my teen clients wittily described herself as getting "hangry." This term, "hangry," which I learned from her, and validated with the Urban Dictionary, refers to "When you are so hungry that your lack of food causes you to become angry, frustrated, or both."

As they grow up, most children mature and learn socially appropriate ways to get what they want. Defiant children, however, adopt and follow inappropriate methods, becoming demanding, oppositional, and difficult. Underlying influences driving oppositional behavior may be feelings of inadequacy due to concerns such as:

- Rejection by one's peers
- Learning problems
- Problems relating to a parent(s)

- Traumas, such as sexual abuse
- Body image concerns
- Sibling conflicts
- The perception that defiance is "cool"
- Being overscheduled
- Internet time and activities competing with demands from schoolwork responsibilities
- Unfavorable self-comparisons through social media interactions that push down self-esteem

Whatever the roots, the destructiveness and disagreeableness of defiant children is purposeful. This is not a phase. This problem will not just go away overnight. Your defiant child is trying to antagonize you. She's not doing it because she's evil, although at times you may wonder if she is. Your child acts this way because she doesn't know how else to handle her difficult thoughts and feelings. This is the key to understanding why your child is being defiant, and it is crucial that you keep it in mind as you're dealing with her.

As you're probably well aware, conventional discipline strategies usually fail when applied to defiant children. Defiant children may refuse to go on a time-out from an early age, and claim not to care about losing privileges. This sets the tone for ever-increasing frustration and conflicts between the child and his parents. When adults resort to spanking, defiant children are often able to manipulate the situation and turn the focus on the parents' behavior. They will say things like "I'll report you for child abuse" to avoid facing responsibility for their own transgressions. As crazy as this may sound, defiant children actually believe they are equal to adults. Many exasperated parents have told me how they tried to shut their defiant child in her bedroom only to have her destroy her own belongings or escape out the window.

Your Child May Have Oppositional Defiant Disorder (ODD)

All kids display defiant behavior from time to time, but it's possible that your child has a condition called oppositional defiant disorder (ODD). Don't be intimidated by the term ODD, which may sound ominous and clinical to parents. ODD symptoms include chronic anger, blaming others for mistakes, being touchy, or easily annoyed and vindictive. To qualify for an ODD diagnosis, your child must do things like talk back, refuse to do chores, use bad language, and say things like "You can't make me" or "You're never fair" nearly every day for at least six months. In other words, kids with ODD have oppositional attitudes and behaviors that are more of a pattern than an exception to the rule. The fifth edition of the American Psychiatric Association's *Diagnostic and Statistical Manual of Mental Disorders (DSM-5)* includes this list of three subgrouped behavior clusters that a child diagnosed with ODD would exhibit:

Angry/Irritable Mood
- Often loses his temper
- Is often touchy or easily annoyed by others
- Is often angry and resentful

Argumentative/Defiant Behavior
- Often argues with authority figures or, for children and adolescents, with adults
- Often actively defies or refuses to comply with requests from authority figures or with rules
- Often deliberately annoys others
- Often blames others for her mistakes or misbehavior

Vindictiveness
- Has been spiteful or vindictive at least twice within the past six months

As you can see, the eight diagnostic symptoms for ODD listed above are grouped into: angry/irritable mood, argumentative/defiant behavior, and vindictiveness, reflecting that this disorder includes both emotional and behavioral symptoms. Children and teens are required to have four or more symptoms for at least six months to meet the diagnostic criteria for ODD. Criteria have also been included to emphasize that the behavior is beyond the norm for the child's developmental age and specifiers for severity have been included. In addition, kids with ODD can also be diagnosed with conduct disorder (a more extreme form of ODD described in the introduction) as a coexisting condition. To meet the official diagnosis of ODD, the symptoms must be present more than once a week to distinguish the ODD diagnosis from symptoms common to developing children and adolescents. The *DSM-5* also reflects research showing that the degree of pervasiveness across settings (e.g., home and school) is an important indicator of severity.

It's important to realize that even if your child displays only one or two behaviors on the list on page 5, or these behaviors are not that frequent, you still need to learn how to keep the situation from getting worse. The expression "An ounce of prevention is better than a pound of cure" could not be more relevant than when parenting defiant children. I have counseled many children who met the ODD diagnostic criteria, and I have also worked with lots of defiant children who fall short of meeting the criteria. A child with any level of defiance can create big problems for himself, his family, and others around him. The strategies in this book will work for all defiant children, whether or not they have ODD. Whatever level of defiance you are dealing with will lessen considerably if you follow my ten-day plan, which is based on what I do with defiant children and their families who come to my office. To keep things clear, from this point on I will use the term "defiant child" to encompass both those kids with ODD and those who are defiant but don't meet the criteria for ODD.

How Defiant Is My Child?

The list below describes eight aspects of defiant behavior. To help get a handle on exactly how defiant your child really is, think about which of the defiant behaviors that I've listed occur in your child, and the degree of impact they have. Using the spaces next to each sentence, rate the impact of your child's behaviors from 1 (most problematic) to 5 (least problematic).

_____ My child often loses his temper.
_____ My child often argues with adults.
_____ My child defies or refuses to follow an adult's requests or rules.
_____ My child deliberately annoys people.

_____ My child blames others for his or her behavior.

_____ My child is touchy and easily annoyed by others.

_____ My child is angry and resentful.

_____ My child is spiteful or vindictive.

Look carefully at how you rated your child's behaviors. It should be clear which defiant behaviors present the biggest problems for you. Now, ask yourself the following questions:

- When did these behaviors start?
- In what setting(s) do they occur?
- Are there negative events in my child's past that could be influencing these behaviors?
- What, if anything, has helped me manage any of these behaviors in the past?
- How have I tended to respond to these behaviors?

Don't worry if you can't answer all these questions yet. Your goal for right now is to start thinking about your child's challenges and how to approach them.

You Are Not Alone

Most parents with defiant children feel extremely isolated, as if they are the only ones in the world dealing with this problem. I can assure you that you are not alone. Sadly, our society is filled with images of "perfect parents" and "perfect families." Unfortunately, many of these "perfect parents" end up in my office in a panic when they realize that their "perfect" child is no longer manageable. As I tell all my clients, no one on this earth is perfect. Looks are deceiving, and you can't compare your family to other families or you will drive yourself nuts.

Most people don't know anything about defiant kids until they have one. The mother of a twelve-year-old boy I worked with shared with me the following:

A few years ago I saw a mother and her son arguing outside a church. The boy made it clear to his mother that he was not going in for the service. I was appalled to see that this boy ended up sitting outside in the lobby and that his parents took turns watching him. I looked at my four-year-old son and felt grateful that he would never be like that boy out in the lobby. Well, I was more surprised than you can imagine when I found myself going through the same thing and many other battles at home once my little angel turned eleven. I never would have guessed my child would become so difficult and defiant!

I have seen defiant children come from both intact homes and broken homes. Some defiant children have been star athletes, musical virtuosos, and even honor students. Of course, many of the defiant children I have seen have struggled with school grades, friends, and family relationships. The point here is that there is no one family mold or background circumstance that fosters defiant children. Defiant children are found in families of all income levels and walks of life. As a society, we have a huge need for the tools and strategies to guide and help them.

How Does Your Defiant Child Affect You?

How much distress is your child's problems causing you and other members of your family? As a parent of a defiant child, you have probably experienced some or all of the feelings listed below. Put a check next to any that you can identify with.

_____ You question why you had children in the first place.

_____ You resent how your defiant child has drained you and the rest of the family.

_____ You feel desperately overwhelmed trying to keep up with all of life's demands.

_____ You feel nothing is going to help your situation.

_____ You feel exhausted.

_____ You feel manipulated.

_____ You feel sad that your marriage or domestic partnership has lost its passion.

_____ You feel guilty.

_____ You feel like a horrible failure as a parent.

This list is not exhaustive. As I discuss in the next chapter, parents wrestle with these views and even extremely negative thoughts (I call them "toxic thoughts") about their defiant children. For now, you need to stop beating yourself up and comparing yourself to other parents. As "golden" as their family life and children may seem, trust me—that is not the case behind closed doors. Every family has problems, and the best thing you can do for yourself and your family is to accept the situation you've found yourself in. I share with my parent and child clients that the expressway to misery comes from overly wanting a life that you don't have or overly not wanting your life as it is at this time. Your child is temperamental, overly reactive, demanding, and draining, and this can be very upsetting. Whether you want to blame his DNA, past life events, your parenting, or the family history, this is how your child is. But by accepting your situation and seeking help as you're doing now, you've put your entire family on the track back to happiness and peaceful coexistence.

Big, positive changes in your child will begin with you making changes in how you view and react to your child. Don't get hung up on any regrets. Accepting your past mistakes and valuing yourself for doing the best you can will lead you to make changes and experience growth as a parent. In the words of Carl Rogers, who was one of the preeminent thinkers in psychology, contributing to education, therapy, and humanistic psychology, "The curious paradox is that when I accept myself just as I am, then I can change."

Coaching Yourself and Your Child to Calm Down and Solve Problems

This ten-day program emphasizes two crucial skills for your defiant child, which are essential for you to learn, model, and coach. These are: calming down and solving problems. Defiant children, more than other children, sorely lack these two skills. The more you learn to calm down and solve problems, the more you can coach and model your child to do the same. The exercises included throughout this program are designed to increase your self-awareness to make the changes in your parenting mind-set and how you engage your defiant child. The more you can begin to see yourself as an emotion coach for your child, the less personally you will be impacted when he is struggling with his own emotions and taking them out on you through bad behaviors.

Making Changes

Now that you have a better understanding of what defiant behavior is and how it applies to your child, you know that you need to make some changes and get control. The first step to gaining control is taking inventory of yourself as a parent.

Like all parents, you have made your fair share of mistakes. The notion that parents are to blame for their child's defiant behavior is often reinforced by the fact that some defiant kids are model citizens away from home. Many defiant kids, though not all, get good grades at school, cooperate with coaches, and are polite to their friends' parents. Some are even able to convince therapists that their problems are caused entirely by their parents. I have certainly heard my fair share of creative, embellished stories from defiant kids during therapy.

Identifying Your Positive Parenting Behaviors

To help you stop blaming yourself and gain a sense of control, let's start with the positives. Read the list below and check off what you have done well as a parent.

_____ Giving smiles
_____ Giving winks
_____ Giving pats
_____ Standing close
_____ Saying "I love you"
_____ Keeping eye contact
_____ Giving hugs
_____ Giving nods
_____ Shaking hands

_____ Attending school
      conferences
_____ Giving praise
_____ Giving compliments
_____ Driving to lessons
_____ Giving rewards
_____ Arranging birthday
      parties
_____ Driving to activities

Give yourself a pat on the back for doing any of the above behaviors. Your child deeply appreciates them, even if he doesn't admit it.

If you feel that you have not exhibited the behaviors on page 10 enough, then there is no better time than now to start. Some may be more consistent with your personality than others. For example, perhaps you are not an overly demonstrative person and you don't feel very comfortable with hugs. In this case, use verbal praise instead.

Practicing these positive parenting behaviors helps set the stage for connecting with and understanding your child, which is one of the key factors in resolving your child's defiant behavior. I discuss this in detail on Day 2.

Identifying Your Negative Parenting Behaviors

Now let's talk about your negative parenting behaviors. Read the list below and check off the negative parenting behaviors you have exhibited.

_____ Yelling	_____ Lying
_____ Sarcasm	_____ Gossiping to other
_____ Teasing	parent(s)
_____ Hitting	_____ Threatening
_____ Ignoring	_____ Putting down
_____ Lecturing	_____ Throwing things
_____ Shaming	_____ Denying feelings
_____ Criticizing	_____ Impatience
_____ Provoking	_____ Unrealistic
_____ Nagging	expectations
_____ Interrupting	_____ Excessive, harsh
_____ Dwelling on the past	consequences
_____ Using guilt	

Don't feel bad if you've checked off a fair number of the behaviors above. We all make our share of mistakes and have done some (or even more than some) of these negative parenting behaviors. While it's never good to do these things, some behaviors are more destructive to your relationship with your child than others.

Yelling and hitting. Nothing fuels defiant behavior like yelling and hitting. When you yell and hit you are showing poor impulse control delivered through a temper tantrum. What kind of life lesson is that to teach? To be sure, most of us have yelled. I have yelled at my kids and even grabbed them in a few past isolated incidents. I am not proud of this, and I encourage you to realize, as I did, that we are bullying our children when we yell at or hit them. While it may feel as if you have succeeded in getting them to stop their offensive behaviors, it's a short-term fix and you've really just succeeded in increasing their defiant and aggressive behavior for the long term. More than hitting, yelling is a very pervasive parenting problem. For this reason, Day 3 is devoted to helping parents understand why they yell and how to stop yelling.

Criticizing. If you find yourself criticizing your child, please stop. Criticism means making negative comments about your child's thoughts, feelings, ideas, or who they are. Children often see such criticisms as put-downs. Put-downs include name calling, ridiculing, judging, and blaming. They really hurt children—it's just that simple. Put-downs are detrimental to effective communication, and they will damage your child's self-esteem. Children who are put down by their parents often feel rejected, unloved, and inadequate.

You should certainly give constructive feedback on your child's behavior, or something he has done, but don't criticize the child himself.

Nagging. Nagging means repeating something that you have already said to your child over and over. I have had many children sit in my office and roll their eyes while their parents talked at them and not with them. The old saying, "In one ear and out the other" is exactly what happens when you nag your defiant child. When you tell your child something once, or at most twice, there is no need to say it again. Nagging can cause children to stop listening or to become more defensive or resentful. Starting today and throughout this ten-day plan, I will give you lots of strategies and examples of how to get your child to hear you without your nagging. My program will help you gain your child's compliance by improving the quality of your relationship and being a more effective parent. As you'll see, your child will be much more likely to follow your requests and do what she's supposed to if she feels close to you.

Interrupting. This is a very common parenting problem. When your child is talking, you should give her the opportunity to finish what she's saying before speaking yourself. This is common courtesy. Children who feel that they can't get a word in edgewise may stop communicating with their parents altogether.

Dwelling on past conflicts. Once a problem or conflict is resolved, you should try not to mention it again. Children should be allowed to start over with a clean slate. Parents who bring up their children's past mistakes are teaching them to hold grudges for long periods of time. Also, children need to know that once a matter is settled it becomes part of the past.

Injecting guilt. It's one thing to ask a child how he would feel if he were in your shoes or someone else's in a given situation. Too often, however, parents push this to the limit and try to make their children feel guilty because of their thoughts, feelings, or actions. Parents who use guilt to control their children run the risk of alienating them. A client of mine named Loretta used to sling loads of guilt at her fourteen-year-old son Harold, who her neighbor found smoking marijuana. For ten straight minutes, Loretta peppered Harold with statements like "How embarrassed do you think I feel now that the neighbors know our problems?" and "Don't you realize how you have ruined my trust in you?" Harold just became agitated and stormed out. I took this time to coach Loretta to put her wounded ego aside and give her son what he really needed—support and understanding. Loretta used the calm, firm, and noncontrolling approach that I teach you in this book to get Harold to open up to her about how he caved in to peer pressure. They reconnected, and Harold soon abandoned his problematic peer group along with his interest in marijuana.

Using biting sarcasm. You are using sarcasm if you say things you don't mean and imply the opposite of what you're saying through your tone of voice. An example would be saying something like, "Oh, aren't you bright," when your child makes a poor choice. The use of sarcasm hurts children. Sarcasm is an obstacle for parents who are trying to communicate effectively with their children.

Lecturing. When parents jump in and give their children a dissertation on how they should do things instead of letting them have some input into solutions for problems, they are lecturing. Overly directing and controlling your defiant child will almost guarantee that he will not listen to you. If anything, he will do the opposite of what you are trying to get him to do. Parents who tell their children how to solve their problems may lead children to believe that they have no control over their own lives. These children may end up believing that their parents don't trust them, or they may resent being told what to do and as a result resist their parents' directions.

Making threats. Threatening any child, especially a defiant one, is rarely effective. In fact, threats often make children feel powerless and resentful of their parents. And with defiant children, threats actually tend to escalate the situation.

Lying. No matter how tempting it is to make up a lie to, say, avoid talking about uncomfortable topics like sex, you shouldn't do it. It's really best to try to be open and honest with your child. This encourages your child to be open and honest with you. Also, children are very perceptive. They are often very good at sensing when their parents are not being totally honest with them. This can lead a child to believe his parents don't trust him.

Excessive, harsh consequences. As I will further discuss in Day 6, Discipline Without Desperation, doling out disproportionate or too frequent consequences usually worsens your defiant child's behavior. While harsh and very punitive measures (e.g., excessive grounding or removal of privileges) may get your child's attention, it is likely that your child will end up feeling resentful, guilty, shamed, belligerent, and even may feel hopeless about ever being able to meet your expectations. Also troubling is that defiant children usually react to these unpleasant, consequence-heavy punishment tactics by escalating their negative behaviors. They often also deny their role in conflicts or the impact of their problematic behaviors. As you will see, guiding your child with appropriate discipline (through taking on a coaching mind-set) is far more effective in managing his defiance than giving him over-the-top consequences to punish him. I will address the difference between punishment and discipline in Day 6.

Denying your child's feelings. When your child tells you how she feels, it's important that you don't make light of these feelings. If, for example, you think your child "shouldn't" feel sad about losing a baseball game, it is best not to say so. In this case, you will do better by saying something supportive, such as, "I know you really wanted to win. It's hard to lose sometimes." With younger children, ages four to six, you can do this by using simple, concrete words (e.g., "Daddy and I can tell you are sad that your rabbit died."). Children need to have their feelings supported by their parents. As a parent, you will give your child a wonderful gift by showing understanding when it comes to her feelings. Being understanding is so important to parenting defiant children that I've devoted the next chapter to this issue.

All of the negative parenting behaviors described above can increase defiant behavior in your child. It's easy to say, "I just won't do that anymore" and still fall into the pattern of repeating these behaviors. Occasional slips may occur. When they do, address these negative behaviors with your child. Sal, a single father I worked with, shared with me a recent breakthrough he had made with his thirteen-year-old son Anthony. Sal was a self-proclaimed "hardass in recovery." He had a history of yelling at Anthony around the house and at soccer games. Sal had made very strong progress in relating to his son in a far less critical manner—until one night, when Anthony and Sal were at a soccer awards banquet and Sal criticized him for looking down when he received his award. I coached Sal not to beat himself up, and he was determined to continue to be less controlling and more open, so he approached Anthony and said, "Anthony, I apologize for being so critical of you. Seeing you up there, getting that award, made me feel honored to be your father." Anthony later told me that "Dad really seems to get it now." The more you model being accountable for your negative behaviors, the more you can influence your child to do the same.

Taking Care of Yourself
Will Help You Help Your Child

You have taken inventory of yourself as a parent by doing the exercises earlier in this chapter. You realize that you have done and said some things well and that there are definitely some things you can do better. I know that I have been far from a perfect parent with my own three children. I have "lost it" and screamed more times than I care to admit. But I also know that by changing my parenting attitudes and behaviors, I have been much more effective in parenting them. I am confident that the same positive results can occur for you, too. The best way you can begin to change your parenting attitudes and behaviors for the better is to start taking care of yourself.

Make time for things that will relieve stress—exercise, having lunch with a supportive friend, watching funny movies—and treat your partner as your ally. Go out together and talk about anything but your defiant child. Try not to worry too much—defiance does put your child at risk for more serious difficulties in the future, but it's a problem that can be resolved if you make the important changes in attitude and behaviors that I suggest throughout this book.

You need to maintain interests other than your child, so that managing him doesn't take all your time and energy. Try to work with and obtain support from the other adults in your child's life besides your spouse (teachers, coaches, etc.) while dealing with your child.

Ways to Relax

Parenting a defiant child has conditioned you to live with anxiety. You never know when the next outburst or crisis will occur. At times you may feel as though your child holds you and your family hostage emotionally. When we are worried, anxious, hurried, or harried, our bodies begin to feel tense. Actually, this "fight or flight" response is a natural reaction. Your body has been given the signal to prepare to respond to a threat. If a real physical danger were present, you would be able to protect yourself by attack or retreat. When the emergency was over, an all-clear signal would be given, and your body would relax and return to its normal state. In our modern times, we are constantly dealing with stress. Constant mental stress keeps our bodies in constant tension, which itself becomes a form of stress. You can handle stress by learning to cope with thoughts and events so they no longer are stressful. You can also learn to relax. When you practice relaxation, you are giving the all-clear signal. As you become better at giving the signal, you are able to trigger the relaxation response so that your body can return to its normal state.

Defiant children influence their parents to feel tension a lot of the time. When they don't get what they want, they feel threatened, typically experiencing the same "fight or flight" response mentioned above. Unfortunately, for defiant children, this response seems to appear as "fight or fight even more."

The fight-or-flight response affects each of us, as parents, differently. Depending on the person, it can cause sleep disturbance, fatigue, increased or decreased appetite, headaches, stomachaches, poor concentration, irritability, or overt emotional reactivity such as yelling. Following the well-known mind–body model, some diseases may be caused or made worse by chronic tension. It can also weaken our immune systems, making us more susceptible to colds and other infections. The following are two proven ways you can use to relax yourself and relieve some of that tension:

Deep Breathing

When you are tense, your breathing can become shallow and rapid. In fact, most of us do not breathe properly, tense or not. Improper breathing robs you of oxygen that purifies your body as well as helps your body produce energy. Fortunately, learning to breathe properly is not difficult. Find a comfortable place to lie down. Place your hands on your abdomen just below your ribcage. Begin breathing slowly and deeply. If you are breathing properly, you will feel the expansion in the abdominal area before your ribcage expands. Spend five to ten minutes several times a day practicing your deep breathing. You will notice that as you become more proficient, your breathing will improve during your normal activities. The beauty of this deep-breathing technique is that you can call upon an abbreviated form to use any time you're feeling angry and want to yell. Taking a few deep breaths is a wonderful way to soothe yourself and set the stage to use other helpful strategies in conjunction with your breathing.

And if you find yourself in an argument, you can also use it to calm down. Deep breathing can be used to prevent, lessen, and recover from emotional overloads and outbursts.

Restoration of Pleasant Images of Your Child

By this point, you have begun to think of your child as problematic and difficult. It is important that you counter this image and get back in touch with pleasant images about him.

One of many skills from dialectical behavioral therapy (DBT), an established approach I use for counseling clients with anxiety and stress, is referred to as safe space visualization. This is typically accomplished by visualizing a soothing, neutral image such as a forest or countryside. I suggest you do this and also include soothing visual memories of your child to help you control your emotions when you are feeling stressed.

To prepare yourself for this exercise, relax your muscles and take a few deep breaths. Then close your eyes and recall a joyful memory of your child. It could be a family picnic, vacation, or favorite activity. Try to fully experience this positive memory. See the sights. Hear the sounds. Feel the air. Smell the smells. Tune in to the sense of well-being and admiration you felt for your child in that moment.

Allow ten to fifteen minutes for this exercise.

Gaining Serenity with Gratitude

I wrote earlier that misery comes from overly desiring what you don't have or not valuing what you have. It is normal to feel beat up and depleted as the parent or caregiver of a defiant child. Shifting yourself to an attitude of gratitude guides you to be in a happier state of being. Thinking about your life in this positive manner also redirects your focus from what is troubling you about your child to being able to see his gifts. Gratitude helps you give love to your child when he is acting unlovable. Tuning in to your gratitude helps reduce your anxiety and allows you to take a flexible, healthy perspective.

Take a Gratitude Shower

I have found that when I have my clients imagine the things they are grateful for as a shower of gratitudes coming down upon them, this can be a very centering experience. I encourage you to do this gratitude exercise. Simply close your eyes and picture the "good stuff" in your life streaming down on you. For example, you can reflect on having eyes to read or ears to listen to this book being read to you. Perhaps you are grateful for your family, your friends, your colleagues, or having rewarding interests in your life. As a way to calm down, when you notice your child acting up, center yourself with reflecting on what you are grateful for.

Make the Commitment to Help Your Child

Your child needs your help to overcome her defiance. Parents and family members have the most powerful impact on a child's behavior, attitude, and approach to life. Put simply, children are persuaded and impressed by the people they spend the most time with and the people who matter most. That means you and the other members of your family.

Your defiant child needs to unlearn his entitlement-laden, impulse-driven way of handling his emotions. The best gift you can ever give him is to be persistent in applying the information and strategies that I have to offer. Most efforts fail because parents abandon them prematurely. As you go through this work, note the progress and celebrate it. If there are rough spots—and there always are—remind yourself that there has also been significant progress. Gather strength from the knowledge that you are helping your child get to a much better place.

DAY
(1) **SUMMING IT UP**

Today you have already learned a lot about defiant behavior in children, and you've begun a very important and rewarding ten-day program that will help you lessen defiant behavior in your child. Stay mindful of the following points as you continue this journey:

- This is not just a stage your child is going through.
- Whether your child meets the diagnostic criteria for oppositional defiant disorder (ODD) or not, you must take action to lessen his defiance.
- The powerful strategies found throughout this ten-day program will work for children with any level of defiance.
- There is no one consistent, identifiable cause of defiant behavior.
- Your parenting methods, for better or worse, have a huge influence on your child's defiant behaviors.
- You need to take care of yourself in order to reach your goal of lessening your child's defiance.

GETTING READY FOR DAY 2

- Stop blaming yourself, anyone else, or even your child for her being defiant.
- Stay mindful of your negative thoughts and challenge them with more positive ones.
- View yourself as an emotion coach for your child to learn how to calm down and solve problems.
- Practice the relaxation and visualization exercises discussed.

DAY 2

Understanding Your Defiant Child

Showing your child love is crucial to effective parenting, but so is understanding him—and that is often the critical and missing ingredient in parent–child relationships, especially with defiant children. Tragically, children who are well loved by their parents often do not feel that love if their parents don't understand them. Parenting without a true understanding of our children influences us to see our kids as we *think* they are rather than as they *really* are. I know very few parents who don't love their children, but I know many parents who don't understand them.

Most parents believe that if they love their children this will magically convey that they "are here and will always be here." But parents who never learn how to understand what is really going on in their defiant children's minds will not be able to grasp how to break the cycle of defiance.

Your Child Feels Misunderstood

The harsh reality is that defiant children feel misunderstood. As you will soon see, defiant children are more complex than you may have thought. We parents become so focused on our kids' external behaviors that we tend to overlook their inner angst. Understanding is one of the most powerful tools available for creating breakthroughs

21

in difficult family patterns, especially for stopping defiance in your child. In the previous chapter you learned what defiance is all about. Now I will give you some powerful ways to deeply and accurately understand your defiant child.

IT FEELS GOOD TO BE UNDERSTOOD

Understanding your child is an important part of helping him become secure and healthy, because it shows him you love him. Please read through the questions below and reflect on them. This activity will help you see how important feeling understood has been in your own life, so you can more fully appreciate the value of understanding your child.

- Who most understood your feelings, needs, and desires as you were growing up?
- How did you feel about the person who understood you the most?
- Who least understood your feelings, needs, and desires as you were growing up?
- How did you feel about the person who understood you the least?
- How did feeling understood help you to behave in an appropriate manner?
- Did feeling misunderstood ever influence you to make poor choices or to behave in an inappropriate manner? If you answered yes, what did you do?

As you'll probably see by your responses to the above questions, feeling understood provides us with the emotional leverage to do our best to make good choices and do the right thing on a daily basis. Demonstrating to your defiant child that you understand him, even if you don't agree, gives him a sense of validation. By validating your child when he is emotionally flooded, you will take him out of "fight or fight harder mode," reduce his defiant behaviors, and help him to calm down.

Keeping yourself focused on validating your child helps you avoid taking his emotional reactivity personally. This will keep you in the helpful role of emotion coach versus emotionally wounded parent.

You may feel that you're already good at understanding your child and at showing that understanding, but as you will see in this chapter, there is a lot involved in the process of understanding, especially with defiant children. The bottom line is that the ways in which you show your child understanding may need improvement.

Listening Is Key

In his best-selling book *The Road Less Traveled*, M. Scott Peck discussed the value of listening. He said that if we listen to our children with the devotion and intensity that we listen to a great speaker, we are giving them a valuable gift. Listening and valuing your child's ideas is what supports your ability to communicate effectively with her.

The hard truth is that most parents do not listen well because they are too preoccupied or too busy—with work, community, religious activities, and home responsibilities. Listening to your child is not the same as giving her advice or telling her how to correct a situation. Certainly there are times when your child will value your advice, but she must be ready to listen to it. And before your child will be ready to listen to you, you'll need to learn how to listen to her.

Listening alone does not ensure understanding. The key is to make understanding your goal for listening. When you listen with the goal of understanding, it changes everything for the better. To fully understand your child you need to put aside any agenda you may have and focus on his agenda. The only way that you can really listen is to do so unselfishly and with the delay and containment of your own judgment.

How to Really Listen

Listening is such an important part of effective communication, but it's a skill that must be learned and practiced. When you listen to your child, you are showing him you are interested and care about what he has to say. Here are some tips for becoming a good listener:

Make eye contact. When it comes to listening, your eyes count almost as much as your ears. Your eyes are a very powerful cue to your child that shows you are interested. If you make little eye contact, your child gets the opposite message—that you are not interested in what she's saying.

Eliminate distractions. When your child expresses a desire to talk or seems open to talking, support him by giving him your full attention. Put aside what you were doing, face your child, and give him your undivided attention. If, for example, you incessantly check your mobile device for e-mails or text messages or continue to listen to your voice mail, wash the dishes, read the paper, or watch TV while your child is trying to communicate with you, he may get the message that you aren't interested in what he has to say. Or he may internalize the belief that what he has to say is not important. If your child expresses a desire to talk at a time that you are not able to, plan a time with your child to talk later on.

Listen with a closed mouth. As tempting as it may be to jump in with your unsolicited parental wisdom, it is best to try to keep the interruptions to a minimum while your child is speaking. You can offer encouragement through a smile or a pat, but don't interrupt her. Your interruptions can break your child's train of thought, and this can be very frustrating for her.

Let your child know she has been heard. After your child has finished speaking, show that you listened by restating what she said, in slightly different words. For example, if your child is complaining about her math class you could say something like, "It sounds like you had a really frustrating day at school." Not only does this show that you've been listening, it provides your child with an opportunity to clarify if you have misinterpreted her message.

It is critical that you don't criticize. I am convinced that a big reason so many children respond with "fine" or "good" when asked about their day at school is because they are afraid of being criticized. Consider the following conversation between a father and his twelve-year-old daughter:

> **Dad:** "Hey, Sarah, how was school?"
>
> **Sarah:** "It was okay."
>
> **Dad:** "Just okay?"
>
> **Sarah:** "Well, I didn't do so well on my math test. I really am mad at . . ."
>
> **Dad (interrupting):** "Hold on Sarah, I thought you were going to prepare for this one. Did you go and get extra help like I suggested? Come to think of it Sarah, I really don't think I saw you putting much time into studying for this test. See, I was right! I never should have let you and mom talk me into giving you that cell phone yet because you obviously never know when to put it down!"
>
> **Sarah (to herself):** "He makes me so upset. I'm never going to tell him anything again!"

As you can see from this example, Sarah's dad not only interrupted, he was critical of her. While he is most likely coming from a place of concern and love, Sarah feels threatened. Her dad's aggressive style of listening and responding to Sarah prevented him from learning how she felt about her poor test grade. Suffice it to say, Sarah's dad lost an important opportunity to understand what his daughter was thinking and feeling.

HOW GOOD ARE YOUR LISTENING SKILLS?

How often have you really thought about how you listen to your child? If you are like the majority of parents I have worked with, you will find the following exercise very valuable. By reflecting on these questions, you will be able to get a strong sense of what you do effectively and what you do that is not so effective when listening to your child.

- What do you do best to support listening to your child (e.g., give good eye contact, ensure no interruptions, or clarify what you are hearing)?
- What do you do that gets in the way of listening to your child?
- At what time of day or under which circumstances are you in the best position to listen to your child?
- What time of day or circumstances leave you in a compromised position to listen to your child?
- What can you do starting right now to be an even better listener to your child?

Be Patient

You have probably heard the expression "Patience is a virtue." When it comes to being a good listener, this is certainly the case. Despite your best attempts to use basic listening skills like those described above, you may find your defiant child is still very hard to listen to, let alone understand. Truly listening to your defiant child means closing your eyes and ears to the whining, swearing, and slamming of doors. It means opening your eyes and ears to his fears, frustrations, and emotional limitations.

Sadly, most parents of defiant children are so discouraged, hurt, and angry that they tune out their defiant child. You have probably felt the same way and even wanted throw up your hands and shout, "I just don't get this kid and never will!"

Listening with your best intention means giving your best attention. Focus your attention on what your child is thinking and feeling and don't let your hurt ego get in the way. During one of my counseling sessions, nine-year-old Simon told his father, Nick, that he wanted to put a bullet in Nick's head. Nick was understandably shaken to hear his son's fiercely hurtful words. Yet Nick happened to be working on becoming a great listener. So instead of telling himself that his child was impossible, a lost cause, Nick began to ask Simon questions about why he felt that way. Simon reminded Nick of his past overly aggressive behaviors and Nick just listened—unselfishly. While this father and son still had a long way to go, they made a huge, powerful improvement in their relationship that day.

Solid listening promotes solid understanding. I can't stress enough that understanding your defiant child's struggles and staying mindful of them will actually reduce your child's defiance. Yes, you read correctly—your understanding reduces his defiance. This is because the more understood he feels, the less he needs to use his defiance to get your attention. Now let's look at things you may do that get in the way of understanding your defiant child.

The Obstacles to Understanding Your Child

Many of the words and actions that you think show your child you understand him actually influence him to feel mad or misunderstood. Following are some examples of things many parents say that undermine their ability to understand their children:

1. Giving unsolicited advice.
   - "What you should do is . . ."
   - "If you would stop being so afraid then you wouldn't have that trouble."

2. Talking about their own feelings and experiences instead of their child's.
   - "I can't understand why you are carrying on."
   - "It makes me angry when you just don't seem to care."
   - "I wonder when you are ever going to learn!"

3. Making their child's pain seem unimportant.
   - "Other families also have their problems."
   - "Why don't you grow up?"
   - "Stop that. You're being ridiculous!"

There are many obstacles to understanding your child. You may use poor listening skills. You may tune out when you feel frustrated that your child hasn't met your needs. Mistrusting your child's motives by always assuming he is being defiant will also lead to misunderstanding. Many parents forget that kids make mistakes, and they lose sight of how their own shaming and blaming can deeply wound their child.

Following are some crucial points to keep in mind as you work toward understanding your child. Remembering these points when you hit rough spots with your child will help you stay calm and focused:

- Defiant children lack emotional maturity.
- Your defiant child wants your love and approval.
- Not understanding your defiant child fuels the defiant behaviors.
- Defiant children feel very misunderstood.

A Lack of Emotional Intelligence

Research on defiant children shows that they tend to lack something called emotional intelligence. A lack of emotional intelligence is basically a lack of emotional maturity. Daniel Goleman popularized the concept of emotional intelligence, which involves our ability to understand, use, regulate, and manage our emotions as key determinants of success and happiness in our lives.

Emotional intelligence appears to be a key predictor of children's ability to make suitable peer relationships, develop a well-balanced outlook on life, and reach their academic potential at school. The term encompasses the following five characteristics and abilities:

1. Self-awareness—knowing your emotions, recognizing feelings as they occur, and discriminating between them.
2. Mood management—handling feelings so they're relevant to the current situation and so that you react appropriately.
3. Self-motivation—"gathering up" your feelings and directing yourself toward a goal, despite self-doubt, inertia, and impulsiveness.
4. Empathy—recognizing feelings in others and tuning in to their verbal and nonverbal cues.
5. Managing relationships—handling interpersonal interaction, conflict resolution, and negotiations.

Chances are your defiant child has lower-than-normal levels of emotional intelligence, which is a big reason life is so difficult for him. The truth is that many of the things your child "chooses" not to do (e.g., be more self-aware, control his impulses) may actually be things he *can't* do. The more you understand your child's emotional immaturity and limitations, the more you can begin to work around them rather than clash with them.

Your Child Wants Your Love and Approval

Years ago I saw a TV documentary about female adolescent gangs. The initiation into the gang called for prospective gang members to take turns going into the center of a circle of their peers. The girl in the center charged different girls on the perimeter, each time taking a beating from a few who ganged up on her to keep her from breaking out of the ring. At the end of the ritual, each girl in the center was hugged and given praise by her peers. Why were these teen girls putting themselves into the center of a ring and getting pummeled by the girls surrounding them? Because they wanted the love and approval of the gang, which had become their surrogate family.

Believe it or not, the roots of your child's defiant behavior are not so different from this gang initiation. Your child's defiance leaves him feeling misunderstood and like an outsider in your family. The truth is that your child is trying to join a gang—your family. He is desperately trying to gain a sense of belonging and approval from you and the rest of the family. The more you use your listening skills and commit to understanding your child, the more he will feel your love and approval for who he really is underneath the bravado of his defiance.

Your child's defiant behavior may lead you to question how much she values you. In over twenty-five years of working with defiant children, however, I can tell you that very few have denied that they love their parents. This includes children who have slammed doors, stolen from stores, spoken to their parents with vulgar language, refused to go to school, broken windows, and physically assaulted their parents.

Remember that when your child is acting unlovable, she is actually desperate for your love and approval. I know it can feel daunting to see through your child's obnoxious and defiant words and behaviors, but doing so will keep you in touch with her underlying feelings of vulnerability. No matter how angry and rejecting she may act, never give up on letting your child know how much you value and love her. Your child watches your every move. Do your best to let her know how much she means to you, whether she asks for it or not.

Misunderstanding Leads to More Defiance

Defiant behavior works in a cyclical way. Think of the defiant behavior as your child's safest language to express his negative feelings. Defiant children increase their negative behaviors when they feel misunderstood. As he becomes more defiant, you become more frustrated. This frustration, in turn, leads you to respond in ways that leave your child feeling misunderstood. As your child feels more misunderstood, he will likely become more defiant, and the cycle continues. This is illustrated in the cycle of defiance figure.

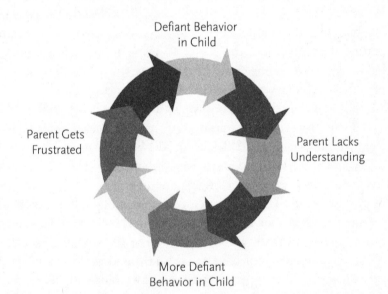

Defiant Behavior
in Child

Parent Lacks
Understanding

More Defiant
Behavior in Child

Parent Gets
Frustrated

This conversation between a defiant fourteen-year-old and his mother is a perfect example of how this cycle of defiance works:

> **Greg:** "I said I'll get ready but you didn't let me finish my game, so now you have to wait or I won't go."
> **Mom:** "You knew all day that we had to go. I have had it. I need you to get ready now!"
> **Greg:** "You blew it! You're trying to force me and I'm not going."

Mom: "I just don't see why you get this way, I try to be nice but nothing works. You are losing your video game privileges for a week."

Greg: "I hate you!"

The words and dynamics of this argument are typical. As you can see, Greg is not willing to take responsibility, Mom is getting frustrated, and the rift in understanding increases.

This dynamic of escalating defiance is one of the most common observations I have made between parents and their defiant children. The child has been locked into a defiant behavior pattern, which the parent does not understand. The child just gets more defiant and the parent responds with frustration, which influences the child to be more defiant. This attitude makes the child feel even more misunderstood, which prompts him to use his defiant behavior to express himself further, and the cycle just intensifies.

Ten Traps That Can Lead to Misunderstanding

There are many obstacles to misunderstanding your defiant child, but once you're aware of them you can avoid them. Below are ten things parents do that get in the way of understanding their children. If you find that you fall into one or more of these traps on a regular basis, don't feel too bad—you're certainly not alone! You *can* change things, and this knowledge will give you the power.

1. Expecting your child to be able to do things before she is ready.

When it comes to understanding your child, your great expectations may lead to great complications. We ask a three-year-old to sit still. We ask a four-year-old to clean his room. Middle-schoolers are not supposed to forget things, and high-schoolers are supposed to know what they want out of life. I remember driving one of my children back to school one night after she forgot a book there—something she had never done before. Just after arriving at the school, I gave my unsolicited fatherly advice about the importance of remembering where things are. The next day I discovered that I had misplaced my car keys!

In all of these situations, we are being unrealistic. We are setting ourselves up for disappointment and setting our children up for repeated failures to please us. In short, we are asking our children to stop acting their age. If your child cannot do something you ask, it's unfair and unrealistic to expect or demand more, and getting angry about it only makes things worse. A five-year-old cannot act like a ten-year-old, a ten-year-old cannot act like a fourteen-year-old, and a fourteen-year-old cannot act like an adult. To expect them to is unrealistic and unhelpful. There are limits to what your child can manage, and if you don't accept those limits, it will cause major frustration for both you and your child.

2. Overgeneralizing occasional misbehavior.

If your child cannot meet your expectations, you may assume that he is being defiant, instead of looking closely at the situation from your child's point of view so you can determine the truth of the matter. While defiant children have a natural tendency to act defiant, this certainly does not mean that they are always being defiant. Every child exhibits occasional difficult behaviors, and you need to distinguish between normal negative behavior and a pattern of defiance. Parents of defiant children often overlook this possibility because they've gotten in the habit of assuming that every negative act is an act of defiance. Denise, the mother of six-year-old Todd, was elated to share with me that once she made up her mind to look for instances of Todd being more cooperative with her requests, the more cooperative he actually became. This follows the popular expression, "Perception is reality." Trust me, once you begin to look for exceptions to your child's defiant behaviors, you will see them a lot more.

3. Preventing your child from acting like a child.

It's so easy for parents to forget what it was like to be children and to expect their kids to act like adults instead of acting their age. A healthy child may be rambunctious, noisy, emotionally expressive, and have a short attention span. All of these "problems" are not problems at all, but normal qualities of a normal child. Rather, it is our society and our society's expectations of perfect behavior that are abnormal. Take a good look at your child's behavior in relation to his age before you assume he is acting defiantly.

4. Expecting your child to meet your needs.

If you are like most parents, you may often expect—and even demand—that your child meets your needs—for quiet, for uninterrupted sleep, for obedience, and so on. Our job as parents is to meet our children's needs, not the other way around. When you find yourself feeling angry or frustrated because your child is bothering you, or not allowing you to do something important, take a deep breath and remember that your child's needs must take precedent. The more you understand your child's challenges (e.g., that his own self-absorption gets in the way of seeing and meeting your needs), the less uptight you will be about it. I am not saying you should let your child treat you poorly or walk all over you. I'm saying that if you relax your expectations, your child will have a better chance of meeting your needs. And if your needs are not met, try to understand why rather than immediately getting frustrated or angry.

Donna, a single mother of eleven-year-old Marissa, discovered that Marissa was snooping in her room and had found her diary. Donna was furious at Marissa because her need for privacy had been violated. I had a counseling session with Donna and Marissa to discuss the incident. Donna followed my advice to try to really understand where Marissa was coming from. Marissa tearfully shared her fear that her mother was secretly dating and that Marissa was worried her mother would meet someone who would take away all of Marissa's time with her mother. Donna listened and understood Marissa, and Marissa agreed to stop snooping in Donna's room.

5. Taking your child's mistakes personally.

Your child has very little life experience, and he will inevitably make mistakes. Mistakes are a natural part of learning at any age. Regardless, it's easy to blame him for his mistakes instead of trying to help and understand him. Please do not fall into the trap of viewing your child's mistakes as a negative reflection on yourself. You will do yourself and your child a great favor by not taking his mistakes personally.

Yes, I know that being called nasty names by your own child and not dwelling on how this hurts may seem like a tall order, to say the least. This is where switching your mind-set from parent to coach can give you some emotional objectivity and help you avoid taking your child's problem behaviors so personally. Do your best not to react to mistakes, challenging of rules, or misbehavior with surprise and disappointment. You know your child will make mistakes, so don't act as if you think he should behave perfectly at all times.

6. Forgetting how deeply your child can be hurt by blame and criticism.

Most parents know that physically abusing their child is wrong and harmful, yet they forget how painful angry words, insults, and blame can be. When a child is verbally attacked, she naturally believes that she is at fault. It's easy to let your child's defiant bravado convince you that nothing bothers her. I can tell you, however, that defiant children of all ages have cried their eyes out in my office when sharing with me hurtful things that their parents said to them. To keep yourself from falling into this trap, imagine how it would feel to be on the receiving end of your words as you react and speak to your child.

7. Miscommunicating and overreacting through texts and other electronic forms of communication.

Janice showed me upsetting text messages exchanged between her and her fifteen-year-old son, Casey. She had sent him what she perceived was a gentle reminder that she'd be picking him up from his girlfriend's house. Casey had texted back,

> "I will let you know when I am ready."

When Casey had written this message, which was clearly not considerate to his mother, he was in the midst of consoling his girlfriend.

Casey's girlfriend had been filled with tears and drama as she was trying to sort out a big misunderstanding between her and two of her friends on social media. Time got swallowed up for Casey and he lost track of how close it was to when he and his mom had initially agreed that he would be picked up.

Janice became quite frustrated when she received Casey's text, thinking to herself, "I went out of my way to drive you there and now you think you are the one to tell who is going to tell me when you are ready! Now I am not only your chauffer but also expected to be at your beck and call!"

Thinking this while being in a riled up state of mind she wrote back,

> "I will decide when you are ready. I am going to leave now and you better be ready to go in fifteen minutes!"

Upon receiving this text, Casey wrote back,

> "Just stop! Why do you always have to make my life miserable?"

The above text exchange example shows that Casey did not intend to be disrespectful to Janice. He was struggling with "taking on" his girlfriend's angst. Janice had no idea this had been going on and how worried he was for his girlfriend. Casey was just trying to get more time and was not deliberately disregarding her authority. In this example, the text messaging may have saved time in communicating logistics but it added frustration and led to a misunderstanding.

8. Overlooking how healing loving actions can be.

It's easy to fall into draining cycles of blame and misbehavior, instead of stopping to give your child love, reassurance, self-esteem, and security with hugs and kind words. Many moving breakthroughs with defiant children have begun with their parents hugging them in my office. I've never had a child complain to me that she was loved too much.

9. Forgetting that your child learns by example.

Your child has been watching you for a long time. It's not what you say but what you do that your child takes to heart. A parent who hits a child for hitting, telling him that hitting is wrong, is in fact teaching him that hitting is right, at least for those in power. In a session one day, Ellie shared with me a personal turning point for modeling good coping skills for her three young children. One day she got angry and threw a dish across the table. Later that week, the most defiant of her three children also threw a dish—but this one cut his sister's head open. Ellie got a quick and powerful lesson that children learn by example. There's an excellent poem entitled "Children Learn What They Live" by Dorothy Law Nolte, PhD, that powerfully speaks to the huge impact parents have in modeling behaviors and values to their children. Here's a short excerpt:

> If children live with hostility, they learn to fight. If children live with kindness and consideration, they learn respect.

The parent who responds to problems with peaceful solutions is teaching his child how to be a peaceful adult. So-called problems can give you your best opportunity for teaching values, because your kids learn best when they are learning about real things in real life.

10. Seeing only the outward behavior, not the love and good intentions inside the child.

When your child's behavior disappoints you, you should always try to assume the best. You should assume that your child means well and is behaving as well as possible under the given circumstances (both obvious and hidden from us), together with his level of experience in life. As you saw in the example on pages 34–35 with Janice and Casey, while Casey needed to be more mindful of time commitments with his mother, controlling threats, fueled by inner negative thoughts, don't resolve conflicts. If you always assume the best about your child, he will be free to do his best. You may recall the Restoration of Pleasant Images of Your Child exercise on page 18, which was designed to help you reconnect with the positive aspects of your defiant child. Use it!

Dealing with Your Negative Thoughts

It's crucial that you don't get bogged down with negative thoughts about your defiant child. It's common for parents of defiant children to become consumed with negative self-talk. Self-talk is those silent comments you make to yourself as you go about your day, such as, *"I can't believe he spoke to his sister that way"* or *"Why doesn't he ever listen to me?"* When you feel down or blue in response to your child's behaviors, you may think to yourself something like, *"This child is impossible."* Occasional negative thoughts about your child are normal. But frequent and intense negative thoughts can cause you to feel overwhelmed, cornered, or threatened by her. What happens in your mind makes you react strongly to your defiant child.

Unless you are really aware of what you are saying in your head, you will have little to no control over what comes out of your mouth. My book for couples, *Why Can't You Read My Mind? Overcoming the Nine Toxic Thought Patterns That Get in the Way of a Loving Relationship*, addresses what I refer to as "toxic thoughts" among partners. These toxic thoughts are rigid and unfair and destroy intimacy. Toxic thoughts are negative thoughts that have lost their reality and have gotten out of control, causing you to lose your perspective. Toxic thoughts are more extreme versions of negative thoughts. Unlike the negative thought, *"I don't like my child's behavior right now,"* toxic thoughts are twisted, distorted, highly negative perceptions that are simply not based in reality, such as *"My child's behavior makes him a lost cause."*

I have found that parents of defiant children are particularly vulnerable to becoming ensnared in toxic thoughts about their child. Examples of such thoughts are:

- "He is going to ruin this family."
- "All he does is suck me dry."
- "Nothing is ever good enough for this kid."

These types of toxic thoughts can also sabotage your ability to see the virtues of your defiant child. It's important for you to counter these highly negative thoughts by thinking of positive exceptions and building on them. One mother of a defiant twelve-year-old boy felt more positive after reminding herself how he voluntarily gave up accepting birthday gifts since age seven. Instead, this particular child donates his birthday proceeds to less fortunate children. Examples of positive counters to toxic thoughts are:

- "He actually can be very protective of his brother when other kids pick on him."
- "She showed consideration for everyone in the family last week by agreeing to turn down the volume of the TV."
- "He came home last week ahead of his curfew time."

The more you recognize your child's positive and appropriate behaviors, the better able you will be to adopt a more positive mind-set. Your positive mind-set will keep your child more positively connected to you. I know that challenging and changing your negative thought patterns takes work and patience, but remember: the payoff will be a far less defiant child. For more guidance on overcoming toxic thoughts in parenting please refer to my book, *Liking the Child You Love*.

Love Is Not Enough

Today I have given you a tremendous tool for connecting better with your child to help reduce his defiance. This tool is understanding. Your understanding is just as important as your love, if not more so, to help your child break out of the cycle of defiance. Over the course of twenty-five years of counseling families, countless parents have told me, "But we love him so much, why does he behave this way?" or "I would do anything for her, but I can't break through her anger," or "I love him to death and I do all these things to help him but he just does not seem to want to help himself—I don't understand him one bit."

I believe these parents do care. Most are well meaning, sincere, and full of love for their children. And yet, I have seen the look of shock, sometimes horror, on these same parents' faces when their children reveal the extent of their hurts, sadness, anger, frustration, feelings of inadequacy, and other emotionally painful issues. The more you lead with understanding, the less your child will follow with defiance.

DAY 2 SUMMING IT UP

You are giving your defiant child a tremendously valuable gift when you seek to understand him. All the love in the world won't help you lessen your child's defiance unless you understand the nature of his struggles. Keep the following in mind as you move forward:

- Defiant children feel desperately misunderstood.
- Defiant children tend to be emotionally immature and consequently they lack the tools to manage strong feelings and solve problems effectively.
- Your child cannot verbalize it, but she greatly values the fact that you understand her.
- The more you show your child that you understand her, the less defiant she will be.

GETTING READY FOR DAY 3

- Keep a journal of when you catch yourself listening ineffectively and effectively to your child.
- Stay mindful of the obstacles that interfere with listening and understanding your child.
- Be careful not to miscommunicate if you communicate through written electronic media such as text messages.
- Stay mindful of your own internal negative and toxic thoughts that can derail your attempts to express understanding and support.

Coaching Yourself
Around the Yelling Trap

Ten-year-old Eddy heard his mom, Jane, tell him to settle down, but he tuned her out. She hoped his raucousness would soon stop but she was unfortunately on the "bottle it up and explode later plan" with Eddy. He and his friends were playing and Eddy's attention was elsewhere. With horror, Jane watched as a crystal vase of flowers toppled over after Eddy bumped into it. As she watched the vase fall to the floor, Jane tried to will herself to stay calm. She even reminded herself that she had forgotten to put the vase in a safer place. But kids have a way of pushing the envelope with even the most patient and understanding parent. Jane started yelling at Eddy. "I told myself that I wouldn't yell, but it didn't work," she told me later in a counseling session.

On Day 2 you learned how important it is to understand your child in order to reduce his defiant behavior. Today we'll work on getting control over the one thing you may do that actually increases your child's defiance—yelling at him.

Think about it: How often have you screamed at your kids, "You get in here right this minute and pick up this mess all over the floor!"? Or, have you ever yelled something such as, "I'm sick and tired of having to yell at you!"? Given the stress of parenting a defiant child, as crazy as this sounds, you, too, may have ended up yelling that you did not want to yell. Don't worry, you're likely not crazy—just stressed out. These are likely the verses of a familiar song. Even when you get to the point where you can understand your child's defiance, frustration can easily lead you to yell when your defiant child is acting out, when she doesn't do her homework, or when you have to tell her something five times. By the sixth time, the request often comes out louder than a fire engine's siren. As you will learn today, there are many reasons why parents scream and yell, but yelling only creates more trouble when you're dealing with a defiant child.

A few years ago, I was in a toy store when I happened to pass by an aisle and see a father glancing at his mobile device while with his three elementary-school-age children. Almost at that instant, I heard a loud crash as several boxes fell off the shelf and onto the floor. The father immediately began screaming at one of his children. The child began to cry, and the father suddenly stopped yelling and looked up at the ceiling for a moment. Then he hugged his child. As he hugged the child, the father suddenly began crying and said he was sorry. Watching this scene, I almost started to cry myself. This father obviously realized that his yelling was a mistake, and he tried to do something about it. My hope is that by reading this chapter you will learn to control and greatly reduce your yelling as well.

My first goal today is to help you understand why yelling is such a big parenting problem, and why it is especially problematic when it comes to parenting defiant children. I will also discuss why so many parents yell and give you plenty of hands-on, easy-to-use strategies to avoid yelling. In addition, I will address particularly difficult situations (i.e., yelling triggers) and show you how to avoid yelling in these circumstances. Let's begin by taking a closer look at why yelling is so detrimental in parenting defiant children.

Yelling Is a Serious Problem

Yelling is a huge problem for parents of defiant children. Studies show that most parents—even the most patient ones—lose their temper and yell at their children. Unfortunately, most children become immune to being yelled at and start to tune it out. Research shows that parents whose general way of disciplining their children is by yelling have children who are more likely to display physical or verbal aggression, social withdrawal, and a lack of positive/pro-social behaviors, such as sharing and empathy. There is also some evidence that yelling, like physical punishment, can lead to feelings of depression in teens. Yelling is very problematic with defiant children because they not only tune out, they also tend to lash out. When you yell at a defiant child, it usually fuels his defiant behavior. Remember that defiant children seek to push your buttons and get you angry. By yelling, you are letting him know that he succeeded in upsetting you.

As a parent, you're trying to be a role model and teacher. Your job is to communicate your ideas to your children in a calm manner. Like the example of Jane described at the beginning of this chapter, many parents try to be calm and not yell but end up doing so anyway. Or some parents yell from the outset out of concern for their child's negative behaviors. Unfortunately, in either case, you show your kids by yelling that you've lost control of yourself. This is clearly not a trait that you want to pass on to your kids. After all, when you yell, you're only teaching them to yell. Whatever your yelling pattern has been, don't be too hard on yourself. We have all yelled at one time or another. Today you will learn how to free yourself from the yelling trap.

The seductive aspect of yelling is that it often seems to work—at least in the short run. This is because it tends to cause a child to obey solely out of fear—the fear of losing your approval or even his relationship with you. You may not realize it, but a defiant child who is yelled at regularly feels unsure of his parent's love. A child feels rejected when he is yelled at, and over time he begins to believe that the love of his parents depends on his good behavior. This is especially frustrating and scary for defiant children because of their difficulty in controlling their reactions and behaviors.

The best way for you to fully grasp the damaging aspects of yelling is to do some personal reflecting of your own. See the box on the next page to help you get in touch with what it feels like to be on the receiving end of yelling.

GET IN THE SHOES OF THE "YELLEE"

As a parent of a defiant child, you are likely doing a good amount of yelling. If you turn things around and think about how you respond when your spouse, boss, or any other adult yells at you, it will be quite illuminating. Consider the following questions:

- When you are yelled at, do you respond to yelling warmly and positively, eager to grant every demand?
- Are you inwardly plotting how you'll pay that so-and-so back?
- Do you feel a sense of inadequacy?
- Is it hard to let go of negative thoughts and feelings that arise after being yelled at?

By reading through and responding to these questions, you've gotten an up close and personal perspective on what it's like to be on the receiving end of the negative impact of yelling. As you can see, yelling harms your child's feelings about himself. The bottom line is that it's important to think about how often you shout at your children, what you say, and what else is happening in their lives. I have summarized below the reasons yelling is troublesome to defiant children.

Why Not to Yell in a Nutshell

- Yelling does not effectively alter your child's behavior.
- Yelling gets in the way of exploring and solving the issue at hand.
- Yelling gives kids the wrong kind of attention, and defiant kids will misbehave to get attention, even if the attention is yelling.
- Defiant children think in concrete terms: "If it's okay for them to yell at me, it must be okay for me to yell at someone, too."
- Yelling often leaves your defiant child feeling resentful toward you.

- Defiant children are more likely to act out in response to yelling.
- The more you yell, the less your defiant child will hear you.
- Yelling sends your child the message that you're mad at her.
- Children who are yelled at learn to respond only to yelling. They don't respond as well to reason, or to calm, rational discussions.
- Yelling is demeaning. It's a way of saying, "I have power and you don't."
- Yelling also conveys the message: "You're not worth talking to calmly. You deserve to be yelled at."
- Yelling lowers your child's trust in you as a safe person to open up to.

Instead of viewing yelling as a way of controlling your child, you need to see yelling for what it really is—an expression of anger. Yelling is an adult temper tantrum. Sure, sometimes you will get angry at your children. After all, you are alive and you will react to situations. But the key here is to realize that you have a choice in how you react. If you feel frustrated or angry and are in danger of yelling, tell your child, "I'm really mad about that now. I'll deal with it when I've calmed down." Later in this chapter you will find twenty-five concrete strategies to help you avoid yelling.

While writing this book I asked a few of my young clients how they felt about their parents' yelling at them. Here are a few responses:

> "I don't like it when my mom yells at me because it makes me cry."
>
> —ROBERT, AGE SEVEN

> "When parents yell it puts pressure on the kid and makes them want to scream."
>
> —EMILY, AGE NINE

> "I don't like when I get yelled at because it just makes my temper rise and it gets me angry."
>
> —LUKE, AGE ELEVEN

> *"It worsens the whole situation because when parents yell it just puts more stress on everyone. Also, when my parents yell it makes me not want to do what they ask."*
> —LAURA, AGE FOURTEEN

Yes, there may be times when you will be required to raise your voice. For example, you may need to yell to stop your child from stepping into the path of an oncoming car. But in most cases, it is counterproductive to yell at your child.

UNDERSTANDING WHAT DRIVES YOU TO YELL

To help you understand what drives you to yell, please consider the following statements and questions and answer as honestly as you can.

	YES	NO
I yell because I get so frustrated and I have no other way to handle the situation.	❐	❐
I yell because my parents yelled and it is what I learned to do when my children misbehave.	❐	❐
I yell because it has become a habit for me.	❐	❐
I yell because I believe it is the only option to get my child to listen to me.	❐	❐

- How often do you yell?
- What types of incidents do you usually yell about?
- How do your children respond to your yelling?
- What thoughts go through your head *right before* you yell?
- What thoughts go through your head *while* you're yelling?
- What thoughts go through your head *after* you're done yelling?

Give yourself some credit for exploring why you yell—it takes courage to examine yourself this way. After all, Socrates said: "The unexamined life is not worth living." I have seen over and over that parents who understand why they yell and learn to limit it greatly reduce defiant behavior in their child. So even if the motives of your yelling seem difficult to examine, please stay with me and keep working on it. Reducing your yelling is a huge way to lower your child's defiance.

The Many Reasons We Yell

Now that you realize how destructive yelling is, it's time to discuss the more common reasons parents yell. While this list is not all-inclusive, here are the main reasons that parents yell.

A response to intense frustration.

For many parents, yelling is their response to intense frustration. As a parent, you are confronted with many conflicting pressures and demands, and frustration is common. And when your defiant child continually challenges you, it can seem impossible to avoid yelling. Keep in mind, though, that yelling generally raises the tension level in the household and creates more defiance-related problems than it solves. The challenge for you is to manage your frustration and learn new and healthier alternatives to yelling. At the end of this chapter, I offer many strategies to reduce your frustration and help you avoid yelling.

My parents yelled at me, so I do it, too.

Many of us were raised with a considerable amount of yelling from our own parents. Some parents may believe, "I had to deal with it, so my kids will have to do the same." Also, many parents feel that children are "too loose" these days and that yelling will snap their children into behaving better.

You may find it amusing to take a look at ancient history. You'll see from reading the quote below that the more people change, the more they stay the same:

The children now love luxury; they show disrespect for elders and love chatter in place of exercise. Children are tyrants, not the servants of their households. They no longer rise when their elders enter the room. They contradict their parents . . . gobble up dainties at the table, cross their legs and tyrannize their teachers.

—SOCRATES

As Socrates noted two millennia ago, "children have been pushing the limits of acceptable behavior for quite some time." Now consider the wisdom of another great mind, Albert Einstein, who said that the definition of insanity is "doing the same thing over and over again and expecting different results." It seems clear that children have had challenging behaviors for a very long time and that years of yelling at them has not been the solution.

Yelling became a habit.

As parents, we want our messages to our children to be clear and powerful. We want them to notice us and to listen. I'm always amazed at how many parents of defiant children tell me that yelling gets their child's attention. In reality, the attention parents gain from yelling at their children is usually fleeting. Yelling gives parents a fast and powerful way to get heard—maybe not listened to, but at least heard. The kicker about yelling is that once you've started doing it, you get used to yelling. It becomes what I call a "conditioned parenting reflex." In plain English, yelling becomes a habit. And the problem with this yelling habit is that you become predictable to your children and they start to expect you to yell. Sadly, it becomes a very toxic habit. Most parents are amazed when I model what I call focused whispering as an alternative to yelling. Whispering often gets and holds a child's attention much more powerfully than yelling. I describe this technique in more detail in the section Twenty-Five Alternatives to Yelling.

Screaming seems to be my only option.

Many parents of defiant children truly believe it when they say, "The only way he listens to me is when I scream," but nothing could be further from the truth. As an example, consider Jody, who felt this way. Sobbing during an initial counseling session, she described to me the aftermath of her yelling just that morning. She relayed to me a scene in which her ten-year-old son lay on the floor, a whimpering mess, as her daughter sat comatose-like on the chair in front of her. The deafening sound of silence reminded Jody that an ugly moment had just occurred. The silence, however, soon ended when her defiant son threw his book bag against the wall and ran up to his room.

Like many parents, Jody's "hot button" was her son's casual attitude about completing homework. (In the next section, I give strategies to deal with what I call "homework hassles.") Jody, a single parent, said that on this morning, her son Sean had not done his homework from the night before. Sean, a fifth-grader with attention-deficit/hyperactivity disorder (ADHD), had forgotten his assignment book at school. Jody told me, "I resented the demands of managing Sean. I just exploded and screamed, thinking that I'd finally make him change his behavior." Like so many parents, Jody felt that yelling was her only option. Fortunately, Jody was able to learn alternatives to yelling.

My child "should" show me respect.

Parents understandably may react strongly and are quite negatively impacted when their children are disrespectful to them. Yet I have often found that defiant children have parents who are hypervigilant about them showing respect. Demanding respect from a defiant child usually fans the flames of his defiant behavior. As I wrote in my book, *Liking the Child You Love,* parents' rigid thinking patterns lead to emotional overreactions and unrealistic expectations. The irony is that the less you demand respect from your child by yelling at him to give it to you, the more respect he will give you over time.

Getting the Right Mind-Set

In the next section, you will learn powerful techniques to avoid yelling. Staying mindful of these three important points will help keep you centered and effective as you integrate these strategies to reduce your yelling:

Don't be attached to the immediate results. Remember that your child has to see that you are serious about sticking with your changes.

He may initially roll his eyes or even scoff at you when you use these alternatives to yelling. But rest assured, your avoidance of yelling will pay off in the long run. It may not happen overnight, but less yelling from you over time means less defiance from your child. While it may not happen the first few times you avoid yelling, trust me when I tell you that most of my clients report seeing significant reductions in their child's defiance within ten days.

Your goal is to join with your child, not be her adversary. The more you realize and remember that you are working with—rather than against—your child to lower her defiance, the more you will make this happen.

Think of yourself as your child's emotional and behavioral coach throughout this program. Being your child's coach in no way compromises your role as a parent. Quite the opposite is the case. Your parenting connection will be increased when you switch into coach mode. Coach mode helps to release you, and your ego, from feeling locked in the role of hurt, disappointed, or stuck parent. Taking on a coaching mentality means staying calm to rationally guide and encourage your child. Keeping your calm is crucial for parents when managing defiant children. Research by Dr. John Gottman offers five key steps to parents for emotion coaching:

1. Become aware of your child's emotions and your own, as well.
2. See your child's negative emotions as opportunities for intimacy and teaching. They are not threats to your authority.
3. Use your heart to feel what your child is feeling. Validate your child by reflecting back his words about his feelings.
4. Use empathy to help your child find words to label the emotion he is having. Saying "I can see you are really frustrated right now," helps him label his intense emotion and talk about it rather than act it out with defiant behavior. Avoid saying things like, "You should not feel frustrated."
5. Set limits and work together to solve problems. I will discuss setting limits in Day 6, Discipline Without Desperation. The main idea is to have a "learner's heart." This means exploring

options to help your child come up with possible solutions to overcome challenges and attain goals.

Twenty-Five Ways to Help You Stop Yelling

Here are some powerful, effective tips to help you avoid the yelling trap.

1. Be an active listener.

If you are in a conflict, draw your child out to see how he genuinely feels. Avoid being overly judgmental, which leaves your child feeling criticized and which will cause him to become defensive. One of my clients, Ken, told me how he found it helpful to ask his twelve-year-old son, Troy, to "Please help me understand why you seem upset." Just that simple question helped Ken remember to listen to rather than lecture his son. Even if Troy did not give Ken an immediate answer, Ken realized that by asking this question he left the door open for Troy to share this thoughts and feelings later on.

2. Use understanding to slow yourself down.

Listening, as described above, helps you to dig deeper and understand what's really going on with your defiant child. This is perhaps the best antidote to yelling. Recall from Day 2 the power of understanding. While understanding alone may not stop you from yelling, it will help. Try to analyze what it is that you'd like your child to change, and then rationally explain it to him. For example, in the case of a messy bedroom, ask yourself what is okay and what you'd like him to stop doing. Kayla, the mother of thirteen-year-old Gordon, realized that she could live with some clothes on the floor but not with two-week-old potato chips in the corner. As another example, is it possible that your son refused to get ready for school because he has a test he is not ready for? Or is your daughter scared of being rejected by her new group of friends and is she taking it out on you? As I discussed on Day 2, understanding what is going on with your child will help slow you down emotionally. The more you slow down, the less emotionally reactive you are and the less likely you will be to yell.

3. Ask yourself whose problem it is.

Maybe your teen is playing music too loudly or your preschooler is playing a favorite "Let's Go to the Zoo" song for the hundredth time and you have a headache. Unless you indicate to them that you have a headache, your children will not know. Yelling at a child for something that is affecting you will not get your problem resolved. One mother I worked with, Colleen, realized that she never told her five-year-old son Ryan how much it bothered her when he tugged on her coat. At first she thought it was cute when Ryan did this, but over time it started to annoy her. Colleen calmly told Ryan to stop tugging on her coat, and this prevented her from yelling. Children need parents to describe what they are feeling in order for them to understand. If you yell at your child because he is showing little or no appreciation for a gift you have given to him, your child will not understand that you are feeling unappreciated or rejected by his reaction. Be aware of how you interpret your child's behavior or reaction. The truth is that defiant children do not always understand how what they say or do affects their parents. Let your child know what you expect and what you want—your child can't guess.

4. Recognize anger as a signal.

It's okay to feel anger—what matters is how you handle it. Anger does not have to mean "I must yell." Recall how earlier I described yelling as a conditioned parenting reflex. It's more helpful to view anger as a "signal" to resolve a problem. While people may differ, the common warning signs of rising anger include:

- Tightness/pounding in the chest
- Negative/toxic thoughts (e.g., "This child is ruining our family!")
- Rapid breathing
- Sweating
- Clenching of fists
- Quivery voice

Please refer to the deep-breathing exercise I described on Day 1, which can help to reduce these symptoms. Reframing the urge to yell as a signal to resolve a problem will help you be more constructive and logical and less likely to yell. For instance, if your son is making a mess in the family room, don't wait until you're going to explode before you mention that he needs to pick up some of the clutter. Should you become angry, you can say both in your head and out loud, "I'm really angry about that now, I'll deal with the situation when I've calmed down." The main idea is to let the emotional overloads simmer down before communicating.

5. Don't take it all so personally.

In his book *The Four Agreements,* Miguel Ruiz writes, "Don't take anything personally. Nothing others do is because of you. . . ." This is valuable wisdom to keep in mind. If you stop and think about it, most of the time when you yell at your defiant child, it's because you are taking her behaviors too personally. Realize that even if she is trying to provoke you, your defiant child is behaving in this manner because of her own struggles, not yours. Remembering this will help you not to get so frustrated, and the risk of your yelling will be much lower.

6. Put a picture in the picture.

Keep in mind that your child's behavior in the moment is not all he is. Like a TV with a picture-in-a-picture feature, make his irritating behaviors the small picture and surround it with a bigger picture of his positive behaviors. This is similar to the Restoration of Pleasant Images of Your Child exercise you tried on Day 1. The more you view your child's defiant behaviors as the smaller picture, and at the same time create and focus on the big picture of his goodness as a fellow human being, the less threatened you will feel and the less likely you will be to yell.

7. Use humor.

One of my clients, Lisa, tried the following experiment I had suggested. Like many parents, Lisa felt exasperated by her ten-year-old daughter Becky's resistance to cleaning up her room. This had become the focus of many arguments, with a lot of yelling back and forth. I coached Lisa one day to playfully tell Becky that one million dollars was set to be delivered to their home; but this could only occur if Becky cleaned up her room. Becky was caught off guard by a humorous request instead of the usual yelling by Lisa. The good news was that Becky complied. Any kind of humor to lighten things up reduces tension and your chances of yelling.

8. Use focused whispering in place of yelling.

As I mentioned earlier, whispering is a very powerful way to get your child's attention. This can also be a powerful way to avoid making a scene in public. Your teenager may find whispering a bit patronizing and corny, so use it selectively with older children. Kylie, like other parents I have worked with, realized that she could use focused whispering anytime she needed to make a point. Kylie used the technique with her eight-year-old daughter Ali when they were at a neighborhood party. Ali was being rude to the parents and kids attending the party. Kylie went over to Ali, paused for a moment once she had Ali's attention, and then calmly and firmly whispered, "Ali, I am asking you please to be polite." Ali complied and Kylie avoided an ugly scene by not yelling at her daughter. I will talk more on Day 4 about using a calm and firm parenting demeanor as part of the strategy to avoid power struggles. I recommend the following steps for focused whispering:

- Get your child's initial attention by calmly approaching him or her.
- Look her directly in the eye and pause a moment before speaking (kneel if you need to).
- If you think it will not physically threaten her, gently place your hand on her shoulder.
- Whisper your request in a brief, firm manner and then walk away.

9. Become skilled in the art of shrugging.

Shrugging is another alternative to yelling. By shrugging, you give a powerful nonverbal message, which states, "I am not going to overreact." Shrugging in a nonchalant manner can be coupled with focused whispering or other strategies listed here. Iris, age seven, told her father, Allen, that she was going to run away and live at her friend's house. Recently divorced and highly sensitive about providing a solid home, Allen had yelled at his daughter when she first said this. However, after I helped Allen with his parenting skills, he learned to shrug at such threats, which Iris had no intention of carrying out. Shrugging helps to neutralize your own excess emotionality and will consequently slow down the melodrama of defiant children (and possibly your own, too).

10. Don't humiliate your child or call him names.

As I mentioned on Day 1, it's important to avoid name-calling. Avoid speaking in a denigrating manner. Always remember that respect begets respect and addressing your child in a negative manner quickly erodes his respect for you. And to make matters worse, yelling occurs more often when you speak negatively. The words hurt even more because the yelling tone is like pouring salt into the emotional wound. It is much more effective to say, "I would like you to clean up these toys before you get anything else out," instead of saying, "You spoiled brat, pick these toys up right now!"

11. Just let it go.

Ask yourself if the situation is important enough to address or if you can let it go. If you need time to yourself, explain to your child that you are not in a good mood and that you will speak to him when you are feeling better. If you have family support, have someone take your child while you sort through your emotions. Whenever possible, no matter how brief, take a time-out for yourself. Do whatever it takes to calm yourself down, such as taking slow, deep breaths, meditating, writing in a journal, calling a supportive friend, or praying. One parent I worked with shared with me that she learned to "just close my eyes and picture myself floating" as a self-calming strategy.

12. Say the Serenity Prayer.

I find this well-known prayer very useful for all stressful situations, and over the years I have heard from many parents that it helps them avoid yelling: "God grant me the serenity to accept the things I can-not change, the courage to change the things I can, and the wisdom to know the difference."

13. Remember that you control the show.

Don't fall into the trap of mirroring your child's moods. Remember that you are the parent and the one who must show a healthy exam-ple of how problems are handled. I have seen parents become very passive-aggressive when they let their defiant child determine their own behavior. If you mirror your child's behavior, acting nicely when he is nice and badly when he acts badly, you are allowing your child to manipulate you.

14. Enough is enough.

If your child has already paid extensively for this behavior through a natural consequence or from someone else's input (police, teacher, coach), ask yourself whether your input is necessary or if you simply want a little revenge. Many parents have a dark side that leads them to provoke their children. This hurts your child's self-esteem. When I say "dark side," I don't mean that these parents are evil, or wish their children harm. Rather, I am referring to the frustrations that can lead you to want to "punish" your child. Examples of this include wanting to remove your child's privileges to an excessive degree or giving him a seemingly endless barrage of lectures about something that is already over and done with. I will talk more about knowing how and when to give your child appropriate consequences on Day 6 when I review my discipline approach called Discipline Without Desperation.

15. Say "Let me think about it."

As I mentioned earlier, a key component of successfully parenting defiant children is slowing down. Defiant children will try to catch you off balance with a ridiculous request. Saying "let me think about it" will help you slow down. Stacey was Gretchen's defiant fifteen-year-old daughter. Stacey had a manipulative way of making requests (e.g., asking to go a friend's house just when Gretchen arrived home from work). Gretchen called me one day ecstatic, saying, "Instead of folding to Stacey's request to go to her friend's, I realized how easy it was for me to say, 'let me think about it.'" Gretchen later saw me in a counseling session and added that while Stacey did not like having to give her mother the time and space to make parenting decisions, the decisions ended up being better ones.

16. Get on a reality TV show.

Imagine that you and your child have been selected to star in a new reality show about the ordinary lives and interactions of families. This means that all of your interactions with your child are being filmed by hidden cameras all over your house, in your car, and wherever the two of you go. Would you want the entire country to see you yelling?

17. Make sure your own needs are met.

Are you addressing your child when you are tired or hungry? Remember that it's hard to work through problems effectively with your child if you are not in a conducive physical state to do so. Try to avoid a diet loaded with refined sugar, which makes your blood sugar go up and down. Are you exercising and getting enough sleep? Most people don't get adequate exercise and aren't getting enough sleep. Proper nutrition, exercise, and sufficient sleep can do wonders to relieve tension and lengthen your yelling fuse. Also bear in mind that conflicts often flare up just before dinner. I suggest either having dinner earlier, having a snack before dinner, or trying to postpone any discussions or conflicts until after dinner. If your basic needs aren't being met, this could be contributing to your feelings of frustration and agitation and your urge to yell. Unless a situation needs immediate attention, eat or rest before speaking to your child.

18. Talk to yourself.

When you feel the urge to yell, say to yourself, "I'm feeling an urge to yell. This is just an urge. I can control it." I recall Wilma, a mother of two defiant elementary-school-age boys, giving me a high five in a counseling session when recounting to me how she talked herself down from yelling. By being mindful of your urge to yell and soothing yourself with this affirmation, you will feel calmer and less likely to yell.

19. Put yourself on record.

Keep a written record of the times you feel an urge to yell. Mark down for each one whether you're glad a couple of days later that you didn't yell, or if you wished you'd yelled. Figure out the percentage. Then remember this percentage next time you feel an urge to yell. Step back and feel good about what you have accomplished. Remember to reward yourself for yelling less often.

20. Think of quiet and powerful role models.

If you visualize other parents who refrain from yelling, you will feel their support to help you avoid yelling. Warren told me that when trying not to yell at his defiant ten-year-old daughter, he pictured his karate instructor's patience, quiet dignity, and grace when working with him. Remembering that other people work to avoid yelling may help you feel that you're not alone in fighting the urge to scream.

21. Be clear and concise with your directions.

Yes, you've asked your child to pick up her clothes several times and they're still on the floor. If your child is elementary-school age, help her to get into the habit of doing the task on a regular basis. Make sure your child is capable of doing the task by herself. Children aren't always going to admit that they did not completely understand what you said. If your child is a teen, help her to understand the importance of doing the task. Make sure you are clear with your statement by avoiding the use of the word "you"; use the word "I" instead. For example, say, "I notice that you did not pick up your shirt," as opposed to, "You keep leaving your shirt on the floor." Avoid words and phrases such as "always," "never," and "all the time." As you learned on Day 2 in the section on toxic thoughts, these words are rigid and unfair, and they foster negative feelings and defensiveness. You don't want to make accusations, just resolve the situation. Let your child know what your expectations are beforehand to avoid problems later.

22. Think about your final days.

When you feel the urge to yell, ask yourself, "What if today turns out to be the last day of my child's life?" A client of mine named Tyrone shared this strategy with me. Tyrone viewed himself as a "yeller in recovery." He credited this powerful mind-set shift with his success in remaining in control.

23. Plan ahead.

Know which issues matter, which ones don't matter, and which are nonnegotiable. Many parents don't take the time to make these important distinctions in advance. The clearer you are about your concerns, the fewer concerns you will end up having. Discuss them and your expectations with your child—and designate preset consequences. Planning ahead will also help you pick your battles wisely, which I discuss on Day 4.

24. Deal with problems as they occur.

Many parents have confessed to me that they yell because they had put off reacting to a problem when it occurred. Sasha was pleased to share with me that she became a more effective parent by not bottling up her reactions and by dealing with issues as they occurred. In the past she would let her nine-year-old son Eli play video games, while resenting the fact that it delayed their getting out of the house in the morning. Sasha changed her approach; instead of stating her concern and yelling, she used the focused whispering technique right away. Being prepared will help you keep from erupting. I will further discuss managing children's excessive video game use and other "screen time excesses" in Day 4 and in Appendix 2.

25. Think "presidential."

If you really have a hard time believing that you can't avoid yelling, then try this. Think how you would behave if the president of the United States were around when you want to yell. If the president visualization is not working for you, ask yourself how you would act if an assailant brandishing a loaded gun cornered you. Would you be rude to some crazy person threatening to shoot you? My guess is probably not. The bottom line is, if you can pull it together and control yourself for certain people and special circumstances, then you can do it other times, too, especially to benefit yourself and your child.

How to Sidestep Stubborn Yelling Triggers

Today you have learned many different tactics for controlling your yelling. This is very exciting because you're on your way to mastering one of the ways to reduce your child's defiance. Now I'm going to give you some extra support for those times when your urge to yell seems especially hard to overcome. All of the strategies I described above can still be applied in these situations, but the following will give you some more specific plans, tools, and strategies for handling some of the more difficult and challenging "yelling triggers" you may come up against.

Morning Madness

"C'mon, let's go, you're going to miss the bus!" Ah, the joy of being a parent on school-day mornings! Many parents have told me how botched morning routines leave them shrieking at their children. As one of my clients so aptly described it, experiences like this make you feel as if your head is going to explode. Let's consider an example. Imagine that it is early morning in your house, and your defiant child is avoiding getting dressed for school. The more you mention it, the more defiant he becomes, throwing tantrums, complaining about clothes, and finding other things to do. Your aggravation builds and you raise your voice, demanding that your child do what you say. You yell at him to get dressed this very instant. He becomes more defiant, and the power struggle intensifies. Power struggles create frustration, anger, and resentment for both the parent and the child. As you may recall from my discussion on Day 2 of the cycle of defiance, the more frustrated you become, the more misunderstood your child feels, and the more his defiance grows.

The following suggestions may help you avoid yelling during morning madness.

- Find out why your child is so sluggish in the morning. Is he tired? (If so, he needs an earlier bedtime.) Is he distracted by toys or by the TV? (If so, put limits on toys and TV.) Or is your child a slow starter? (If that's the case, you may need to wake him up fifteen minutes earlier.)
- Map out a morning strategy. During a calm period in the evening, tell your child what's expected of her. Agnes, a mother I worked with, found it empowering to say to her daughter, "After you wake up, I would like you to come downstairs for breakfast as soon as you can." Agnes realized that proactively stating her request made her feel more in control right off the bat. You may also tell your child that if she does not follow your requests, there will be consequences, such as not being able to watch a favorite TV show later on. To help reduce defiance, it may be helpful to ask your child to help choose an appropriate consequence for noncompliance. This will help her feel more in control.
- Manage your own expectations. Remember that mornings can often be stressful, even under the best conditions. Morning madness goes on in many homes, not just yours. Reminding yourself of this may help you not to overreact and not to yell when things don't go as planned.

Homework Hassles

Every night, in millions of homes across the country, the age-old story of children and their homework plays out. The characters may vary, but the script is usually the same. With defiant children, numerous power struggles and problems exist around homework. Parents are easily embroiled in homework power struggles because they're afraid that homework problems will sabotage their children's success in school. Suffice it to say, homework issues are usually fraught with powerful negative emotions from both children and parents. In an attempt to cope, parents will use trial and error, bribery, threats, reasoning—anything they think might work. Consider the following basic guidelines when handling homework challenges. They will help create a more rewarding homework situation for both you and your child.

- Avoid giving negative nonverbal messages. It is very important that you don't set a negative tone by sending a negative nonverbal message. Grimaces, body stiffness, sighs, raised eyebrows, and other types of negative body language can be very powerful nonverbal messages. Defiant children can be quite sensitive, and they will pick up these messages. This will only add to the tension of the homework situation.
- Help your child devise and try out a set homework schedule. The responsibility of deciding when to sit down and do homework may be overwhelming to some defiant children. The more overwhelmed a defiant child feels, the more defiant he becomes. Strive to gain cooperation by discussing with your child a time that can be adhered to as realistically as possible. This will also relieve the problem of having to "hunt down" or "corral" your child to get him to do his homework. Unless it is mutually agreed upon, no interruptions should be allowed during homework time. Phone calls, TV, and everything else should wait until the work is completed.
- Prioritize the assignments. For some defiant children, the decision about what to do first becomes a major source of tension. They may dwell on this choice for a long time and become anxious and overwhelmed. Other children may give all work the same level of importance. Most children will do best if the more challenging work is tackled early on. For some children, however, getting an easier assignment done first will get them in the groove to work on the harder challenges. See what works best for your child.

- Don't nag or hover over your child during the homework session. Nagging is often a very big problem for parents and usually just leads to more defiance and refusal to do homework. If you nag, you are setting yourself up for tremendous frustration and anger. You are also fostering "learned helplessness," as your child will become overly dependent on you.

- Find the correct answers first. Parents sometimes have a habit of zeroing in on the incorrect answers. The next time your child brings you schoolwork to look over, focus first on how well she did in solving problems and spelling words correctly. Focusing on these "mini victories" can do wonders to increase your child's motivation to tackle more challenging problems. For the answers that are incorrect, calmly and encouragingly say something such as, "I bet if you go back and check these over you may get a different answer." I can't stress enough that your goal is not only to manage your defiant child's negative feelings but also your own. If you focus first on the incorrect answers and become angry, when the child returns to her work she will likely be more involved in dealing with the loss of your parental approval than finishing the task.

- Don't let homework drag on all night. Sometimes parents will allow their children to work on homework for several hours or until they finish. This is fine if the performance of the child is consistent or the assignment realistically calls for such a commitment of time. However, in the event your child is no further along after one or two hours than he was after ten minutes into the assignment, I suggest that you stop the homework activity. It's important for your child to learn sensible time boundaries. Lingering over homework hour after hour can lead to increased feelings of inadequacy. Stay constructive and look for other ways to get help if your child is repeatedly stuck. If necessary, arrange a meeting with the teacher to explore reasons for your child's learning difficulties or motivational problems.

Don't finish assignments for your child. Some parents will complete an entire assignment for their children. This is called enabling, and it creates in your child an unhealthy dependence on you. While your goal may be to help your child finish a difficult assignment, the end result can be very destructive. He must learn to depend on himself, not on you, to finish his homework. If your child cannot complete an assignment, and he has honestly tried, write the teacher a note explaining the circumstances. I have found that most teachers will understand the situation. If your child has severe learning problems or a high tension level, he may be dealing with tremendous frustration, anger, and disappointment. Additional academic support services may be needed. See Appendix 1 for suggestions on how to seek an evaluation of your child's learning strengths and challenges.

Sibling Rivalry and Fighting

"Sibling rivalry" refers to the competitive feelings and actions that often occur among children within a family. Consider the following situation between Jeffrey, age nine, and his younger brother Scott, who's seven.

> **Jeffrey:** "He took my video game."
> **Scott:** "He stepped on my foot!"
> **Jeffrey:** "Stop looking at me!"
> **Scott:** "No, you stop looking at me!"

If you find yourself wanting to howl at the moon when facing situations like these, you're not alone. Fortunately, there are many ways you can help reduce rivalry between your kids:

- Treat each child as an individual. Help your children understand that they are treated differently by you and have different privileges and responsibilities because they are different individuals.
- Respect each child's space, toys, and time when he wants to be alone and away from his sibling.
- Avoid labeling or comparing one child to the other. This feeds their competitiveness.
- When a new child comes into the family, adequately prepare the older sibling for her important new role. Make her feel like it's her baby, too.

- Play detective. Watch and note when siblings are not getting along (before dinner, in the car, before bed) and plan separate, quiet activities for those times.
- Watch how you treat each child to see if you are contributing to the rivalry. Make sure you are not playing favorites.
- Have realistic expectations of how your children should get along, cooperate, share, and treat each other. Remember that a reasonable amount of sibling competition and struggling for recognition is normal.
- Offer positive reinforcement when they are getting along or when they resolve their own conflicts. This helps to dispel their perception that "we fight all the time."
- Make each child feel special and important. Try to spend one-on-one time with each child every day.
- Take time out to reenergize yourself. Do things just for you. This may include meeting with friends, engaging in a hobby, or reading a good book—maybe even one that is not about parenting!
- Stay centered by realizing the sibling rivalry will eventually abate.
- I doubt that as late teenagers your children will be arguing over who gets to sit next to Dad in the front seat or who can have a grape-flavored lollipop. Remind yourself that sibling competitiveness waxes and wanes and usually lessens over time.

Phone Frenzy

Children instinctively know when your concentration is divided. Defiant children can be especially tuned in to this and use this time to become even more demanding. When you're on the phone, your defiant child sees that you're giving attention to someone or something, and not to him. To help you cope with the phone frenzy tensions, the following may be helpful:

- Remember that your child may not understand that you're temporarily unavailable because his own self-absorption gets in the way of his appreciating that you're talking to someone on the other end of the phone.

- When he interrupts, say "excuse me" to the person you're talking to (so that you model how you'd like him to behave) and tell your child, "I'm talking to someone on the phone. I'll be busy for five minutes, and when I hang up, I'll listen to you and help you." Of course, if your child is really losing it, you may have to end the phone call. But yelling or threatening punishment will only increase your child's anxiety, making it harder for him to cooperate.

- As always, prevention is the best strategy. For a younger child, set up some activities he can do while you're on a call—drawing, coloring, working on a favorite puzzle—or put a toy telephone and some office supplies next to the phone and encourage him to make a call when you do.

Testy Texting: Another Form of Yelling

Electronic communication is increasingly being used as a means for parents, older children, and teens to interact. The convenience of text messages can be compromised, however, by them missing the in-person communication cues of a face-to-face conversation. It is important to be aware of how the perception of yelling (intended or not) through electronic communication, such as text messages, can be damaging to the process of conversing with a defiant child. As you will see in the examples below, a calm, firm, and noncontrolling style of communicating can help to manage this process.

> **Dimitri:** "You need to stop making dumb choices already! And smarten up! We talked about you taking a break from this group of friends. You're better than them!"

> **Doug:** "You're always yelling at me and telling me what to do. Stop trying to control my life!"

Dimitri: (calm, firm, noncontrolling) "Not my intention to seem like I am yelling. I am just frustrated because I am worried about you getting into trouble. Let's talk later. Pls text me in a half hour to let me know you are okay. I realize we need to figure out how to discuss this without fighting . . . let's work on it . . . ok?"

Doug: "ok fine . . ."

Doug: (twenty minutes later) "Dad can you please come get me now. I have to get home to do some homework."

In the brief text exchange above, Doug experiences Dimitri's (father) frustration as yelling. This is an example of what I call "testy texting." Note the calm, firm, noncontrolling text that Dimitri uses at the end to stop the escalation of the conflict.

Now consider this second example, a longer text exchange between a teen, Patty, and her mother, Juliet:

Patty: "omg mom! are you freaken kidding? I am so not ok with this. I don't want you there!"

Juliet: "Enough Patty! I am so sick of your attitude!"

Patty: "My attitude! How about yours????? You are being rediculous. I am in ninth grade mom and there is no way you are going to be a chaperone at this dance! You have to control everything and destroy my life."

Juliet: "How about that dress I just got you for YOUR Dance goes back to the store where it came from? I did not need to spend all that money, especially to have you treat me like crap!"

Patty: "See mom. You always have to make everything about money and every time I talk you make me feel guilty!"

Juliet: (calm, firm, noncontrolling) "Patty, this back and forth is not going to help either of us. I can see how you feel surprised. I feel you were attacking me but I think I also attacked you. If you don't want me to be a chaperone then I won't."

Patty: (5 minutes later) "It's fine mom. I don't care if you are there but just pls don't pressure me with pictures like you do sometimes, ok?"

Juliet: "I understand, Patty. Ok."

As you can see in this text message exchange between Juliet and Patty, when Juliet softens her interaction, becomes less reactive, shows empathy, and backs off, then Juliet feels less threatened, less reactive, and more flexible with her mom being a chaperone at her dance. While these are just brief examples, I have seen over and over in counseling teens and parents how the calm, firm, and noncontrolling approach prevents, reduces, and eliminates conflicts through electronic communication as well.

Bedtime

Bedtime may run more smoothly if you understand how hard it is for your child to stop what she's doing when she's enjoying herself. Put yourself in her shoes: Why would anyone want to turn off a great TV show or stop playing a computer game to brush her teeth?

- To ease the transition to bedtime, it's wise to give your children a good half-hour's notice that they'll have to stop their activities, and then lure them to their rooms with a fun—but quiet—activity.
- Do something nurturing and supportive for yourself immediately before starting the bedtime routine. You will handle it better if you are not so wiped out. Even taking ten to fifteen minutes with a good book can calm you before you usher your child to bed.

Just in Case You Slip and Erupt Like Mt. St. Helen's . . .

If you slip up and yell, discuss the incident with your child. Remember that defiant children can be quite adversely affected by yelling, so try to reduce any tensions by apologizing. Ask your child questions about the incident and allow her a chance to talk about it if she'd like. While your goal is to avoid yelling, owning up to it if you occasionally slip will model the important life lesson of taking responsibility for your own actions. Move on and learn from the experience, and don't beat yourself up about it.

Try Self-Compassion If You Feel Like You Are Failing to Give Up Yelling

Dr. Kristen Neff discusses the value of self-compassion. Based on her research on this important concept, she writes about emotionally healthy ways to cope if you make a mistake. For example, if you yell at your child or teen, self-compassion will help you not beat yourself up.

To have self-compassion, you have to listen to what you say to yourself. The way you talk to yourself—especially when you've failed in some way—has an impact on your health, mood, and even your relationships with others. The central point of self-compassion when you make a mistake, according to Dr. Neff, is to remind yourself that you're only human and you'll try harder next time. She adds that making mistakes, fumbling, and losing your cool are an inevitable part of the human experience—but most of us turn these slip-ups into an opportunity to beat ourselves up for being less than perfect. When we see ourselves as a hopeless failure, we close our heart down to ourselves and to others. Self-compassion isn't self-pity (*Poor me, I shouldn't feel this bad!*) or irresponsibility (*I messed up? Who cares!*) or even self-esteem (*As long as I succeed, I feel good*). It's about recognizing that feeling down is part of the shared human experience and mindfully refraining from judging yourself.

So if giving up yelling is hard, you are probably making it hard by not having self-compassion. Just remembering that you have the right to self-compassion will help you stay calmer and yell less.

A No-More-Yelling Success Story

A client of mine named Cindy had two strong-willed children, Steven, age twelve, and Jennifer, age seven. "They just do what they want and they can be so darn defiant," she complained. Cindy found herself "yelling all the time." She explained, "I yell at Steven for getting dressed too slowly, and I yell at Jennifer for touching boxes on the shelf in the grocery store. I yell at both of them when they're fighting in the backseat of the car, and I yell at them for yelling back at me."

While Cindy had a right to give her children feedback on appropriate and inappropriate behaviors, she also realized after working with me that she was blaming her kids for the fact that she yelled. She also began to see that she contributed to the problem, too. In Cindy's case, she simply expected too much from her children. Cindy made powerful changes by looking at how often she issued commands and then deliberately cutting back. She learned the value of picking her battles. She backed off a little on the smaller issues, and focused on the larger ones.

Next, Cindy explained to her kids the importance of following her instructions. She discovered that she could give them a chance to explain why they didn't want to listen, and if the objection seemed reasonable, she could decide to relent. She also realized that when necessary, she could deliver consequences appropriate to their inappropriate actions but without yelling. Cindy was amazed at how these strategies lessened her children's defiant behaviors, and you'll experience the same great feeling once you've mastered today's strategies.

DAY
(3) SUMMING IT UP

Today you learned why yelling is so problematic in parenting your defiant child. Reducing your yelling will give you a much greater sense of control as you manage your defiant child. Please remember the following main points about yelling when it comes to defiant children.

- Yelling is counterproductive with defiant children because it tends to increase their defiant behaviors.
- Yelling emotionally distances you from your defiant child in an unhealthy way.
- It's important for you to understand the reasons you yell so you can reduce this negative behavior.
- There are many hands-on, easy-to-use strategies to effectively keep yourself from yelling.

GETTING READY FOR DAY 4

- Stay mindful of the negative impact of yelling on your child's self-esteem and overall emotional health.
- Think of yourself as a calm, guiding coach versus a controlling, yelling parent.
- Make a list and stay aware of your yelling triggers and be sensitive to electronic communication exchanges that lack face-to-face cues.
- Practice self-compassion.

DAY 4

Rising Above Power Struggles

There's almost nothing worse than getting into a power struggle with your child. You know what I'm talking about—those times when you've taken one position and your child has taken the opposite position and neither of you is willing to change your position, so the struggle to "win" (or, more accurately, the struggle to gain power) begins. Power struggles are usually pretty intense, emotional, and ugly, and since you've got a defiant child, you probably get caught up in them quite a bit. Today you will learn what it is about defiant children that drives them to create power struggles. I am also going to show you why power struggles are so problematic when dealing with defiant children, and the role you play in these struggles.

You may think that power struggles are impossible to avoid. After all, think about those tense standoffs you've had over the time your child spent on the computer or phone versus cleaning up his room, getting homework done, and going to bed, or about your child's choice of friends. These are all likely to be thorny issues as you set boundaries for your defiant child. You are not alone if you feel locked into these battles where no one wins and no one surrenders. The key to sidestepping and rising above power struggles is to free your mind of the need to win. You will save yourself a lot of aggravation and grief by learning how to avoid power struggles with your defiant child. The fewer power struggles you have, the less defiant your child

71

will be. I have helped many parents and children end their power struggle wars. The good news is that you can end yours, too. Power struggles are almost never about the issue that you're fighting over. They generally occur because your child (and very likely you) is feeling powerless and wants to feel more in control. A power struggle is really about your defiant child (and again, quite possibly you) trying to compensate for her feelings of inadequacy.

Facing power struggles can be daunting. Many parents have shared with me their fears about the repercussions from power struggles with their defiant children. Believe me, I can understand where you're coming from if you can identify with these parents. It can be scary to think about how defiant children, who feel overpowered or powerless, will often seize power through revenge. They will seek to hurt others and will often engage in behavior that ultimately hurts them. For a young child of two or three, revenge may take the form of talking back and spilling or throwing food. At age five or six it may mean refusing to pick up toys. Then the consequences become more serious. Children age ten or eleven may verbally lash out at you, hit you, or break things. And worse yet, revenge from a defiant child at age sixteen or seventeen can be even more upsetting. It could mean drug and alcohol abuse, destroying property, pregnancy, school failure, staying out all night, running away, and even attempts at suicide. When defiant children act out, they are most often feeling powerless and discouraged about their own self-worth. The key to stopping this from happening is to learn how to sidestep power struggles. Consider the following statements, heard in the homes of defiant children everywhere.

"You can't make me!"
"I'm not doing it!"
"Stop always telling me what to do!"
"Leave me alone! I hate you!"

These are the words of defiant children driving their parents into intense power struggles. Defiant children can often seem to be in a good mood and then all of a sudden the power struggle switch is flipped. Like volcanoes erupting, these power struggles are often laden with hotly charged, overflowing negative emotions. On Day

3, you learned why yelling is such a problem and how it fuels your child's defiant behaviors. By making the commitment to control your yelling, you have made a huge positive stride in reducing your child's defiance. That's good news, because reducing your yelling will lead to less intense and less frequent power struggles. Unfortunately, they will likely still occur even if you don't yell. Defiant children tend to make provocative, rigid, challenging statements, like the ones on page 72, completely out of the blue, and they may seem to be about senseless, minor concerns. Today you are going to learn some highly effective strategies for avoiding power struggles. Once you're able to sidestep power struggles, you'll be able to reduce your child's defiance even further. Keep in mind that the skills you'll learn today should be used in conjunction with the ones you've mastered from Day 2 and Day 3. Each day builds upon the previous day, and you're gaining more and more skills to reduce your child's defiant behavior.

Defiant Children Have Unrealistic Expectations

The driving force behind the power struggles of defiant children is that they have unrealistic expectations about what they are entitled to. This is because they consider themselves equal to their parents (see Day 1) and tend to lack emotional intelligence (see Day 2).

In addition to all the hurt, anger, and resentment that result from power struggles, a defiant child may feel less loved by his parent after it's over. While he may not verbalize it, your defiant child strongly wants to feel your love and approval. At the same time, he yearns for the freedoms and choices of an adult. Most defiant kids I've worked with are confused—intellectually they know that they are loved, but they don't feel loved. When you yell at your child, disapprove of her behavior, and get caught up in power struggles with her, she can wind up feeling unloved by you. And she may hold on to the belief that she is not loved even after the dust of the power struggle has settled. It is the emotional immaturity of your defiant child that predisposes her to make these flawed assumptions. This can also be confusing for you as a parent. Clara, the grandmother of fifteen-year-old Odessa, had been raising her alone after Odessa's parents died suddenly in a tragic accident. As Clara described it to me, "I can see Odessa's wheels turning.

She can be so oppositional, demanding, and downright mean to me, but she also secretly wants me to tell her how wonderful she is."

Your Child Isn't Thinking Straight

Here's a good example of a child who pushed for power struggles. Nine-year-old Tony was brought into my office by his mother for counseling after he punched her in the stomach. During one of our sessions, Tony shared with me his skewed perception that his parents did not love him. Our conversation went as follows:

> **Jeff**: "Tony, so you are telling me that you are always getting in trouble?"
>
> **Tony**: "Yeah, because my parents are always yelling at me."
>
> **Jeff**: "Tony, I thought we agreed that since you have been coming here with your family, your parents have pretty much stopped their yelling."
>
> **Tony**: "Yeah, but for no reason they still never let me do what I want."
>
> **Jeff**: "Do you really think that is true, that they never let you do what you want?"
>
> **Tony**: "Well, maybe not never, but most of the time."
>
> **Jeff**: "Well, why do you think that is?"
>
> **Tony**: "Because they don't care about me. They just want me to be perfect."
>
> **Jeff**: "Tony, that's pretty huge to say. Why do you think that is?"
>
> **Tony**: "Because they don't love me."
>
> **Jeff**: "Really?"
>
> **Tony**: "Well, maybe they do, but it seems like they don't because I can never have fun because of their stupid rules."

Like most defiant children, Tony's mind was loaded with exaggerations and distortions. He felt his parents were out to get him and deliberately tried to keep him from enjoying things. My interviews with his parents suggested otherwise.

Twisted, unrealistic thoughts such as Tony's fuel power struggles that lead to defiant behaviors. As you learn not to get sucked in to power struggles, your child will feel more unconditional love from you. The challenge for you as a parent is to maintain your integrity and parental values while not getting caught up in the power struggles. Just stay with me and you will see an exciting new world of parenting without power struggles. Remember, however, that most good parenting strategies fail because parents give up too quickly. So please be patient and determined. Now let's look more closely at what occurs in these maddening wars for control.

Power Struggles Can Hit You Hard and Fast

Twelve-year-old Sylvia and her mother, Robin, had been working with me for a few months and had made great strides in reducing the amount of conflict in their relationship. It was no coincidence that the progress coincided with Robin yelling less frequently. Then one day, seemingly out of the blue, Sylvia reacted to her mother in the following way.

> "You're being a bitch, I hate you. I am, too, going to wear my jeans! You promised me I could wear them yesterday, and if I can't wear them today, I'm not going to school!" Sylvia had been arguing about the jeans for the past forty minutes. It was 7:55 a.m., Robin was running late, and Sylvia's jeans were filthy. Robin continued to do her best not to yell. In her most contained voice she replied, "Oh, really? Well, there is no way you are wearing those jeans." Sylvia then predictably escalated. "Yes, I am and don't even TRY to stop me."

When Robin shared this incident with me, I explained how Sylvia had been determined to create a power struggle—a very emotional one at that! Sylvia was bent on trying to defeat Robin and she was relentless in doing so. In the past, Robin's screams in situations such as these only escalated Sylvia's belligerence and defiance. But as Robin learned (and as discussed on Day 3), yelling shows your defiant child that you have lost control of your emotions. When Robin lost control of her emotions in the past, Sylvia's anxiety and frustration would rise along with her defiance. As she became more defiant, the situation escalated and they were caught in an endless cycle of conflict.

Sylvia ended up wearing the dirty jeans that day. Robin was naturally upset and concerned because in her mind she had lost this power struggle. In fact, Robin, like many parents of defiant children, wanted to give Sylvia consequences for her outburst. She came to my office for support to learn how she could have handled things differently.

Before we continue with Robin, I'd like you to do some deep reflection using the activity in the box below.

HAVE YOU HELPED CREATE POWER STRUGGLES?

Please read through these questions and use your answers to evaluate the role you play in the power struggles you have with your child.

- What do I fear will happen if I give up trying to control my child?
- What am I thinking during a power struggle with my child?
- What do I usually think or feel when I refuse to give my child choices?
- What are the messages in my head that prevent me from remaining calm when my child becomes oppositional?
- Why do I sometimes react to little things too strongly?

Your answers to these questions may reveal that you feel threatened and have negative reactions to your defiant child's attempts to overpower you. You are in the company of many other parents who have felt disempowered and threatened during power struggles. Read on for tips and tools that will help you start avoiding power struggles with your child.

Parenting Without Power Struggles

You can overcome power struggles with your defiant child, and there are more ways to do so than you may think. Let's get back to Robin and her daughter Sylvia. In helping Robin prevent future power struggles, I coached her using the following observations and suggestions:

- Robin first needed to understand what was going on. Sylvia had purposely created a power struggle over wearing those dirty jeans. She did this because she lacked the maturity to address what was *really* bothering her (it wasn't about wearing jeans at all), and she expressed this as belligerence. Sylvia was lost in her own emotions and self-absorption and her goal was to escalate the conflict until her mother was no longer the one in control.

- Robin did not yell, and this was a victory. If Robin had yelled, then Sylvia would have seen that she had pushed Robin's buttons. Had this occurred, Sylvia would have seen that she had gained control of Robin's emotions and therefore had won the power struggle.

Robin told me that at the time of this conflict, she was determined to give Sylvia consequences but she held off. She wanted to consult me first. I explained to Sylvia how forgoing consequences in the heat of this battle was a smart move. Administering and following through on consequences for defiant children can be difficult. This is because giving consequences presents yet another opportunity for conflict in which you are likely to lose power. If you present consequences in the midst of your child's power struggle, it will most likely result in more frustration for you and your child. (I will discuss further how to use consequences in my Discipline Without Desperation approach, described on Day 6.)

I advised Robin to modify her mind-set. My goal was to help Robin be genuine in responding to Sylvia but also to prevent the escalation of a power struggle. I suggested for future situations that Robin take a few deep breaths and then calmly yet firmly say something to Sylvia such as the following:

> "Sylvia, please don't talk to me this way. In the past, I'd have yelled at you but I am not going to now because it won't help either of us. I am asking you not to wear those jeans, but if you do I won't try to stop you. Just know that I think they detract from how attractive you are."

Sure enough, the dirty jeans issue resurfaced about a month later and Robin responded to Sylvia in a manner similar to that above. Initially, Sylvia just stared blankly at Robin and then she stormed out of the room. What happened next was a huge breakthrough. Robin walked into the living room and saw Sylvia sobbing. Sylvia shared with her mother that she thought she looked "fat and ugly" in everything she wore except those jeans. Expressing a sense of shame, she showed her mother pictures of models wearing jeans on some popular teen Web sites and shared that she felt deeply inadequate by unfavorably comparing herself to them. Had Robin not tried to understand her daughter, not resisted yelling, or been preoccupied with giving consequences at that time, Sylvia would likely not have opened up in this manner. Sylvia then apologized to her mother. She also told her mother about other things that had been bothering her, including her parents' divorce and feeling rejected by someone who had been a close friend. Robin and Sylvia went out that evening and shopped for jeans and other outfits that Sylvia felt more comfortable in. Robin wisely used this time to discuss with Sylvia the negative influence of airbrushed, glamorized Internet and billboard images of ultra slim models wearing jeans. She explained to Sylvia how these distorted and unfair representations of what young people are "supposed" to look like are not realistic or healthy. Sylvia appreciated her mother's calming reassurance.

How Al Also Passed Up Power Struggles

"Jeff, I just have so much trouble letting him win," Al said to me. Al was reacting strongly to my attempts to coach him not to continue to be a sucker for his nine-year-old son Ben's standoffs. He added, "When I hear him tell me 'no,' I just want to grab him and shake him."

Al was concerned that Ben was getting away with too much defiant behavior. I had Al make a list of every incident where he directly challenged Ben. Al's list had the following conflicts:

- Getting ready for school
- Doing homework
- Willingness to practice between drum lessons
- Getting along with his brother
- Going to bed at night
- Going to church on Sundays

In every one of these situations Al's way of handling Ben had been to yell, command him to go to his room, or take away privileges. Al was focused on winning these battles. When Al focused on winning, it usually meant overpowering Ben. The problem was that the more overpowered Ben felt, the more powerless he felt. The more powerless, the more defiant he became. One day Al came in to see me and reported a huge epiphany. His wife, Lois, smiled widely as Al told me the following:

> "Last night I really tried a different approach with Ben, and it worked. I told Ben that I really was disappointed in his choice not to get ready for bed. I didn't yell, I just told him that I was concerned and I walked away. Jeff, it was like he became a different kid. After about five minutes, he stopped playing his video game and he came and gave me a hug and told me he was going to bed. All the time that I was pushing him, all I was doing was making it worse."

So, who loses in a power struggle? The parent! If you continue to feel helpless and you get more frustrated thinking that you can't control your child, you will just get sucked in.

Al and Robin both had to *unlearn* their intense need to defend themselves. In each case, they realized that their defiant children had used antics to push their parents' buttons and gain power. Both of these parents learned that they did not have to defend themselves or try to convince their children that they were *right*. By avoiding emotional power struggles, they did not lower themselves to the emotional level of their defiant children. The most important lesson to learn from these parents' stories is that *they gained control by giving it up*. They produced different and positive results in their children's behavior and reactions to them.

Changing Your Mind-Set

Since what you think impacts what you say and do, your first step toward ending power struggles is to change your thinking. To help change your mind-set, consider the following:

- With a defiant child, it is not about overpowering her, it is about empowering her to feel better about herself.
- When expressed calmly and firmly, your views and beliefs are more likely to be heard by your child.
- No adult has ever reported a horrible childhood because his parents were too understanding.

Unfortunately, many parents have not realized that they may cause or prolong power struggles by the way they react. As you will see in the next section, keeping your calm while being firm (but not rigid) in your responses is very important.

Learn to Be Calm and Firm

Al and Robin discovered that the way to handle their situations successfully was to be *calm and firm*. They both got their message across but did not lose their own composure while doing so. The lesson learned here is that if you are patient and willing to view the situation through your child's eyes before reacting, you'll be better able to control your emotions. Even when provoked, you need to do your best to avoid responding to your child with hostile words or actions. You can still say what you mean, just say it calmly and firmly instead of yelling and threatening consequences. Al-Anon, an organization providing support to family members of alcoholics, uses the slogan, "Say what you mean but don't say it meanly." I love it because it so aptly applies to parenting defiant children.

In the example above, Robin was calm because she took some deep breaths and prepared herself for the interaction with Sylvia. Robin was firm because she let Sylvia know that her tone and words were not acceptable. Al was also successful using the calm and firm strategy. The chart on the next page will give you more tips on how to be calm and firm.

Ways to Be Calm	Ways to Be Firm
Remind yourself that being calm is your choice.	Allow a silence when gaining eye contact.
Remind yourself that your negative feelings are okay but reacting to them in a negative manner gives your child a negative example to follow.	Hold solid eye contact.
	Speak in a genuine and serious tone.
Take three deep breaths before responding.	Say what you mean but don't say it meanly.
Talk slower instead of faster. Remember that saying what you mean is more important than being agreed with.	Use "I" statements rather than "you" statements.
Don't raise your voice.	

Many parents feel so threatened in a power struggle that they are not able to be calm and firm. Usually, these parents are bent on trying to win the battle. Trying to win in power struggles with your defiant child guarantees that you will lose. By learning to be calm and firm and using the additional strategies I provide later in this chapter, you will have all the tools you'll need to avoid power struggles with your child.

Calm and Firm Will Not Feel Natural

As I've said in previous chapters, embracing the skills that I am giving you may initially feel unnatural and awkward. The same applies to my calm-and-firm approach. Al certainly felt awkward giving up his tough, old-school approach. And if Robin hadn't given up her old ways of dealing with power struggles she would never have learned what was really troubling Sylvia. On Day 2 I discussed how your defiant child lacks the emotional intelligence to manage his moods and problems. This lack of emotional intelligence not only creates power struggles but also perpetuates them. Keep in mind that emotional intelligence also refers to the skills to soothe oneself and communicate effectively. Since your defiant child lacks these skills, he's left with impossibly demanding and belligerent methods to attempt to get what he wants. Yes, it may seem unnatural to stay calm and firm at first. It also may seem counterintuitive, as though you are giving up your parental power by not joining in the escalation. Just remind yourself of the truth—your natural instinct to escalate will just take you to an ugly place with your child.

Your natural instinct to escalate in the face of your child's defiance comes from your fight-or-flight response discussed in Day 1. When you feel threatened, you get a surge of adrenaline. It is natural to feel some strong unusual and discomfiting feelings when your child is defiant. Just feeling your chest pound or hearing your voice quaver can be alarming. And, not surprisingly, the more the power struggle escalates, the more intense your physical reactions. Below are more suggestions for remaining calm and firm so you don't go ballistic or say things to your child that you will regret later.

Ways to Stay Calm and Firm

- Remind yourself that feeling "pumped up" by the threat of a power struggle is normal. You're experiencing the body's normal way of dealing with what it initially perceives as threatening and stressful.
- Remind yourself that your child will grow up and that this issue will not last forever.
- Feel good about yourself for taking responsibility for your own feelings and your own emotional reactivity.
- Make a mental and written list of the times you have resisted power struggles and read it when you question your progress.
- Remind yourself that the more power you give away, the less power you leave for your defiant child to try to take away. Trying to win just makes power struggles worse.

Don't Be Controlling

In addition to my calm-and-firm strategy, I also recommend using William Glasser's choice theory. Glasser stresses that the only behavior we can control is our own. When Glasser's theory is applied to people with children, especially defiant ones, the message is clear and simple: don't try to control your child. Being controlling won't work, and all you will succeed in doing is alienating her and destroying your relationship with her. Think about it. When you realize that someone is trying to control you, don't you get frustrated? At the very heart of Glasser's choice theory is the idea that forceful methods prevent children from acknowledging their own responsibility. If your child does not take responsibility for his actions, then he will blame others for his mistakes and unhappiness. Below are some examples of controlling and noncontrolling ways to speak to your child.

Controlling	Noncontrolling
"I told you to pick up those toys. Do it now!"	"I have been frustrated by all the toys not getting picked up. I am asking you to please pick them up. I can help get you started if you like."
"Either you apologize for teasing your sister or you lose your video games for a month."	"I know you were frustrated but I really have a hard time with the way you treated your sister. I am asking you to please apologize to her."
"You stay away from that new friend of yours, he means trouble."	"I'm your Mom and as you know I get worried. Please let me get to know your friend a little better. It would help me feel more relaxed about your spending time with him."
"You never eat breakfast, and obviously I need to make you start doing it."	"It is your choice, but I am asking you to please consider eating breakfast. When you don't eat properly it can leave you feeling wiped out."
"I don't want to hear about you needing to get to the next level of your video game. You better stop playing right now!"	"Let's find a fair way to work together and balance your time to get things done and your time to play video games. Help me give you time to play by first getting your chores done and completing your homework. I am willing to be flexible about a video game break down the road once we both see a pattern of you keeping up with your homework and chores. I really want to support you having some time to play your game, but I need your help, okay?

Each of these examples illustrates how you can sound less controlling. Keep in mind that calm, firm, and noncontrolling represents a parenting mind-set and not a set of prescribed lines. The examples shown on page 83 are only meant to guide you. Be patient with yourself if you initially make some blunders with your words. Remember to stay calm, firm, and noncontrolling with yourself as you learn to do so with your child.

As you combine being noncontrolling with being calm and firm, you will pave the way for some exciting, positive changes. Being calm, firm, and less controlling will dramatically reduce the power struggles with your child and his overall defiance toward you.

Still skeptical about this philosophy and approach? Let's look at Sharon's situation. Sharon was in the kitchen preparing dinner. Her son, eight-year-old James, came in and asked for a cookie. Their dialogue:

> "Not right now James. We are going to be eating dinner in forty-five minutes."
> "Why not? I'm hungry now," James insisted.
> "You know we don't eat cookies right before dinner, James," Sharon said with growing frustration.
> "Yeah, but I'm starving. Come on, just one cookie." Sharon stopped what she was doing and turned angrily toward James while holding back her scream. "I told you no junk food before dinner and that's all there is to it."
> "But I'm hungry. Why can't I have something to eat when I'm hungry?"
> "You are not going to eat a cookie before dinner. You know the rules in this house. You can go to your room now."

As Sharon and I discussed this incident I asked her if she had ever munched on anything while she was preparing dinner. Sharon guiltily looked down and then smiled. She admitted that she had certainly snacked while making dinners. Yet, she felt that as the mother she should set rigid boundaries and not allow snacking before dinner. But Sharon realized while speaking to me that her own "taste testing" was modeling to her son the exact behavior she didn't want him to exhibit.

She also realized that her commanding tone just escalated James's desire for the cookie. More important, Sharon was able to see that it was not so much about James wanting a cookie as it was about his wanting to "win" over his mother's resistance to his having that cookie. We came up with the plan that James would be her taste tester in similar situations. When Sharon gave James this privilege, he decided that snacking on junk food would interfere with his being a good taste tester. As you can see, Sharon effectively avoided a power struggle with James. She redirected James in a calm, firm, and noncontrolling manner to nibble on the food that she was preparing. Sharon also influenced James to eat something healthier than a cookie. By not going toe to toe with James and trying to overpower him, she empowered herself. James was able to delay his need for immediate cookie gratification thanks to Sharon's sidestepping her need to win the argument.

Now you have learned the philosophy of being calm, firm, and noncontrolling, and this will greatly lower the chances of your getting caught up in power struggles. The next important step is to pick your battles wisely.

Pick Your Battles Wisely

Your defiant child finds it very difficult to be challenged and to handle frustration, so trying to control too many aspects of your child's life fuels his defiance. The benefit of being calm, firm, and noncontrolling is that you will lower your chances of overreacting to any request, comment, or interaction with your defiant child. Even so, I suggest that you focus only on one or two of your child's behaviors that you want to change—such as not using foul language, or not hitting—and discuss and negotiate with him how this can be achieved. To help pick your battles more carefully, try to think about each situation from your child's point of view:

- Are you being unreasonable in your requests?
- Are you provoking your child by using a commanding tone and making a rigid request?
- Are you trying to control her the way you would a much younger child?

Beth, the mother of seven-year-old Teresa, used the following reasoning to remain calm, firm, and noncontrolling, and to pick her battles wisely. When she was trying to decide whether to let something go, Beth asked herself one simple question: "Will this really matter to her or me when she's thirty?" Beth said to me, "This really helps me look at the big picture. Then I put things into perspective and decide if something's really worth the fight." For example, when Teresa insisted on drawing pictures of her Barbie dolls before starting her homework, Beth realized that Teresa really did need that time to relax. Beth decided not to fight this battle anymore. Beth used to push Teresa to stop drawing these pictures, to fierce protests from Teresa. Beth told herself to stop interfering. She also told herself, "I'm sure at thirty, she probably won't want a whole heck of a lot to do with Barbie dolls."

Beth did not by any means become a wimpy parent. She just made a wise choice about what issues were important to focus on. When it came to issues of safety, Beth had a stronger bottom line. For example, she gave Teresa a clear message that she had to sit in the back of the car and wear her seat belt. Teresa got the message very clearly that her mother would definitely fight this battle if it ever became one.

To help chose your battles more effectively, take a look at the following hierarchy of issues to address with your child:

Priority of Battle Importance	Example
1. Behaviors, activities, or problems that are dangerous to your child's physical and emotional well-being	Walking in dangerous places without supervision
2. Behaviors, activities, or problems that are dangerous to others' physical and emotional well-being	Throwing potentially harmful objects at others
3. Behaviors, activities, or problems that are against the law	Stealing, and threatening to harm others
4. Behaviors, activities, or problems that interfere with your child's education	Refusing to do homework
5. Behaviors, activities, or problems that interfere with the running of the household	Destroying property in the house
6. All other negative behaviors, activities, or problems that you need work on	Slamming doors, refusing to take out trash

Start at the top of this chart and work your way down. Consider solutions for one issue before addressing another one. The only time you should break this rule is when you are getting nowhere after months of work. Then you should focus on another problem for a while and go back to the first problem after the new one is solved. The bottom line here is that you shouldn't sweat the small stuff, but make sure to be in charge of the important issues of safety, health, and physical acting out (such as hitting).

Nineteen More Ways to Avoid Power Struggles

Here are nineteen additional easy-to-apply strategies for sidestepping power struggles. These tips come from the trenches—from parents of defiant children that I have worked with over the past twenty-five years. Use the same mind-set I shared with you on Day 3 for applying these strategies. Don't be attached to immediate results, and focus on joining with your child rather than being her adversary.

1. Think "prevention."

Focus on what makes your defiant, easily frustrated child melt down. Be mindful of the triggers that lead to incidents, and try to identify any warning signals. By now you probably have a good idea of which situations are likely to cause power struggles. While there may not always be a rhyme or reason, you may find your child's defiance is more likely to spike with issues such as these:

- Your reactions to his clothes
- Your reactions to her friends
- Your request to him to discontinue being on the Internet, playing a video game, or watching TV
- Your requests for him to clean up his room
- Your requests for homework to be completed
- Disapproving of any of her choices

Try to discuss these difficult situations with your child during a calm moment and ask him for help in solving the problem. One of my clients had a fourteen-year-old son named Dan who complained and refused to take his medication for his attention-deficit/hyperactivity disorder (ADHD) at 7:00 a.m., which was the time his parents felt he should take it. Tensions had been mounting. Mindful of the idea of prevention, Dan and his parents came in for a counseling session. I acknowledged Dan's resistance to the medicine and asked him what he thought could work. Dan asked to take the medicine at 7:20 a.m. instead of 7:00 a.m. His parents agreed, and the power struggle was over.

2. Think about responding, instead of reacting.

Buddhist teachings offer the wisdom of "respond, don't react." I like this phrase because it is very consistent with the calm, firm, and non-controlling approach that helps parents bypass their child's (and their own) emotional reactivity. This is essential for influencing your child to become less challenging and more cooperative. Readers who have completed this ten-day program share with me that this Buddhist-like approach is key for them to avoid overreacting and fueling power struggles with their defiant children, allowing them to stay calm and emotionally centered while managing their stress.

When you react you are usually having a gut reaction, often based on fear and insecurities. Afterward, you likely realize that this is not the most rational or appropriate way to act. Opting to respond instead of react, however, involves viewing the situation as it is, and deciding the best course of action with compassion and cooperation.

Check out the responding versus reacting example below between Blair, age nine, who is full of anxiety about going to his first day of summer camp and is consequently being disrespectful to his mother, Shirley.

Blair to Shirley: "I hate this! You always make me do things I don't want to do. You never care what I want. Please, mom, just let me stay home and relax! All the people there are going to be stupid."

Shirley reacting: "You are being unbelievably difficult. Why do you have to make this so hard. You were the one who picked this camp instead of the others. How dare you give me attitude! You are going to be late and also make me late for work!" Shirley is clearly reacting by getting angry. She is yelling and this upsets Blair, and strains their relationship.

Shirley responding in a calm, firm, noncontrolling manner: "Blair, I can't accept you being rude to me. I understand, though, that you are feeling stressed out. Meeting new kids and counselors may feel uncomfortable at first, and I hear you that don't want to go to camp. I do think, Blair, that you will feel better about this after you go today. Let's go over your checklist to remember the things you need to bring for today. Doing this will help both of us stay calm."

As you can see in this example, when Shirley responds instead of reacts, she offers a validating and soothing acknowledgment to Blair. While there is no guarantee that this will make Blair's anxiety "go away," Shirley's response guides and coaches Blair to collect himself to face, and hopefully work through, his underlying anxiety by not feeling so alone in it. Shirley stays calm, firm, and noncontrolling and this allows her to see Blair's anxiety rather than getting sucked into a power struggle by blindly reacting to his defiance.

3. Suspend yourself from the ceiling.

Now hold on a minute! Before you sprint to get a ladder and start climbing, let me clarify that what I mean is to metaphorically picture suspending yourself from the ceiling. If you struggle with being able to understand your child, I suggest that you watch yourself and your child/teen interact from above. Doing this promotes mindfulness. Many parents express to me that their own raw emotions (usually fears) and consequent reactivity get in the way of understanding, *really understanding*, their kids. Here is one strategy that you can quickly use to stop yelling: you may recall on page 41 I mentioned the father who was in the toy store who looked up at the ceiling to help himself re-center. Observing him taught me a valuable lesson that I share with my counseling clients. The next time you feel like you want to yell, get some imaginary tape and fasten yourself to the ceiling. By self-monitoring how your child and you are interacting, you will have more control to make a better choice. I have found that when many of the parents I work with imagine looking down on the interaction with their children, they can rise above those thorny emotional struggles that sabotage mutual understanding. This paves the way for parents to give their children the validation and empathy that they so strongly need. I recall some years ago one of my own children really giving me the business. I felt angry and hurt and wanted to yell. Instead, I remembered the father I had seen in the toy store, and pictured myself taped to the ceiling. Doing this gave me the ability to see both her perspective (despite her abrasive delivery in how she expressed it) and my own reactivity, which would have just created more shared frustration and *anger*.

If you are feeling too initially reactive and overwhelmed to picture yourself on the ceiling, it may help to first take a few centering breaths to keep yourself calm. Once you are calm, you can truly rise above a fruitless power struggle with your child by imagining that you are observing from above. Give this a try and you will hopefully yell much less.

4. Give notice of time and transitions.

Give notice of time frames and time remaining before carrying out plans or actions. Many children react badly when interrupted and told to get their coats and shoes on. A five-minute warning works wonders. I have had some parents even use a kitchen timer, which becomes the reminder of when to get ready. If you take your child with you on errands or to some kind of meeting, tell him ahead of time how long it will take and when he can expect to leave. Try to prepare your child for any changes in routine. Defiant children tend to be inflexible. When possible, give your child advance notice of changes in plans and activities.

5. Watch what you model.

Remember that as the parent you are always teaching your child, for better or for worse. If you scream, throw a saucepan, or put your fist through a door, you are teaching your kids to be what you don't want them to become.

- Give respect so that you are more likely to get respect.
- Show flexibility and you will be more likely to receive it.
- Be a good listener.
- Discuss ways to solve problems without fighting.
- Inspire your child by the quality of your character.
- Stay calm, firm, and noncontrolling in expressing yourself.

6. Watch your pace.

To stay in a balanced, supportive mind-set and be a guiding, supportive emotion coach for your child, it is important to stay mindful of the pace of your discussions. You can stop a power struggle from accelerating by picturing yourself on a racetrack with your child. Do not let your child be the pace car! If you envision yourself as the pace car, the one setting the intensity and speed of interacting, you will keep better control over your emotions and your child will likely follow suit. In human relationships, when there is conflict, words can fly out of our mouths like race cars accelerating around a track. The faster you go, the more likely you or your child will metaphorically crash and burn. Instead, mindfully maintain a manageable emotional pace. If you feel yourself emotionally accelerating, note this and respond versus reacting, by easing your foot off the metaphorical gas pedal.

7. Be consistent in your boundaries.

I am honored to have a photo in my office of me with B. F. Skinner at a psychology convention many years ago. I was an undergraduate student majoring in psychology, and I was thrilled that this famous psychologist took the time to answer a few of my questions after his seminar. Dr. Skinner's theories on reinforcement suggest that we need to be consistent in setting boundaries with our children. Saying "No, no, well maybe in a minute . . . okay just this time" will give your child a very different expectation than if you say "no" and stick to your guns. Think about it. If you are playing a slot machine in Las Vegas, are you more likely to keep playing if you consistently don't win? Yet, when you don't know if you'll get what you want because you get it randomly, you'll keep pulling that lever. Your children are the same way.

8. State your case and then back off.

After you've verbalized your concerns in a calm, firm, and noncontrolling manner, don't get hung up on trying to get immediate compliance or a positive response from your child. Plant the seed and then let it germinate. This is a great way for you to practice not being attached to getting immediate results. For example, a client of mine named Leslie told me, "I used to try to get my Grace [her fifteen-year-old daughter] to acknowledge me when I was making a point but all that did was to get her angrier. Now, when I don't appreciate her tone or her behavior, I just calmly and firmly state how I feel and slowly walk away. More often than not, Grace will come up to me later and apologize. She never used to do this!"

9. Be courteous when you make requests.

I have found that many defiant children respond much more readily when the parents say "please" and "thank you." You may think it's futile to use these strategies in the face of your child's disrespectful words. But based on what I have seen, these courtesies really do reduce your child's defiance. This is especially true when your child may be used to your speaking in a more commanding and less courteous manner to him.

10. Think "compromise."

When you see a power struggle beginning, tell your child, "I really want us both to feel as good about what we agree on as possible." This conveys the message that you want to join with your child rather than be her adversary. When your child sees that you are interested in seeing that her needs are met, she may be more willing to cooperate and to go the extra mile to respect your needs, too. I advise you to brainstorm solutions to the struggle and never discount someone else's idea. Write all the suggestions down and then hand the list to your child first. She can go through them and cross off the ones that she doesn't like. Then you get the paper and the opportunity to cross off the ones you don't like. Usually there will be two or three suggestions left that the two of you can come to an agreement about. This is a great problem-solving method, and with enough practice, it can be done without writing anything down.

11. Avoid negative labeling.

Whether you just think them or actually verbalize them, negative labels are destructive to good problem solving, so try to reframe negative labels into more positive ones. For example, defiant children are often labeled "stubborn," so consider using "determined" as an alternative. Be careful not to impose the "stubborn" label or, if you already have, stop using it. Another important label to avoid is "liar." Instead, think of your child as not feeling emotionally safe or confident enough to accept responsibility for the truth. In addition, I have seen the label "lazy" hurt many children as well. As an alternative to "lazy," I like the term "motivationally blocked." Below are more alternatives to negative labels.

MORE ALTERNATIVES TO NEGATIVE LABELS

Negative Labels	Positive Reframing Labels
Stubborn	Determined
Selfish	Valuing himself
Jealous	Caring and protective
Controlling	Confident
Stingy	Cautious
Calculating	Deliberate
Anal	Careful
Pushy	Enthusiastic
Nuts, or crazy	Unique
Obsessed	Focused

12. Work on your own confidence and self-esteem.

The better you feel about yourself, the better able you will be to dodge power struggles. Give yourself credit for reading this book. Remind yourself that parenting is not easy and that you are trying your best. Think about all the challenges in your life that you have met. Above all, don't beat yourself up for your mistakes. Everyone makes them. Find support for yourself from mental-health professionals, other parents who may have been through a similar experience, or parents of children of a similar age who seem to be coping well. They may have some good ideas you could try.

Darlene, a single mother whom I saw for a few counseling sessions to address her self-esteem issues, triumphantly shared with me a three-word phrase that she found helpful to keep in mind: She said, "To coach myself and model self-esteem to my kids, I often think or verbalize, 'Know Your Value.' I say this when life gets tough because reminding myself to know my own value is comforting and it encourages self-pride to my kids, especially when I make decisions in their best interests that they may not like too much." Keep in mind that, as I discussed in Day 3, having self-compassion is also valuable to give yourself support when you fall short or even feel helpless or hopeless. Remember that working on your own self-esteem and self-compassion will enhance your ability to remain calm, firm, and noncontrolling amidst power struggles with your defiant child.

13. Use humor.

Despite my own children telling me, "Dad, you're not funny," I have found that occasional humor works to reduce tensions. Many parents have found that when attempted in good taste and without ridicule or sarcasm, humor can diffuse power struggles.

14. Give your child appropriate ways to feel powerful.

We all want to feel powerful, and if we don't have opportunities to do it appropriately, we will create inappropriate ways to feel powerful—such as power struggles or picking on siblings. In the middle of a battle with your child, stop and ask yourself, "How can I give my child more power in this particular situation?" It might be as simple as asking him for his help or giving him a particular job to do that he is totally in charge of.

15. Remember that less is more.

Please watch your tendency to nag. Use fewer words when you speak. An example of nagging is, "Why do I always have to remind you to hang up your coat? What do you think I am? A butler?" In this situation, you will likely get much further by keeping your request short and sweet. Say something like, "Please put your coat away. I appreciate your realizing that it's important to me." And make sure you say it in a friendly voice and with a smile.

16. Give choices and ask for input.

If your child is being overly negative and demanding, tell her in a calm, firm, and noncontrolling manner that she has two choices. If she wishes to stay around, she can change the subject and stop complaining; or, she can go somewhere else in the house to complain if she chooses. Choices help your child feel empowered. In the same vein, let your child know how valuable she is to you. Tell her that you'd like her to stay around. The more valuable to you she feels, the less likely she is to misbehave. In the spirit of the "joining together" mind-set, ask her advice on buying clothes or how to decorate your home. Ask her for new ideas to celebrate the holidays.

17. Say, "I understand; however . . . "

Should your child choose to escalate the situation, it's time to use three powerful words that can cut through any argument. These words are "I understand; however . . . " For example, "I understand what you're saying; however, I can't allow you to walk over to his house alone." Using these words repetitively (like a broken record), in a calm, firm, and noncontrolling manner will serve to de-escalate the situation without allowing your child to draw you into the power struggle. If "I understand; however . . . " is still met with resistance from your child, try saying, "We each see this differently, so let's talk calmly to better understand one another." Both of these responses put you in the guiding and coaching mode and get you out of the parent power struggle trenches.

18. Empower your child.

Don't be afraid to teach your child to say "no" to you in a respectful way. Your child has a right to opinions and choices that are different from yours. The key is to teach your child that this does not have to thwart an eventual compromise. I have worked with many adults who as children were not allowed to say "no." Most found a way to say "no" in a number of other ways such as rebelling or doing a job halfway. Teach your child to say respectfully, "No, I would not like to do the dishes, but I will sweep the floors and vacuum the rug." This creates an atmosphere of cooperation and support.

19. Not everything is a power struggle.

Consider that not *everything* is a power struggle. Despite his pattern of defiance, sometimes your child may actually *not* be trying to drive you crazy. He is simply thinking of his need for satisfaction and he wants some space from you. Don't view all actions as a rebellion against your authority.

Special Considerations About
Screen Overuse and Screen Addiction

The following are representative quotes from children in my practice expressing their views on screen technology use:

> *"There is like a fine line between using technology to be entertained and also to communicate way too much with other kids. It's cool to go online though because it just makes it easier to hang with friends even if you are not actually there with them. But sometimes I get way too many friends hitting me up with messages and I forget what I am supposed to be doing."*
> —ADDISON, AGE SIXTEEN

> *"Practicing math on my computer is so much fun! My mom and I found a math Web site that is so awesome. It is so much funner than listening to my teacher."*
> —CAYLA, AGE EIGHT

"I would rather go online and play a game with someone I have never met instead of hanging out with the jerks I don't like who live nearby."
—LOGAN, AGE FOURTEEN

"I see a lot of kids my age basically using text messages to spread rumors about other kids hooking up. Kids get really upset how fast bad stuff gets spread around!"
—ABBY, AGE FIFTEEN

"My mom—she just does not get it! I am getting teased—really bad—on a daily basis, actually I mean hourly basis! Those other girls are like so mean, saying and spreading all this crap about me. They won't stop spreading nasty rumors. I hate my life and I act like a bitch to my mom because she will never understand how humiliated I feel!"
—SHELBY, AGE THIRTEEN

"It's amazing how much attention people can get on the Internet, especially girls around my age. They upload pictures on Instagram and are flooded with likes. Girls my age become addicted to the attention they get online." (Disturbingly, as I have seen frequently in my practice, when Cody was in counseling with me it was largely to help him cope with the anxiety and stress of trying to "rescue" a girl he met online who was doing self-harming acts.)
—CODY, AGE SIXTEEN

"You get to like connect with cool people you would not see or meet in person but you don't get face-to-face experience." When I asked Audrey about the downside of not having face-to-face experience, she said, "It sucks though because you don't know as much how they really feel because they are not really in your life the same way that someone is that you go to school with."
—AUDREY, AGE FIFTEEN

"I've been around the growing and evolving technology for my entire life, and my parents taught me to pull it in myself. Within limitation there is a psychology that drives people, even adolescents and children to break free from control. It's a self-owning sort of mentality that tells us not to let ourselves be possessed. Technology however can be this controller over us if we let it be, which is why we, ourselves, must learn to moderate our own usage of it so that we do not let it become too large and dominant a point in our life."

—ISAAC, AGE SEVENTEEN

"I am fine with kids having your phones, tablets, and laptops. But when they let these things control their lives, I really worry about that. Technology is a tool. It should not be a hindrance."

—NINTH-GRADE ENGLISH TEACHER

On Day 9 I discuss what I call "stubborn obstacles" to outsmarting your child's defiant behavior. One of the concerns I mention in Day 9 is addictions and how they can drive defiant behavior in children. The ubiquitous presence of the screen-based technology with its relentless pull and potentially addictive influence on children and teens is a growing concern for parents. It is therefore important to give this topic separate attention in the context of power struggles.

With so many forms of enticing online and screen technologies available to children like never before, conflicts are common between parents and children over amounts of mutually agreed upon screen time. This concern especially presents significant challenges for defiant children who are prone to push boundaries and defy rules. The influence of screen technologies, while ever present, presents new parenting challenges never before faced.

Massive and Progressive "Screening" with Each New Generation

The most recent generations have witnessed colossal changes in how we communicate as a society. Each new generation is born into a faster rate of digital technology changes and advances. There have never been so many competing choices for kids to choose to focus on. Technology, in this sense, can also create huge distractions for children.

In past generations, parents were exposed to societal changes before children. In recent generations, however, children are exposed to the ongoing digital revolution(s) at the same time or even before their parents. To this point, I recently heard some parents joking about recruiting any available eight- or nine-year-olds to help them set up newly purchased "smart technologies."

RECENT GENERATIONS: FROM DIGITAL IMMIGRANTS TO DIGITAL NATIVES

Generation	Dates born	Description
Generation X	Mid 1960s to Early 1980s	Not born into the digital age, varying ages of adopting computer use.
Generation Y	Early 1980s to Late 1990s	Familiar with digital technology and media.
Generation Z	Early 2000 to 2010	Digital technology/social media is a natural, primary form of communication.
Generation Alpha	2011 and Beyond	Likely ambitious and driven. Will be part of an even faster changing world.

The above table, adapted from the book *Closer Together, Farther Apart,* by Robert Weiss and Jennifer Schneider, breaks down the generations born before and after the technology boom. The group of people born and raised before the widespread use of technology is called "digital immigrants." In contrast, the generations known as "digitally native" are those born during or after the general introduction of digital technologies. In considering what these terms represent, it is clear that beyond face-to-face interactions, our basic forms of interpersonal communication and social connections have been radically reshaped in the last few decades.

Those in Generation X (Gen X) mainly use technology for convenience. They have largely adopted use of digital screens. While they weren't born "holding a smartphone" like some members of the digital native generations, they are the first generation to come of age along with the Internet.

Generation Y (Gen Y) also known as "Millennials," are more familiar with interactive communication, media, and digital technologies than prior generations. While there are no precise dates when Gen Y starts and ends, the literature tends to cite Gen Y as overlapping the birth years from the early 1980s to the early 2000s. The single most defining characteristic of Gen Y is that its members use digital technology as a primary resource for communication, interaction, and information.

Generation Z (Gen Z) is also known as the "Always On" generation. This group has birth years ranging from 2001 to 2010. Children born in these years have never known a world without high speed Internet. In observing children and listening to their stories about how they communicate, engaging with each other through social media is as natural to Gen Zs as breathing. These children were born into a world of multitasking. Many have bragged to me about their speed of texting on cell phones wedged deeply in their pockets! Of course, the neurological, developmental, social, and educational impact of living with these kinds of technologies from birth onward is not known.

The next foreseen generation grouping appears to be Generation Alpha, which is the name designated for those children born from 2011 and later. This generation will face the most rapidly shifting technological advances ever.

A New Way of Life or Way Too Much Technology?

Research studies vary on findings of the amount of time that kids spend on technology on a daily basis. Some studies have indicated teens spend over ten hours a day and others cite children, preteens, and teens spend a more "modest" seven hours per day using technology. This includes computers, TVs, mobile phones, and video games and other electronic devices. Often children are using two or more technologies simultaneously. As pointed out in *Closer Together, Farther Apart*, somewhere between 71 and 76 percent of children's days are now digitally engaged or digitally enhanced. Dr. Shirley Turkle, a distinguished researcher on the societal impact of technology and author of *Alone Together: Why We Expect More from Technology and Less from Each Other*, speaks about the need for people to limit the use of popular technological devices because of their adverse effects on face-to-face communication.

The terms "Internet addiction," "technology addiction," and "screen addiction," have all been, to varying extents, used synonymously to describe the threat of children overusing technology. The line can be fuzzy about the extent to which screen use among children is normal, becomes excessive, or reaches an addictive level. You will likely be the best judge on the extent to which your child is negatively influenced by screen technology. The goal of this section is to illuminate this issue and provide some guiding advice on making these determinations. I will also provide recommendations on how you can help your child. In addition, I discuss further related suggestions in Appendix 2, Further Considerations with Age-Specific Guidelines for Managing Your Child in Cyberspace.

The general consensus among mental health professionals about what constitutes an addiction is best described as any behavioral pattern that interferes with healthy daily functioning. The same criteria seem reasonable for screen addiction. That said, addiction experts disagree about at which point any behavior pattern actually becomes problematic or still represents normal functioning.

Keeping Our Eyes on Screen Benefits

Before I discuss concerns related to screen technology, it is imperative to keep in mind that today's information age provides a myriad of benefits for our children. Knowledge of all kinds is readily available. A seven-year-old in my practice, for example, made a few taps on his mother's mobile device and enthusiastically shared with me intriguing information about the breed of his family's new dog. A nine-year-old taught me about her wonders of the world project that she had researched "just for fun." A teen client of mine discussed with me what he learned on line about the human body and how this sparked his interest to become a physician. In sessions many of my clients have used their mobile devices or my computer to build a connection with me by sharing music and sports interests. There is instant availability of limitless information to be gleaned from our virtual world.

The Internet is also a vast entertainment medium in addition to being a limitless forum for knowledge. Children share and show me exciting details of the thrilling and challenging games they play against other players from all corners of the globe. Teens tell me about digital screen connections with peers that have enhanced their self-esteem. These include positive interactions with peers with whom they connect via mobile apps, phone text messages, or other forms of instant messaging or video chatting. In many cases they have never met in person yet they feel personally connected and valued.

Emotionally Vulnerable Children
Are More Negatively Impacted

While the Internet can be a highly interactive, rewarding experience for children, it can also become a problematic escape from daily life. This is especially the case for those with self-esteem issues, including defiant children who may be more vulnerable to losing themselves in a world of screens.

The Internet can cause overstimulation and interfere with meeting the demands of day-to-day life. With one tap, click, or swipe, children can enter a different world where the problems of their real lives are no longer present. Excessive technology use and addiction among children is a problematic and growing concern.

In my practice I have encountered new pressures children face as a result of the cyberbullying, sexting, harassment, and stalking that exist in cyberspace. Particularly alarming for many of the parents I work with is the exposure of their children to pornography and their fear of their children's vulnerability to sexual predators. Similar to addiction to drugs and alcohol, the Internet offers children and adolescents a way to escape painful feelings or troubling situations. I have seen children who have sacrificed needed hours of sleep to spend time online and who have withdrawn from family and friends to escape into a comfortable online world that they have created and shaped.

Dr. Kimberly Young, director of the Center for Internet Addiction Recovery and an international expert on the topic of screen addiction, has shown that children who lack rewarding or nurturing relationships or who suffer from poor social and coping skills are at greater risk of developing inappropriate or excessive online habits. There is also speculation that children diagnosed with ADHD are at higher risk for Internet overuse and addiction. In my practice I have seen many children with ADHD struggle to break free from the clutches of screens that seem to pull them in. I have also seen this especially be the case for children who have autistic spectrum disorder (see page 239) and anxiety-related issues. Because they feel alone, alienated, and have problems making new friends, children with the above concerns turn to fictitious, video game characters and invisible, remote strangers in online video games and in social media forums looking for the attention and companionship missing in their real lives.

One depressed teen I worked with spent hours and hours online because his virtual friends were, in his words, "less dysfunctional than my crazy family." He explained that he felt a sense of solace in using social chat forums to distract himself from the chaos of his brother's drug addiction and consequent family upheaval. In contrast, I counseled another child in a similar family situation. He was, however, able to play sports as his expressive outlet. He added that at times in the past, "When I was spending too much time online it was making me a social loser."

As Shirley Turkle points out, relationships that begin and end through instant messages are edited and avoid the face-to-face vulnerability element that makes us all human. I continue to be amazed at the number of teens I see in my office who ask each other out and break up via text messages. This can make it challenging for children to relate to their peers in an emotionally intelligent manner. I even had an adult client I had been working with whose husband announced via text message that he was divorcing her and inquired how she wanted to receive the divorce papers!

I have increasingly listened to accounts of more and more parents struggling with prying their children away from the home computer screens, video game consoles, and all kinds of mobile technology devices. On page 104 is some information about what I refer to as screen overuse issues and screen addiction. Even if after reading the information below, you do not sense your child is experiencing concerns relating to overuse or addiction to any type of screen technology, this section may still be of value for preventing your child from escalating his use of technology to unhealthy levels. You can also find further strategies for excessive screen use issues in Appendix 2.

Is My Child Overusing or Addicted to Screen Technology?

It is important to acknowledge that most children and teens who use screens for doing such things as text-messaging peers, or using social media, or playing video games, learn to keep these activities from overtaking their ability to function within their families, at school, and in the community. They eventually learn to manage the inherent distractions, and "rush," that comes with technology. They attend school, participate in activities, hold jobs, and go on to college.

At the same time, many children become mired in screen technologies and this has a detrimental impact on them. On Day 1, I mentioned the *DSM-5*, which contains descriptions, symptoms, and other criteria for diagnosing mental disorders. This most current version of the diagnostic manual now lists Internet gaming disorder in Section III, the section of the manual titled "Conditions for Further Study." This section describes Internet gaming disorder as a "Persistent and recurrent use of the Internet to engage in games, often with other players, leading to clinically significant impairment or distress."

In addition to problematic video game use, I see in my counseling practice the problems caused by excessive cell phone use and excessive time spent by teens on social media. This is manifested in children not getting adequate sleep, avoiding and resisting doing homework and chores, refusing to participate in family meal times, and even neglecting personal hygiene. Dr. Kimberly Young identifies several potential warning signs for children with problematic or even pathological use. These are:

- Loses track of time while online
- Sacrifices needed hours of sleep to spend time online
- Becomes agitated or angry when online time is interrupted

- Checks Internet-based messages several times a day
- Becomes irritable if not allowed access to the Internet
- Spends time online in place of homework or chores
- Prefers to spend time online rather than with friends or family
- Disobeys time limits that have been set for Internet usage
- Lies about amount of time spent online or "sneaks" online when no one is around
- Forms new relationships with people he or she has met online
- Seems preoccupied with getting back online when away from the computer
- Loses interest in activities that were enjoyable before he or she had online access
- Becomes irritable, moody, or depressed when not online

Additional signals of problematic screen use can include:

- Unsuccessful efforts to cut back on Internet use
- Use of the Internet as a means to escape problems or sadness or anxiety
- Loss of significant relationships or educational or social activities because of excessive Internet use

By staying mindful of the red flags listed above, you will be aware of the multiple influences of technology on your child's finite capacity for attention and level of functioning. Drawn to the riveting allure of technology, preteens and teens are filling their free time with social networking, texting, instant messaging (IM), reading blogs, downloading and watching entertainment, and other electronic screen distractions.

Setting Screen Use Boundaries in a Calm, Firm, Noncontrolling Manner

On pages 106–108 are fourteen strategies to encourage your child to reclaim control of his life from the online world and screens. Having worked over the years with many children struggling with these issues, I can tell you firsthand that parents who guide and coach their children to manage screen use are more likely to have their children cooperate versus parents who impose unilateral sanctions in a demanding and rigid manner, which often leads to children rebelling with defiance. Some of these strategies may fit for your situation better than others. Use the ones that are most helpful. As you will see, the calm, firm, and noncontrolling approach underlies all of them:

1. Calmly tell your child that you are concerned about some of the changes you have seen in his or her behavior and refer to those changes in specific terms such as: fatigue, declining grades, giving up hobbies, or social withdrawal.

2. Empathize with your child about screen overuse and acknowledge how he feels threatened at the very idea of limiting screen time. Remember that validating his perspective will, in turn, help him see yours.

3. If you have a spouse or intimate partner, be mindful of your child seeking to exploit differences between the two of you. Children can learn how to appeal to the more skeptical parent and create divisions. If you are a single parent, take some time to think about what needs to be said and to prepare for the likely emotional response from the child. I discuss tips for single parents further in Day 7.

4. If you feel guilty about setting boundaries with your child for screen time use, consider that this is likely because of your own anxiety over your child being upset with you. Remember that defiant children can be masterful in having on-the-spot emotional outbursts filled with accusatory phrases designed to make parents feel guilty or inadequate.

5. Stay calm, firm, and noncontrolling in your demeanor. Say something like, "I am looking for you to help me give you back more computer time. To do this I am asking you to please work with me and not fight me on setting manageable boundaries for both of us."

6. To ensure that you stay calm, firm, and noncontrolling, keep yourself focused on responding without reacting, as discussed earlier. Meditation practices encourage this way of being. If you react to the emotion—or worse yet, get sidetracked and deliver a soliloquy to your child about her disrespect, this will

only escalate the power struggle. The bottom line is: acknowledge your child's feelings but stay focused on managing her screen use.

7. Be supportive and remind your child that you love him and that you care about his happiness and well-being. Parents often report to me that their children interpret questions about their screen use as blaming and criticizing. Engage in a conversation about what interesting things your child has been doing online versus demanding a rigid accounting of how much time he spends online each day and which Internet activities he engages in.

8. Remind your child that with TV you can monitor her viewing habits more easily, but with the interactive, online world you need her help and cooperation to become appropriately involved. If your child has gone into inappropriate Web sites, express your concerns in a nonshaming manner. Encourage your child to have an honor system to keep a log of Internet use for a week or two to build trust between you. Realize that if your child shuts down or balks at the idea of your monitoring his use, then you are likely dealing with his denial of problematic use or even addiction.

9. Become more Internet savvy. If you or your child encounter inappropriate behavior online, whether it's violent video games, cyberbullying, or online predators, don't ignore it. Act on the misconduct by talking to your child about the issue, openly but tactfully bringing up the subject with another child's parents, or reporting it to the appropriate authorities.

10. Take an active interest in your child's online activities. Calmly inform your child that you will check online history folders. Learning about monitoring software and installing filters requires a degree of computer savvy. Discuss with your child that you will be doing this, otherwise you will destroy the trust you are trying to create or enhance.

11. Do not fall into a shaming and controlling way of reacting to your child if you see signs of Internet addiction. I have seen too many parents react impulsively and rashly take the computer away as a form of punishment. This usually only leads to

your child pushing back—very hard! Most troubling with this rigid approach is that your child will internalize the message that he is bad. You can possibly gain cooperation in an Internet power struggle with your child by having a collaborative stance. If, however, you are reactive and controlling with your child, he will look at you as the enemy instead of an ally.

12. If your child continues to struggle with Internet overuse, make the computer visible. Perhaps you could move your child's personal computer out of his or her bedroom and into a common area such as the family room.

13. Ask your child to share his thoughts and feelings about his Internet interests and experiences. Keep the communication flowing.

14. If your child has a true Internet addiction, he will struggle with real withdrawal symptoms of nervousness, anger, and irritability. Seek help from a qualified mental health care professional if this is the case. Professionals with this expertise will work with you and your child to encourage and establish clear boundaries for limited Internet usage. I have often seen children restricted to an hour per night after homework, with a few extra weekend hours. Stick to your rules, collaborate with your child's therapist, and remember that you're not simply trying to control him or her—you are working to free him of a psychological dependence.

DAY 4   SUMMING IT UP

Today you have learned many powerful ways to avoid power struggles with your defiant child. Keep in mind the following key points as you move forward:

- Defiant children are emotionally immature and they seek out power struggles. You fuel these struggles when you try to win.
- Breaking free of your rigid internal beliefs is very important when you feel yourself being drawn into a power struggle. When you are stuck, try to approach the situation from a new angle.

- Presenting yourself as calm, firm, and noncontrolling along with choosing your battles wisely are keys to avoiding power struggles. Also, being attentive to your child in spite of his provocative behavior can defuse tension.
- There are many strategies you can use to avoid power struggles. Try to remember to use them in the heat of the moment and don't give up too early.
- The massive ongoing infusion of digital screen technology offerings can have a negative influence on children's ability to focus and manage daily activities and demands.

GETTING READY FOR DAY 5

- Stay mindful of the fruitless efforts of engaging in power struggles with your defiant child.
- Remember that it takes two to have a power struggle. If you don't allow yourself to get sucked into pointless debates and arguments, then there will not be any.
- Practice speaking and responding in a calm, firm, noncontrolling manner with your child and ask for feedback. If your child is too young or not verbally expressive enough to give you feedback, practice in the mirror, with your partner, or with a trusted friend.
- Look for the underlying concerns, often driven by anxiety, that may be influencing your child to be particularly rigid about certain wants and needs.
- Stay mindful of the rapidly changing technology temptations that compete for your child's time and attention.
- Take an active and supportive role in discussing and monitoring your child's exposure to online and technology influences.

DAY 5

Reinforcing the Positive Changes in Your Child

You are now almost halfway through my program, and you are probably already seeing less defiant behavior in your child.

If so, I know you're feeling good about the progress. If not, now is not the time to throw in the towel. It takes some children longer to lower their defiance than others. You must be realistic in your expectations, so please don't give up. If you continue to practice what you've learned so far and push forward with my ten-day plan, you and your child will be moving in the right direction. To get some perspective on how far you've come, let's take a moment to briefly review what you have done so far. You've:

- Faced the realities of your child's defiant behaviors
- Used the power of understanding to better appreciate your child's frustrations and limitations
- Learned to control your urge to yell and drastically reduced doing so
- Realized that seeing yourself as your child's emotion coach can help you avoid taking his negative behaviors personally
- Avoided power struggles by being calm, firm, and noncontrolling and by picking your battles wisely

All of what you've learned so far has been focused on stopping and preventing your child's defiant behaviors. Today we're going to take a different tack and focus on how to encourage your child in more positive behaviors.

The Power of Positive Reinforcement

This may be hard for you to believe, but your child really wants to feel good. After all, she seems to be angry, even nasty, so much of the time. As the parent of a defiant child, it's tempting to believe that on some level, not only does your child *not* feel good, she must *enjoy* not feeling good, otherwise why would she act this way so much of the time?

As the Dalai Lama said, "The very purpose of our life is to seek happiness . . . the very motion of our life is toward happiness." Whether we call it happiness or pleasure, all of us, even defiant children, like to feel good. So I ask you to take this leap of faith and believe that what I'm about to tell you is true: your five-year-old who refuses to do anything he is asked, or your surly fifteen-year-old who can barely stand to look at you, does actually want to be happy and feel good.

But even though defiant kids want to feel good, they don't always know how to do it. They've had a lot more practice not feeling good. Most defiant children have self-esteem issues because of their difficulties in relating to others. So it's your job to remind them *how* to feel good. One very simple way is by rewarding the five-year-old who gets dressed by herself in the morning and the fifteen-year-old who makes curfew.

Rewards work as an incentive for good behavior in both adults and children. If you think about it, any time you really desire doing something, it's because doing it will be pleasurable for you (a reward).

Young and old, we are all pleasure seekers. When your child gets something pleasant, whether it's a smile, a compliment, or a hug following a positive behavior, this reward feels good to him. The process of giving rewards to strengthen behaviors in the future is called "positive reinforcement." It's a powerful tool that can begin working to further encourage your defiant child to want to behave better, or more cooperatively, almost instantly. While it's important to reward all kids for positive behavior, defiant kids especially need to be rewarded. They need the extra positive incentive to compensate for their negative feelings about themselves.

When Is a Reward a Bribe?

Because positive reinforcement is associated with rewards—both verbal and nonverbal—parents sometimes confuse "rewarding" with "bribing" or "spoiling." Janet, the mother of seven-year-old Ben, recently asked me, "But aren't I just setting Ben up to expect rewards for doing what he should be doing normally anyway? Won't he get spoiled or expect me to give him rewards all the time?"

This is a great question and one I hear quite a bit from parents of defiant kids. I asked Janet to think about herself for a moment (something parents of defiant children need to be reminded to do).

> **Jeff:** "I see you have your gym bag with you. Are you working out at the gym?"
>
> **Janet:** "Yes, it's my one outlet. I try to go four times a week, at least."
>
> **Jeff:** "So you go and work hard because it helps your stress level?"
>
> **Janet:** "Yes, I guess so."
>
> **Jeff:** "And I recall you telling me your weight was important to you, so what about keeping your weight down?"
>
> **Janet:** "Well, of course, that's one of the biggest reasons I work out."
>
> **Jeff:** "So you could say that going to the gym is good for you because it helps your stress level and helps you keep your weight down."
>
> **Janet:** "Absolutely. It's worth the effort."
>
> **Jeff:** "So you could say that you're rewarded for your effort. Big difference from being bribed to go."
>
> **Janet:** "I see what you're saying. My stressing less and looking trimmer are my positive reinforcements. I'm getting rewarded, just the adult version."

Janet got my point exactly. In the world of work, most people go to their jobs every day, show up on time, work hard, and are rewarded, not bribed or spoiled, by a paycheck. They deserve it for all their hard work. And, wherever you are, if you are kind to others you are usually rewarded when their kindness is offered back to you. The common theme here is that all of these "rewards" feel good and increase the chances that you will continue to choose these positive behaviors. These are examples of positive reinforcement in action.

And as I'll discuss a little later on, rewards don't always have to be, nor should they always be, the nonverbal or material kind. In fact, the most powerful kind of reward a parent has to offer is simple, doesn't cost anything, and is always at hand—it's verbal praise. Think also about its power and value to withstand the test of time—I have yet to meet an adult child who complains that his parents gave him too much encouragement and praise during his childhood!

Stop Focusing on the Negatives

In general, parents tend to take their children's positive behaviors for granted and parents of defiant kids are no exception. "But Jenna is *supposed* to unload the dishwasher, so why should I notice or even say 'thank you' when she does her chores?" asked Katherine, a frustrated mom.

When it comes to parenting defiant children, parents tend to hyperfocus on the negative behaviors—the failure to cooperate, the failure to do homework, the failure to be home on time. Your hyperfocus makes complete sense. These negative behaviors drive you nuts! You got used to the defiant behaviors of your child; it became easy for you to think, "Why wouldn't Jason throw his food on the floor? He does that every time." Or "Why would today be a breakthrough day with Alice? She always acts like she hates us." Meanwhile, your defiant child has learned that you're more focused on him when he's throwing food on the floor and when he's slamming doors. Parents everywhere struggle with accepting this truth, but kids really start to believe that you only really notice them when they do something wrong. Your child may not consciously realize that when he misbehaves he gets a lot of your attention. But guess what? He knows it nonetheless. Kids may not always be rational, but they are very good at finding ways to get what they want most—your attention.

Parents struggle with the idea that their focus on bad behavior contributes to bad behavior because it seems so illogical. Why would Alice want to be yelled at? Why would it be preferable to just walking in from school and saying hello, or even to being ignored?

Unfortunately, human behavior is often not rational and kids don't necessarily make sense. Your child goes for the negative attention because he gets a powerful and often quick response from you. Parents struggle with this idea because, again, it implies that they have done something wrong—they've tuned out the positive and tuned in the negative. They have caused the situation. They are the mature ones and should have known better. Therefore, they are bad parents. But that's *not* the case. Your child's emotional immaturity and inflexibility have led him to cope in ways that create problems. You don't need to feel any more guilt. And you should feel good about the fact that you're actively trying to solve this problem and make life better for your child by reading this book.

You have been through a lot with your defiant child. You've had your patience tested, your feelings hurt, and your fantasy of yourself as a patient and understanding parent smashed. At times, you may even feel abused by your child. At the very least, you probably feel beaten up, and of course, as we discussed earlier, you are feeling like a failure or like something is wrong with your child.

Today's skills and strategies are so very important. By following today's steps and using praise and other rewards, you will inspire your child and yourself to focus on the joys that come with positive behaviors. Back in Day 3 I mentioned visualizing a TV with a picture-in-a-picture feature and making your child's challenging behaviors the small picture and surrounding this with a bigger picture of his positive behaviors. Today you will see how you really can change the picture to end this destructive pattern of your defiant child seeking negative attention. You can stop feeling guilty and stop worrying. My proactive approach is very liberating for parents and, best of all, it's so simple to use, and you can start right now.

The Time Is Right for Positive Reinforcement

You are learning about positive reinforcement today for a reason. Had I asked you to use positive reinforcement on Day 2 or Day 3, you might have thrown this book down in frustration. Two or three days ago, you probably would have had to work really hard to find opportunities to give rewards to your defiant child.

But by this point in my program, I'm betting that you're already seeing fewer instances of defiant behavior. Once the defiant behaviors decrease, you are now in a new and better position where you can "catch" your child's positive behaviors. When you "catch" and reward your child's positive behaviors, you increase his chances of doing more of them.

One of today's most important messages is that the more you encourage positive behavior in your child, the more defiant behavior is discouraged. This is true because:

- Your child can't be both compliant and defiant at the same time. So the more compliance, the less defiance.
- The more you and your child notice positive behaviors, including increased compliance, the more both of you will be ready to accept and support them.

Before you started my program, you had probably grown to expect what your child would do "wrong" every day. You just knew the bad behavior was coming. This always makes me think of the phrase that I first heard from one of my past colleagues whom I looked up to: "That which gets noticed gets repeated."

Your child's defiant behavior is prominent on your radar screen because it's something you find upsetting and frustrating. So you've paid close attention to it. Believe me, this tendency to zoom in on the bad is very common, and not just in parenting. I see hyperawareness of the negatives in employee/employer, husband/wife, and brother/sister relationships. Think about it: when your boss calls you into the office, your first thought isn't "I'm going to be praised." It's usually "Uh-oh! What did I do wrong?"

In my first book, *Why Can't You Read My Mind?*, I showed how couples tend to get caught up in and focused on negative perceptions of one another and how, alternatively, they could learn to see one another more positively. The same can be said of the parent–child relationship. You have to make a conscious decision to see the positive amid the negative.

Rewards Do Work

In my experience, over and over again, I have seen parents turn their children's behavior from negative to positive simply by offering sincere and consistent rewards for positive behaviors. Yet many parents still insist, "Rewards just don't work for us."

When parents insist that rewards don't work to encourage positive reinforcement in their defiant children, I ask if they are using rewards to stop inappropriate behavior rather than to encourage appropriate behavior. When one of my daughters was in preschool, I remember a parent trying to coax her crying and clinging child to calm down by saying: "If you stop crying, I will take you out for ice cream later."

Though I totally understand why parents do this—it's uncomfortable and embarrassing to be the parent with an out-of-control child in public—using a reward this way is a form of bribery and it simply never works.

The problem with this way of giving reinforcement is that your child will realize that if he cries at school, he'll get ice cream if he stops. Your teen will quickly realize that if she keeps her room a mess, eventually she'll be offered a reward, whether it's a trip to the mall or a video game, for cleaning it up.

When parents give a positive consequence to stop an inappropriate behavior, it almost always backfires. Because verbal praise isn't an option at the moment the negative behavior occurs, parents often turn to the nonverbal, material rewards, like toys or candy, to rescue them. When this happens, you are using bribery and encouraging your child to keep up the inappropriate behavior.

On the other hand, rewarding a child for her positive behaviors after they occur is quite the opposite and much more powerful. This is the parent who says, "I am so proud of you for this morning. You didn't cry and cling to Mommy, you went right into school. You are such a brave girl." And the parent who remarks to her eleven-year-old son, "I really appreciate how you ignored your sister when she provoked you" is catching him doing something very appropriate.

Rewarding a desirable behavior is not the same as bribing, and therefore it's successful. There are a few people I have met who strongly believe rewarding children for positive behavior is still bribery. I disagree. Your defiant child was on course for a lifetime of disappointments and rejection by behaving inappropriately. You're taking steps to help your child become more emotionally mature because you love him and want the best for him. Providing rewards for compliant behaviors is a positive and necessary part of that process.

Beware of Your Own Emotional Baggage

Some parents need additional support in order to reward their children. You may have received negative messages from your own parents about rewarding, such as: "We don't say those kinds of things . . . " or you may come from a family where there was a great deal of yelling going on. Here's something you need to keep in mind: verbal praise and yelling at your child for bad behavior cannot exist side by side. Yelling at your kids undoes the good work of praise.

The Power of Praise

Frank came to me an open skeptic about what he termed "wimpy, warm, fuzzy parenting." He had married his second wife, Judith, a few years earlier. He and his eleven-year-old daughter, Heidi, had a history of clashes, which often seemed to focus on Heidi's messy room. Judith was a stabilizing force in this small stepfamily, yet, as you will soon see, she felt the strain and tensions as well.

In the first session I reviewed my recommended methods for reducing defiance. Frank's rebuttal did not leave me feeling inspired. He said, "Well, doc, I can tell you that I am a yeller and that's probably not going to change. And my parents certainly didn't bother giving me any compliments as a kid, so don't expect me to be sugar-coating everything for my daughter."

I calmly, firmly, and in a noncontrolling voice (yes, the strategies in this book have even helped me with clients) explained to Frank that I did not believe I could help him if he kept up his yelling. I also told him that I thought parental praise was very important for parenting all children, including defiant ones. We agreed to put our counseling sessions on hold. Frank called me three weeks later sounding very emotional and asked to come in to see me. Exasperated with his daughter's ever-growing defiance, Frank had tried to stop his yelling and follow the other strategies in this book. Judith, as a wise stepmother, had been a relatively passive player in the family struggles. She had told me that her main coping skill when Heidi was acting defiant and belligerent was to grit her teeth. This, however, often left Judith feeling emotionally drained. With Frank's newfound support, however, I empowered Judith to use my calm, firm, and noncontrolling approach to express her own feelings to Heidi. The result was that there was far less tension in the family than when we started.

Only a few weeks had gone by before Frank saw for himself that he was becoming a more effective parent by praising and not yelling. One day, Frank walked by Heidi's room and almost lost his balance when he looked in. All of the clutter had been picked up. Frank's first instinct was to think that Judith had cleared it away, but she was just as shocked when he told her. As it turned out, Heidi, "out of the blue," had decided to clean up her room. Heidi explained to me privately that since there was so much less yelling and fighting at home she "thought it would be a nice thing to do for a change."

In a follow-up session, Frank told me that he was proud of himself for breaking the patterns of his upbringing by saying to his daughter, "Wow, Heidi, your bedroom looks really great. You picked all the clothes up off the floor, cleaned up your desk, and made your bed. How about I take you to pick out that new outfit you wanted?" Frank was shocked to hear what his daughter said in response: "Thanks for saying that Dad. I really don't want any new clothes today. Maybe next week. It's just nice to hear you like my room. I thought you believed I was just a slob and could never change." Both Frank and Heidi, along with Judith, had truly turned a corner in their relationship.

This is what can happen when you replace yelling with praise.

Your Expectations May Be Too High

Some parents refrain from rewarding their kids because their expectations of them are too high.

The first time I met with thirteen-year-old Michael, it was immediately clear that he felt disempowered by his parent's expectations of him. Michael had "accidentally" broken a stained-glass door that had just been installed a month earlier and his parents were very upset. Michael's father, William, was a successful real estate developer who looked like he had just walked off the cover of a men's fashion magazine. Michael's mother, Evelyn, was no slouch either. She was a very attractive woman with a commanding presence, the head of a large medical supply firm.

William and Evelyn both had complained to me that Michael was "lazy" and "every passing day just gives us more attitude. He didn't even seem sorry about breaking the stained-glass door last week." Michael's school grades were declining, and William and Evelyn told me he just didn't care about anything.

When we had time alone, Michael shared that his older sister, Eileen, a skilled soccer player and honor student, was the "star" of the family. He felt that nothing he did was good enough for his parents.

Michael was initially reluctant to tell his parents how he felt, but with my supportive urging he did so. William and Evelyn began to see their son as struggling to keep up with the family's intensity and achievements. Using a strategy from Day 3, I asked William and Evelyn "What if today turns out to be the last day of Michael's life? Would you want him to feel this way about himself, knowing that you could have done something about it?" Both parents began to cry and realized they had been playing a significant role in Michael's defiant behaviors.

I encouraged William and Evelyn to adjust their expectations. Michael was astonished when his mother and father told him they were proud of him for getting a C+ on a recent math test. Math had been Michael's most difficult subject and hearing praise for what used to be a huge bone of contention left him feeling relieved and inspired him to be more motivated. Michael later went on to become a solid "B" math student, admitting to me that once he felt his parents support, and then having significantly reduced fighting with them about his math assignments, he was surprisingly able to surpass even his own expectations!

Why Verbal Praise Is the Best Kind of Reward

Both of the examples on pages 117–119 illustrate an important point about the nature of rewards: you don't have to offer a material reward. In fact, Heidi even turned down her dad's offer of a new outfit. Why? Because she had already gotten the reward she so dearly craved: her dad's admiration.

Verbal praise is the best kind of reward because it doesn't come from a store. It doesn't cost anything. And most important, it's more meaningful to your child than getting a toy, a treat, or another trip to the sporting goods store. Of course, giving other kinds of rewards, such as more video game time or a new toy, or candy, or ice cream, to cooperative kids is not necessarily inappropriate or wrong. In some situations, it can be an appropriate and effective way to further encourage positive behavior in defiant children. (See the section How to Use Other Rewards Effectively, further on in this chapter, for more advice on giving material rewards.)

I have never met a child or an adult who did not, deep down, want her parents to say, "We're so proud of you," or, "I really admire the time and hard work you put into that." People of all ages crave the approval of their parents. You are a powerful person to your child. You always have been and you always will be. Praise from you has weight. It means something. And whether your child is eight months, eight years, or twenty-eight years old, he always wants to know that you're proud of him.

How to Verbally Praise Your Child

Now that you know how effective a reward praise can be for your child's positive behavior, it's important to make sure your praise is meaningful. When giving praise, it's critical to keep the following points in mind:

Sincerity counts. Even though defiant children view themselves as your equal, they also hold feelings of shame. Most defiant children that I have worked with have a hard time believing their parents praise because they often view it as insincere. Using the power of understanding from Day 2, you now can be sincere more easily because you view your child in a much more positive way. You have realized that his emotional immaturity and defiant behaviors were not behaviors he chose to have. To be sincere all you need to do is be honest and speak from your heart. Say something like *"I'm proud of you for being home on time."*

Your praise also will be perceived as more sincere and powerful when you make it specific. Telling your child what you are specifically praising him for helps him to know exactly what he is doing so well. A comment such as "Thanks for saying please and thank you" helps your child know exactly which positive behaviors they are using. This is more effective than just saying, "You had good manners today." Saying, "I really liked how you helped me load and unload the groceries with no complaints" is more specific than "I liked your behavior when we went shopping."

Less is more. To keep your child from thinking that you are being insincere, make your positive comment and then stop talking about it. Keep it simple: "You were so patient and helpful in the store today." Don't lessen the impact by talking on and on about it. If she shrugs it off as if she doesn't care, don't be fooled. You don't have to convince her by saying, "Oh, no really! I couldn't get over how much better you were."

She heard your praise and it made her feel good. Trust in the power of your positive words and let it go.

Show the contrast. It's important that you let your child know what exactly he did that was different from before and why it was helpful.

"Thanks for clearing your books off the table without my asking you. It really helped me focus on getting the kitchen cleaned up while you did that."

"I really appreciated how you went over and put food in the dog's dish while I was on the phone."

The sooner the better. Try to deliver praise as soon as possible after spotting the right action. The longer the delay, the smaller the impact will be on motivating more desirable behaviors. Naturally, a few moments might pass you by, especially in the beginning. It's still okay to bring it up by saying, "I meant to tell you that I noticed how you shared your toys with your brother today. That was very considerate of you."

Be varied and random. Avoid saying the same thing every time you praise your child. The more varied your verbal rewards, the more captivating they will be. Think about this for a minute. When someone passes you every day and says "hi" with the same tone and demeanor, you may start to get distracted by other things. If, however, the person acts more animated or asks you questions, you may become more tuned in. If you say, "Great job," every time your child does something good, that compliment will start to lose meaning. She'll think you're on autopilot, and she'll be right. Varying your comments will help your child continue to perceive your praise as honest and heartfelt.

Don't hold back. Some parents fear that if they praise too much, their child will rebel against the praise. As long as you are speaking from your heart and not going overboard, I don't think there's such a thing as too much praise for the positive moves your child makes. (See the box on the next page for some suggestions on when to praise.)

Praise Can Quickly Work Wonders

Marilyn and Alex were the parents of a defiant seven-year-old boy named Bobby. I had worked with this family for a few sessions, and they had made some very strong progress. When they first came to see me, Bobby was taking his frustrations out by hitting the family cat and throwing major temper tantrums. But as Marilyn and Alex followed my program, Bobby reduced his aggressive behaviors. During one of our sessions I asked the parents if they had been praising Bobby. Both Marilyn and Alex looked down sheepishly and said, "Not as much as we could be." When I asked why, they explained to me that they were afraid to "rock the boat." I helped them see that giving Bobby praise for positive behaviors would make the boat stronger and more seaworthy.

Bobby came in to see me a few weeks later with his parents for a follow-up visit. He was beaming, giggly, and very cheerful. When I asked Bobby why he was so happy, he told me how his mother had caught him doing something really good for a change. Marilyn and I both had a laugh as she said, "Out of the mouths of babes! . . ."

Following is a chart of positive behaviors that deserve praise. Feel free to photocopy it and place it somewhere for easy reference. It should serve as a helpful reminder for you to identify and reward your child's positive behaviors. Blank lines are provided at the bottom so that you can include any behaviors specific to your child.

SAMPLE BEHAVIORS TO PRAISE AND REWARD

Making the bed	Waking up on time	Using humor
Sharing toys	Being friendly	Finishing homework
Asking for help	Being spontaneous	Apologizing
Cleaning his room	Being conscientious	Brushing teeth
Being honest	Being creative	Being calm/relaxed
Being patient	Forming new interests	Inspiring
Being flexible	Stopping a tantrum	Complying with curfew
Being altruistic	Making eye contact	Being intuitive
Being independent	Starting homework	Using good manners
Expressing feelings	Walking softly	Complying with
Not needing to be the	Taking out the trash	screen time usage
center of attention	Speaking softly	expectations
Not interrupting	Being encouraging	Showering
Speaking quietly	Being motivated	_____
Walking the dog	Accepting differences	_____
_____	_____	_____
_____	_____	_____
_____	_____	_____
_____	_____	_____

Use a Positives "Catch Book" to Keep the Praise Alive

I have found that children appreciate parents keeping track of their praiseworthy behaviors and reflecting on them. Many parents have followed my suggestion to start a positives "catch book" to record their younger children's positive behaviors and review with them. As a tip, let your child help decorate and design this "catch book" to help him feel part of the "caught you doing things" process and to own its value. It is important that your praise include times when your child's positive behaviors may not be ideal, but still move in a positive direction. For example, if your son starts teasing his younger brother but then stops and apologizes, or starts to "give you attitude" but then backs off, let him know that you appreciate his quicker recovery compared to the full-blown bullying or past all-out shouting matches with you.

Send Occasional Positive Praise Text Messages to Your Preteen or Teen

If your older child or teen has a mobile device, you can send her messages to reinforce her positive behaviors and accomplishments. Text messaging among teens has become their primary form of communication. Texts from parents are often perceived by preteens and teens as annoying, especially when parents are asking for reassurance that they are safe or on the way home. Sending occasional, random, encouraging text messages will likely change your child's initial response to your message from "What do they want/what did I do now?" to "That's cool to hear."

One caution is not to be attached to receiving an immediate response. This can interfere with your attempt to be encouraging and supportive. If you send a text with strong expectation for a fast response, you may quickly feel frustrated. This can possibly trigger you going into reacting versus responding mode (as discussed previously in Day 4). Check out the sample texts below that I have coached parents to send to their children. I can tell you from what children share with me that they really appreciate these positive and encouraging communications.

Sample Text Messages:

"I am really glad we talked earlier and I like how we heard each other out."

"Your compassion for your brother really impresses me."

"I like the way you kept trying even when you knew you were losing the soccer game."

"Hang in there, I know your English teacher is demanding. I believe in you."

"KYV ... ... Know Your Value ☺"

Praise Penetrates Even Barriers of Rough Exteriors

Carl was sixteen and one of the most defiant teens I had ever met. Carl liked to be different, and his black nail polish and eyeliner screamed this out to the world. Carl was doing poorly in school, was hanging out with a rough crowd who frequently were in trouble, and insisted on his right to smoke cigarettes. Of most concern to Carl's mother, Delores, however, were Carl's threats to kill himself when the two had arguments. More often than not, the arguments resulted from Delores asking Carl to complete his schoolwork.

Carl and Delores came to see me after Carl had gotten himself in trouble and then made more statements about killing himself. A security guard at a nearby specialty store caught Carl shoplifting merchandise. When we met alone, Carl bragged to me that he had stolen other merchandise in the past but had not been caught. After a long silence, Carl said, "I know I shouldn't be doing these things, I just get so upset and then I act stupid."

Carl assured me that he had no serious intent to harm himself. He also told me, "I hate myself when I get in Mom's face, but she's on my case so much and then she starts going psycho and yelling at me. She always tells me I'm irresponsible. She also nags me to call her and then she took away my cell phone because one time I forgot. Dude, she even reads my texts and really pisses me off." I assured Carl that he was not stupid and praised him for his courage to be open with me.

In a session a few days later, Delores said, "Maybe it's just me trying to overcompensate for being a single parent, but I have this pattern where I nag Carl and then I go ballistic on him." I assured Delores that she was not the only nagging parent on earth. Then, after explaining to her the principles in this book, I asked Delores to resist yelling and to become more calm, firm, and noncontrolling with Carl.

I kept in mind what Carl and his mother had individually shared with me and then saw them together for a follow-up session. Good things were happening. Delores said, and Carl confirmed, that she had given up her nagging and picked her battles more wisely. Delores also stopped abruptly confiscating his cell phone and reading his text messages. Carl said, and Delores confirmed, that he was less argumentative, and more open with his mother when she gave him reasonable limits and boundaries with far less micromanagement.

We agreed that Carl would abide by a reasonable curfew. Carl, in good faith, promised to call his mother when he was out with friends. Delores phoned me a few days later to share some more good news. She had praised Carl for calling her to check in when he was at the mall, and Carl had told her that he appreciated her recognition of him. Over the next few months, Delores was pleasantly surprised to see that she and her son had less conflict and that Carl had pulled away from his peer group and was hanging out with better-adjusted friends. He also completed without complaint the community service work the court assigned him for shoplifting.

How to Use Other Rewards Effectively

Though I think praise is the best reward a parent can give on a daily basis, there are times when other rewards can work in conjunction with praise to further encourage positive behavior in your child. A new action figure, a bottle of nail polish, a video game, or an item of clothing keeps things interesting and unpredictable. You may recall on Day 4 that I mentioned I had the honor of meeting the famous psychologist B. F. Skinner many years ago. His theories about positive reinforcement are quite complex, but there are two major conclusions he reached that are germane to your situation. First, Dr. Skinner showed that behaviors are controlled by rewards. Second, when we don't know what the rewards are, we get even more motivated. This is why kids like surprise boxes and many adults like gambling casinos.

Follow these six steps when giving nonverbal rewards to your child:

1. Tune in to what your child values. It's easy to give kids candy or ice cream as a reward, but this can lead to too much sugar and even encourage obesity in some kids. It's helpful to know what your child values besides sugary foods. Extra TV or computer time, more phone privileges, a sleepover with friends, a Saturday at the mall—most kids enjoy these things and will perceive them as powerful incentives.

2. Involve your child. The most powerful rewards are those that are genuinely desired. Ask your child to sit down with you and review the lists in the charts on page 128. Come up with a few options together and agree to use them. This gives your child a goal to work toward.

3. Don't use nonverbal rewards to replace verbal ones. Use other kinds of rewards as complements to your verbal praising when you feel your child has shown a strong, positive change or accomplishment, such as making the honor roll at school, getting a B (or even a C+) on a difficult test, or not arguing with his brother for two weeks. Many younger children find candy rewarding. Again, please use moderation when considering candy. In the boxes on page 128 are suggested rewards for preschool/elementary-age children and teenagers.

4. A reward should follow good behavior. To avoid the bribery scenario, give your child a reward only after she does what you have asked her to do.

5. Be unpredictable. The more that rewards are occasionally unpredictable, the more powerful they are. Catching your child starting his homework early or studying some afternoon and spontaneously giving him a music gift card or that long-awaited new snowboard will further motivate him.

6. Finally—and this may seem basic—if you say you're going to give your child a reward, make sure you do it. You'd be surprised at how many parents renege on their agreements with their kids and then freak out later when those same kids don't do what they promised.

SUGGESTED REWARDS FOR PRESCHOOL/ELEMENTARY-SCHOOL-AGE CHILDREN

Playing with clay or Play-Doh

Helping Mom or Dad

Going out for ice cream

Going to the park

Playing a board game with Dad or Mom

Exploring fun child-oriented Web sites with mom or dad

Bouncing on the bed

Staying up later

Playing with friends

Going someplace alone with Dad or Mom

Having a longer time in the bathtub

Playing in the sandbox

Going to the library

Playing outside

Going to the zoo

Riding on Dad's shoulders

Helping plan the day's activities

Playing a game on your mobile device

Riding a bicycle with Dad or Mom

Feeding a pet

Making noises with rattles, pans, or bells

Drawing with crayons

Going to the movies

Getting a new video game

Eating out

SUGGESTED REWARDS FOR PRETEENS/TEENS

Getting a new or more recent model cell phone

Finding a part-time job

Going to summer camp

Being allowed to sit alone when the family eats out

Having her own checking account

Changing his room around

Computer time

Watching a video

Redecorating her own room

Listening to songs

Taking the car to school for a day (for teenagers with licenses)

Getting a special haircut or hair style

Inviting a friend to eat out

Concert tickets

Participating in activities with friends

Making a trip alone that is deemed safe

Getting to stay out later than usual

Getting to sleep late on the weekend

Going shopping with friends

Going to Disney World or some other amusement park

Purchasing a new video game

Skateboarding

Receiving money for a new purchase

Don't Forget to Focus on Their Efforts

Though we've talked a lot about behavior and accomplishments, your child's efforts are just as important. Praise and other rewards are powerful positive reinforcement tools to help increase any demonstrated positive behaviors. I also want to stress how important encouragement is. Encouragement focuses on your child's efforts. Praise focuses on results. Both are valuable in reinforcing appropriate behaviors. To help give solid encouragement to your child, try the following:

Show unconditional acceptance. As in the earlier example with Michael, parents who are high achievers sometimes, wittingly or unwittingly, send the message that they accept their children only as long as they perform to their parents' standards. Because all children have a fundamental need to belong, to feel accepted and wanted—especially by their parents—having your acceptance be conditional on achievements can undermine your child's self-esteem.

Be supportive with failures. Self-esteem, as I mentioned earlier, is often a core, problematic issue in defiant children. Self-esteem is built on having positive reflections on achievements. At the same time, self-compassion (as discussed earlier in Day 3) is about how we support ourselves in the face of our failures, which is also very important for your child's emotional health. Keep coaching your child to see her shortfalls and failures as opportunities for growth.

Show confidence. All children can learn, though some may take longer than others to master a concept or a skill. Your confidence in your child's ability to keep going when she experiences frustration and defeat, your confidence that she'll eventually succeed, your confidence that she'll make something useful of her life—this is the encouragement that can make the difference between success and failure. To show confidence, you really have to believe that your child is capable of success. If you don't believe in her, then she has to overcome your doubts as well as her own.

Look for past examples of strengths to encourage your child to take the next step. We all do well by recalling our past successes.

Anchoring yourself in past successes can provide motivation for new challenges. Defiant children tend to dismiss what they did well in the past. You can encourage your child by reminding him in a calm, firm, noncontrolling way about what he has done well in the past. This is demonstrated in the example below:

"You did a great job writing that paper on Abraham Lincoln. I know you can tackle this one."

Break larger tasks into smaller ones. Defiant children lack flexibility and can easily become overwhelmed, as when they're given more involved school assignments. Here is an example of how words of encouragement can be used to reduce the demands and the stress that come with difficult challenges.

"I know this assignment is longer than you are used to, but I'll bet if you break it down into sections, it will come out really well when you are done."

Keep the Love Flowing

I think by now you've tuned into my number one parenting philosophy: there's no such thing as being too loving toward your child. It's important to do your best to let your child know through your words and actions that you love and value her. Now that you have gained considerable skills in curbing and reducing defiant behaviors, try to keep your acceptance as free and unconditional as possible. Statements such as these will be deeply appreciated by your child:

- "I really enjoy being with you."
- "I love hearing that great laugh of yours."
- "I know you're disappointed about not making the team, but you tried your best, and that's what's important."
- "I'm glad you're my son."

Be liberal in showing your understanding and love. Try to be patient and understanding about her mistakes and any temporary setbacks. Don't criticize her in front of others. Take time daily to listen and talk to your child and show interest in her activities. Change up the ways that you interact with your child and give affirming messages. As mentioned earlier, text messages can have a powerful impact with kids as they often see text messages as being "important" not to miss. Use texts to communicate the bullet points on page 130.

At the same time, don't dismiss the sanctity of face-to-face, real-time, unedited connections. There is no law that everything has to be communicated electronically. Even though teens seem to favor this medium, and even though you can easily join that "screen world" with your child, I suggest you also "keep it real" by *being real*. Never minimize the power of those face-to-face, shared physical space moments when giving your child praise. And, of course, don't be afraid to touch, hug, and kiss your child. Let her know that no matter what happens, you will always love her.

Positive Reinforcement Can Help You, Too

The focus of this book so far has been on skills that you can use with your child, but it's just as important that you praise and reinforce yourself as well.

I want to congratulate you right now for reaching the halfway point of my program. Think of the thought and energy you are putting into your parenting! You are willing to try to improve yourself as a parent, and that is something you should be very proud of. By giving yourself credit you are also helping your child. I tell the parents I work with, "Gold floats downstream and so do other things." The better you feel about yourself, the better your child will feel about herself.

GIVE YOURSELF CREDIT AS A PARENT

Go through the list of positive behaviors below and pat yourself on the back for all the ones you can check off.

_____ Helped with potty training	_____ Taught to tie shoes
_____ Cooked meals	_____ Helped teach to read
_____ Picked out clothes	_____ Helped with homework
_____ Gave baths	_____ Took to playdates

_____ Read stories at night

_____ Attended teacher
conferences

_____ Took bowling

_____ Hosted sleepovers

_____ Provided affection

_____ Attended school concerts

_____ Watched school sports
events

_____ Expressed love

_____ Decorated house for
the holidays

_____ Listened to briefings
of the day

_____ Loved despite
defiance directed
at you

No matter how many of the above positive parenting behaviors you have done, you should feel good about them. As you will see in the next section, how you talk to yourself plays a big role in how you feel about all the great things you have done and the mistakes you have made.

Reward Yourself with Positive Self-Talk

Self-talk is the conversation you have with yourself in your mind. We all do it, and more often than we are aware. Your self-talk may be about what to get when you go shopping, when to get your car's oil changed, planning your next activity, or reflecting on what others are doing. When your self-talk is positive, you are likely to be calmer and more relaxed. For example, if you say to yourself, "I feel good about how I handled that conflict" or "I'm glad I did not yell," you are praising yourself and you will feel less stressed.

Negative self-talk, such as "I never should have been a parent" or "I'm hopeless," will do the opposite and reduce your confidence. Pay closer attention to your self-talk and do your best to keep it positive. Many people assume that others around them produce these feelings. A perfect example of this is when your defiant child says something like "You make me angry!" as if you have control over how he feels. The reality is that people can't *make* you feel anything. It's the way you *perceive people's actions* that causes you to feel what you feel.

You will feel much better about your parenting efforts if you stay mindful of all the positive things you have done for your child. I also encourage you to be wary of any negative self-talk messages you may give yourself, such as:

- "I'm a mean mother."
- "I never get a moment to myself."
- "I just am not cut out to be a parent"
- "Everyone takes, takes, takes, and no one gives to me."

As you may recall from Day 2, if you give your child a negative label, he will live up to it. The same applies to you. Trashing yourself as a parent in the face of a setback or problem only makes matters worse and diminishes all your previous efforts and the changes you have made. If you make it a point to avoid these negative thoughts about yourself and your parenting situation, you will feel better.

As an alternative to those negative messages, here are some examples of positive self-talk:

- "Even though I made a mistake, I can still try to be the best mom I can be."
- "I can take some time for myself and not feel guilty."
- "I feel good about being calm, firm, and noncontrolling in stating boundaries even if they aren't immediately accepted."
- "Although it's nice to be appreciated, I don't have to have my child's approval to feel good."

As you can see from the negative self-talk examples, they are overgeneralized and focused on the downside of parenting. And as you know from dealing with your defiant child, it's easy to focus solely on the problems. Here are some positive self-talk statements that will help you focus on your strengths as a parent:

- "This is an opportunity to teach my child something new."
- "I just need to take one step at a time and do what I can."
- "I can stay calm when my child is being difficult."
- "Being calm, firm, and noncontrolling helps me stay centered and less reactive."
- "Just because I slipped and yelled today does not mean I have to keep doing it."
- "I can pick my battles wisely to gain my child's cooperation."
- "I am a good parent."
- "I do the best I can."

- "I may make mistakes, but that doesn't make me a less valuable person."
- "It's okay if I feel frustrated or anxious."
- "I am not helpless. I have people and resources to call upon if I need to."
- "In the big picture, this is really not a big deal."
- "I won't put pressure on myself to be the perfect parent."
- "I can still enjoy life, even if it is hard."

Give Yourself Other Rewards

I encourage you to reward yourself once in a while in material ways as well. Being a parent of a defiant child is very depleting. Even though this book is aimed at reducing your child's defiant behavior, your job as a parent will still be filled with demands and challenges. Think about it this way: by giving to yourself, you are giving a better self to your child. Some examples of rewards you might enjoy include:

- Getting your nails done
- Taking a soothing bath
- Purchasing a new song or album
- Going out for dinner
- Getting away for an overnight or weekend without children
- Upgrading your cell phone
- Exercising
- Staying connected to your spirituality
- Taking a new adult education class
- Buying a new outfit
- Reading a new book you've been interested in

DAY
5

SUMMING IT UP

Today you learned about the power of praise and other rewards to reinforce positive behaviors in your child. Remember how much progress you have made since Day 1. Keep in mind the following key points about reinforcing positive behaviors in your child.

- Praise, if given in the correct manner, can significantly increase your child's positive behaviors.
- Increasing positive behaviors lessens the frequency of defiant behaviors.
- Other rewards can be combined with praise in recognizing your child's positive behaviors.
- Encouraging your child's efforts and freely expressing love are very important gifts to give.
- Reinforcing yourself for your positive parenting efforts and actions is very valuable to both you and your child.

GETTING READY FOR DAY 6

- Remind yourself and stay aware of how much verbal praise means to you and your child.
- Speak from your heart and trust the process of encouraging and praising your child.
- Remember to focus on your child's efforts as well as accomplishments.
- Be creative in sharing your praise. Make it a point to give praise face-to-face and also to include reaching out through other means, such as text messaging.
- Give yourself positive reinforcement for being the best parent you can be and still striving to be even better.

DAY
6

Discipline Without Desperation

Welcome to Day 6 and the world of discipline. By the time you are finished reading today, you will understand how to apply Discipline Without Desperation and when and how to use consequences with your defiant child. You have already learned that viewing yourself in a coaching role helps you to avoid and get out of the emotionally reactive booby traps that are easy to fall into as a parent of a defiant child. What you will discover today builds on using discipline in a far more collaborative, encouraging, and effective—versus punitive and ineffective—manner.

As the parent of a defiant child, you've probably tried to use many forms of discipline. You're not alone if you've found the topic of discipline (and trying to administer it) very confusing. Many parents attempt to discipline their children when they're upset and end up wondering if they did the right thing or if they were too hard or soft on their children.

To make matters worse, an overwhelming sea of information exists about discipline. So many books and so many experts! As you try to make sense of it all, you can easily end up with even more maddening confusion about what to do. Well, here's the good news: today you can begin to relax, because I am going to give you a clear and extremely reliable approach to disciplining your child.

I have met with countless parents who offer me a litany of ways they have tried to discipline their defiant children. Often, as they describe their discipline strategies, they throw up their hands in exasperation and say, "Nothing works!" Or they tell me that they're there to see me because they're just not sure how to discipline their child.

In describing her frustration about discipline, Debbie, the mother of defiant eleven-year-old Rubin, said, "I give him consequence after consequence and they just don't seem to faze him at all!" Debbie represents what I term, "consequence ravenous" parents. These are the abundant number of parents who become so frustrated and desperate that they keeping pushing, seemingly powerful at the time, yet in actuality, feeble, consequences on their child—later realizing that they are to no avail. Have you ever been there? Most of us have, at least to some extent. It is easy to become frustrated and desperate after doling out increasingly severe consequences that are ineffective in the eyes and ears of your defiant child.

Discipline Without Desperation integrates and builds on the calm, firm, noncontrolling approach to help you work smarter rather harder in managing your child's challenging behaviors. Managing your own stress levels as you go forth setting limits, boundaries, and consequences is key to feeling in control. Thinking of yourself as a coach and guide will help you employ Discipline Without Desperation. Taking care of yourself as a parent and making discipline a connecting versus disconnecting experience to help your child learn from his mistakes is what this chapter is all about.

I have also seen the stress that couples go through in their own relationship when they see their attempts to discipline their child fail. Many parents, when discussing with me what forms of discipline they have tried, end up arguing with one another in the counseling session. I watch them get increasingly frustrated as they try to make sense out of what's been happening.

One night (coincidentally, during the time I was writing this chapter), Beverly and Andre came in for a session with their twelve-year-old son, Brian. During my initial phone call with Beverly, she told me that Andre was too strict and that she was too easy on Brian. Yet, when they came in to speak with me, I discovered it was really the other way around. Brian just smirked while each parent became more and more confused trying to make sense of things. Brian freely admitted to me that he would privately complain to each parent that the other was not fair. He leaned back in his chair and said, "Yep, I've definitely got their number."

You may feel that no discipline of any kind has ever worked with your child. If so, you are certainly not the only one who feels that way. Remember that compared to other children, defiant children are very challenging and very resistant to discipline. This is because they are emotionally immature, inflexible, reactive, and have difficulty working through conflicts. And let's face it, up to this point, discipline has probably been a pretty emotional area for you as well. In light of these complexities, it's time for you to learn some smart discipline techniques that will work for you in even the toughest of situations. Stay mindful that the best discipline you can give your child is having your own self-discipline to respond to him in a calm, firm, and noncontrolling manner!

Before reading further, please complete the activity in the box below so you can begin to better understand what discipline means to you.

WHAT DOES DISCIPLINE MEAN TO YOU?

As you answer the following questions about discipline, draw from your own experiences growing up; what you have read, and what you have learned.

- Describe your definition of discipline.
- What experiences in your life shaped this definition?
- What gets in the way of you disciplining your child?
- How has your child responded to your discipline attempts?
- How have you felt before, during, and after you discipline your child?

Now that you have a better handle on your own views of discipline, I'd like to share some of my ideas on the subject. Consider for a moment the term "discipline" and its definition. Discipline comes from the word "disciple," which means to teach. To use discipline effectively, you have to view it as a way to teach and support your child. Effective discipline takes in-depth understanding and practice, especially with defiant children. You need to look at your defiant child in a different way. Your child is emotionally immature and needs all the help she can get with her impulsivity, overreactions, and problems in communicating her feelings. Each day of this program I have been challenging you to work with your child differently and manage her emotional limitations. Discipline Without Desperation is just another piece of the puzzle.

Remember on Day 4 when I talked about the importance of joining with your child rather than being his adversary? That's a key component in making Discipline Without Desperation work for you. Parents often think of discipline as a way to "show my child who is boss" or "make him pay for his mistakes." I'm all for supporting your parental authority and having your child be accountable for his negative actions, but you must begin to consider discipline as a way to teach and support your child rather than a way to win back control. This is the only way to make discipline work for you.

When it comes to disciplining defiant children, parents tend to get hung up on what they believe should work rather than on what is actually effective. For example, many parents model disciplining their children on how they were disciplined by their parents or on what they think is the "right thing to do." Often this involves using punishment, or applying a penalty in a harsh way. If you operate like this, you're telling your child, "I'm going to make you see that you are wrong by making you see that I am right." But then you'll never understand why your child misbehaved in the first place and what you can do realistically to prevent such misbehavior from occurring again.

The bottom line is that punishment does not teach or support your child to make important positive changes. Instead, a punishment approach uses shame, control, and intimidation to influence your child to behave differently. Nothing will fail more quickly when trying to encourage positive changes in your defiant child than blindly and rigidly adhering to this approach.

What I'm asking you to do is view effective discipline just the way you would effective teaching. This means striving to encourage and support your child to learn and make good choices. And when he does not make a good choice, help him learn from his mistakes instead of overzealously punishing him.

Mastering the art of discipline starts and ends with a strong and positive relationship between you and your child. Defiant children are much less likely to misbehave when they feel understood and not controlled. As you will see as you read on, keeping your relationship strong with solid understanding and love empowers you to be patient and to avoid overreacting. This also allows you to set reasonable boundaries. Once you think of discipline in this manner, it will become much easier to carry it out.

I have developed an approach to discipline, which I call Discipline Without Desperation, that I've found works wonders with defiant children. So what does Discipline Without Desperation mean?

Discipline Without Desperation Is About Love and Understanding

You know by now that I am a big advocate for giving your child all the love and approval you can. Discipline works best when you and your child have a strong mutual understanding. Discipline Without Desperation means using that understanding to guide your child without emotional upheavals and drama.

Your defiant child may very well continue to "test" just how understanding you are. Parents of defiant kids can get very upset because they don't believe their children are remorseful for their misbehavior. You are not alone if this is the case with your child. Defiant children tend not to show remorse as often as their parents would like. But the problems will only escalate if you become distraught about this lack of remorse on the part of your child. Trust me: many defiant children in my practice express remorse to me but they initially tend to feel too vulnerable to express this to their parents. As I said on Day 2, defiant children lack emotional maturity and coping skills, and this leads them to test you. If you become emotional about this it will prevent you from giving discipline in an effective manner. The best way to avoid this trap is to stay mindful that a lack of remorse is part of the whole defiant-child package. In other words, don't take it all so personally! As you have been following my plan, hopefully you have continued to see a reduction in your child's defiance. The more you understand your child's misbehavior, the more effective you can be in disciplining her.

I'm going to share with you some of my thoughts about why children misbehave, using examples from my counseling sessions with defiant children and their families.

Andrea wanted attention. Andrea, age nine, told me that her mother had started a new job and "she never has time for me anymore." Seeing her mother spend more and more time on the phone and checking her e-mail left Andrea feeling left out and neglected. Already prone to defiance, Andrea messed up the papers on her mother's desk and "accidentally" lost a few in order to get her mother to pay attention to her.

Cody was caught up. Sixteen-year-old Cody, quoted back in Day 4, had never felt "successful" in relating to girls. He had met Scarlet, age fifteen, on a social media site. Though they had never met in person and lived two thousand miles apart, they had formed, in Cody's animated words, an "instant, amazing connection." He told me that Scarlet "is the only person that gets me." Cody felt pressure to keep up with his schoolwork but he was falling dreadfully behind because he was consumed with hours upon hours of communicating with Scarlet.

Ian felt inadequate. Fourteen-year-old Ian confided that he felt inferior to his older brother, who was a local sports star. Ian's way of dealing with these feelings was to hide his brother's football uniform on the day of a big game.

Robert wanted revenge. Eight-year-old Robert admitted to me that he tried to steal money from his mother because he felt angry after she took away his video game. Robert's mother had taken away Robert's game after he received a poor progress report from school.

Jake was jealous. Jake, age fifteen, admitted that he was jealous of all of the attention his parents gave to his younger brother who had problems with anxiety and depression. Jake started smoking cigarettes to express his jealousy.

Stephanie felt scared. Ten-year-old Stephanie felt scared when her parents mentioned that they might move to another neighborhood. She had difficulty making friends and her only friend was her next-door neighbor, so she threw out the information about the new house that her parents had carefully set aside.

All of the examples above have something in common—there is a deeper issue brewing below the surface of these kids' misbehavior. Each of these children is wrestling with strong feelings that they have not been able to resolve, and they want attention. As a result of misbehaving, they usually get a lot of attention. Even though this attention is negative, it's better than no attention at all.

Physical Concerns Count, Too

Sometimes parents forget that a kid's misbehavior may stem from physical problems. While in most cases physical issues are temporary and don't cause an ongoing pattern of defiance, it's important for you to stay aware that physical factors do lead to what I call "flashes of defiance." Trevor, age eight, went through a period of a few weeks when he was much more irritable and obstinate. What Trevor's parents did not realize at the time was that he was starting to feel feverish. Trevor was on his way to developing a full-blown cold and strep throat. In this case, Trevor's parents soon recognized that physical problems might be influencing his defiant behavior. A visit to the doctor helped Trevor feel better physically, and once he did, he was much less defiant. So if your child is going through a rough patch, consider a physical illness as a possible culprit. To name a few:

- Being feverish
- Having an upset stomach
- Having an earache
- Being hungry
- Experiencing menstrual tensions and pains
- Having allergies
- Feeling overly physically stressed in response to worries of any kind

Keep in mind that it is your love and understanding that empower you to look beneath your child's outer layer of defiance and determine what core issues may be bothering him. Understanding where your child's concerns are coming from is a huge part of Discipline Without Desperation. The better you understand what is troubling your child and why, the better equipped you are to deal with the situation constructively and effectively.

Now that you've gotten a handle on why your child may misbehave, I want to discuss another source of confusion when it comes to discipline: giving consequences for negative behaviors. One way in which parents unwittingly give negative attention to a defiant child is when they are reckless in giving him consequences for his actions. As you will see in the next section, the consequences you give for misbehavior and the way you give them have a direct connection to how your child will behave in reaction to those consequences. And it's just as important not to allow the consequences to impinge on your child's self-esteem and his relationship with you. The core of Discipline Without Desperation is the quality of your relationship with your child.

Be Careful About Giving Consequences

When most parents hear the word "discipline" they think of "consequences." This usually means taking away privileges. I have seen countless parents over the years give consequences without stopping to learn why their children's problematic behavior occurred in the first place. You must understand why your child is acting the way she is in order to give effective consequences for her misbehavior. Consequences alone won't teach your child the values and skills that are important for self-worth, problem solving, and self-control. Consequences without your valuable guidance will not work. The core of Discipline Without Desperation is love and guidance. Teaching children what you will accept and won't accept is important. But with defiant children it's equally important to help them learn how to take responsibility for their actions, to learn from their actions, and to relate positively to others. Your consequences can either help or hinder your child's road to less defiance.

As the parent of a defiant child, you know firsthand how unpredictable and difficult using consequences can be. This is because poorly administered or overly severe consequences end up
being perceived by the defiant child as punishment. Since defiant
children tend to see themselves as your equal, they rebel against
punishment.

If your child does not regret or even acknowledge his actions, he
will direct his anger at the one who inflicts the consequences or, as
he sees it, punishment—you. Instead of making a commitment to
change, defiant children tend to show no remorse and to express intense anger and act out right away. This is because as the defiant
child feels controlled and pressured by consequences, his thinking
becomes even more distorted. Specifically, he reasons that he did
nothing wrong and that any consequences are unfair. He lashes out
while thinking or even saying something such as, "See, this is what
you get for making me be the one in trouble." Or defiant children
may learn to avoid punishment by hiding their misbehavior from you
or other authority figures. If you overdo the unpleasant consequences
for misbehavior, your child (and possibly you) may end up feeling excessively guilty. In each of these situations, kids end up with damaged
self-esteem, which will actually increase the likelihood of continued
misbehavior.

The bottom line is that you need to give careful thought to the
use of consequences with your defiant child. The use of consequences
is often a judgment call.

WHEN ARE CONSEQUENCES NECESSARY?

It's not always easy for parents to know whether to give consequences for misbehavior and which ones to give. Following is a
series of guidelines aimed at helping you determine when and if
you should use consequences with your child.

- Did your child break a rule you both agreed upon? Are you
  just burned out or tired and overreacting, or is there a real
  problem here? Are you looking at the situation fairly? If
  your child did not break a known rule, then consequences
  are not needed.

- Are your expectations realistic? Can your child really do what you expect of her? Sometimes parents lose perspective. If your expectations are unrealistic given your child's age or emotional maturity, then consequences are not needed. If you are not being fair, change your expectations and don't give consequences.
- Did your child know at the time that she was doing something wrong? If not, explain why it was wrong but don't give consequences. Help her understand what you expect, why, and how she can accomplish it. Offer to help her.
- If your child knew what she was doing was wrong, and she deliberately disregarded reasonable expectations, and your child continues to show no interest in accepting responsibility for problem behavior, then I suggest using consequences. Ideally, if you can effectively discuss the concerns with your child in a calm, firm, and noncontrolling manner, then I encourage you to try to agree upon the consequences together.

Use Consequences Infrequently

The most important thing I can tell you about using consequences with defiant children is to do it as little as possible. Consequences are important, but the only way they work with defiant children is if you've already used all of the other skills and strategies you learned from the previous days. When you can, try to reason with your child and consider your child's point of view even if you don't agree with him. Modeling and coaching your child to acknowledge the alternative perspectives of others will help him learn this valuable skill to apply in his own life as well.

Here are some examples of things you might say:

"I know you feel it was justified, but I cannot agree that you had the right to push your sister."

"Yes, you have the right to think you should be able to stay up much later. And I do hear you when you tell me your friend is allowed to do this. At the same time, I am asking you to please get ready for bed. You can read for a few minutes up there, though."

"I understand that you want new sneakers this weekend. Yes, you have the right to your opinion that you should have them. At the same time, I am not willing to spend the money right now. But I am willing to talk about some kind of compromise, if you're interested."

I used to counsel a man named Stan, the recently divorced father of Scott, age eleven, and Audrey, age ten. Stan had told me that his two kids would often misbehave on the way between his and his ex-wife's houses. Scott in particular would act out, sometimes even hitting Audrey. Stan had been using way too many consequences with Scott in the past. In fact, Stan had even admitted that he had grabbed Scott and held him up against a wall one time after Scott hit Audrey. So when Stan picked up his kids one day and saw Scott punch Audrey in the arm again, his response was to start yelling at Scott to apologize. Scott snapped into defiant-kid mode and told his father to "make me." Stan took a few deep breaths and remembered to be calm, firm, and noncontrolling. This battle was definitely worth fighting, but he knew he had to go about it differently.

Stan turned to his son and said, "Scott, in the past I would have continued to yell or tried to force you to apologize. I am not going to do that today because it won't help you or me. So, Scott, I am asking you to please apologize to your sister because treating her like this is not acceptable behavior. I have seen other situations where you've handled your frustration quite well, so today I feel disappointed that you hit her. I know you can continue to learn to make better choices when you are frustrated and angry." Stan stopped talking and began to think about what to take away from Scott as a consequence, but his thoughts were interrupted when Scott turned to his sister and offered a sincere apology. Discipline is teaching. Stan taught, Scott learned, and in this case, consequences were not necessary. Stan showed that crucial sense of self-discipline, as I referred to earlier in this chapter, the ability to respond without reacting. Stan's response was measured, and he was in control of his own emotions. This served to coach and influence Scott to reflect on his bad choice and take responsibly for it.

The point is that frequent use of consequences is ineffective because children, especially defiant ones, gradually adapt or adjust to a certain intensity of them. Over time, parents who use consequences frequently will have to become more and more severe to achieve the same level of influence. Consequences can then escalate out of control, to the point where a child's fear, resentment, and anger overwhelm any potential for learning.

Always Be Calm, Firm, and Noncontrolling When Giving Consequences

Discipline Without Desperation worked for Stan because he was calm, firm, and noncontrolling when he dealt with Scott. What makes my approach to discipline work, what makes it so dependable, is that you're removing the emotion. By removing the emotion, you can be calm, firm, and noncontrolling when giving consequences. Perhaps you're wondering how you can give consequences and be noncontrolling at the same time. Good question. The answer is that as long as you think about teaching and not overpowering while disciplining, you will come across as noncontrolling. Trust me—the more emotion you take out of discipline, the more effective it is.

Most parents deliver consequences in a heated, emotional manner. This is Ineffective Discipline. Below are examples of Ineffective Discipline (ID) contrasted with Discipline Without Desperation (DWD). You will immediately see the difference.

ID: "You hit your sister and obviously you can't control yourself. Get up to your room right this minute!"

DWD: "I am very concerned that you just hit your sister. I'd like you to please go up to your room and think about what you did. I'd like to discuss this after we all cool down."

ID: "It's been two hours and you have not left that TV. Now you blew it—no more TV for a week!"

DWD: "The TV seems to be getting in the way of your getting other things done. I need you to not watch TV for the next two days. Let's discuss this and see how we can come up with a better way to handle the TV."

ID: "How dare you speak to me that way! Now you're not going to the mall this afternoon."

DWD: "I can't accept your talking to me in that manner. I will not take you to the mall because doing that feels like I'm supporting this poor behavior. I am asking you to please sit down with me and help me understand why you have been so angry when we talk."

ID: "I have had it with you coming in late! Now you're not going to the dance this Friday night."

DWD: "Look, we really need to talk. I'm not sure what's going on with you being late for your curfew. I'm really concerned about your safety and I have some second thoughts about your going to the dance on Friday. What ideas do you have to make this work?"

Use Consequences That Make Sense

This may sound ridiculously simple and obvious, but you'd be surprised how easy it is for parents to forget that children cannot learn from consequences if they do not know that what they did was wrong. While it's true that many defiant children know that their actions are inappropriate, this is not always the case. Also, the self-absorption of many defiant kids often gets in the way of their appreciating the impact of what they did, even if they knew it was wrong. So before you respond with hair-trigger consequences, ask yourself, "Is my child aware that he has done something wrong and does he understand the extent to which it creates a problem?"

In many cases your child will have to deal with natural consequences. For example, if your child refuses to eat dinner, she'll get hungry later and dinner will be long gone. Or if she plays too rough with a fragile toy, she may break it and no longer be able to play with it. If your teenager stays up too late, he'll probably be exceedingly tired the next day. These are what are commonly called "natural consequences" because they occur automatically. Natural consequences help your child learn a lesson especially well because she will usually care about the consequences.

Logical consequences occur when you, the parent, step in. Whenever possible, use consequences that do not require the cooperation of your child. Rules and consequences must be clear to both you and your child—I suggest putting them in writing before conflicts occur so there will be no debate over what will happen while you're in the heat of the moment. If Joey continues to play video games and refuses to do his homework, Mom and Dad, in a calm, firm, and noncontrolling manner, may have to take away the video game and lock it up. If your child breaks the rule about where he can go on his bike, you may have to take away the bike for a few days. When your child does not do her chores, and you have addressed it more than once in a calm, firm, and noncontrolling manner, then you need to take away her privilege to spend the night with a friend or to rent a movie. Having logical consequences for misbehavior, if they are applied selectively and nonaggressively, can help your child learn that he is accountable for his actions. Discussing with your child what he needs to do to restore privileges is also part of Discipline Without Desperation because this allows him to continue to learn responsibility and accountability. By keeping your emotions out of giving the consequences, you do not run the risk of damaging his self-esteem.

Be Consistent

As I've mentioned before, B. F. Skinner showed that when we are uncertain whether we'll get a reward or what it may be, we go after our goal with serious enthusiasm. Think about it. A kid in the grocery store sees the candy and begs his mom for some. She tells him, "No, and stop bugging me or you will not get to go outside when we get home." If the child continues pleading and his mother finally feels worn down and gives in and the child is still allowed to go outside, then she is teaching the child that if he nags he will not get the consequence he has been threatened with. Thus, he is encouraged to repeat this behavior over and over.

So if you were to tell your seven-year-old child, "If you keep leaving your shoes in the middle of the floor, you will have to straighten up the whole mud room," you must enforce this consequence the next time he leaves his shoes in the middle of the floor. And if he does it again the next day, you have to follow through with the consequence again.

Consistency is important. If you give an "if, then" statement, you must follow through with the "then" part. Many parents complain to me that they are just too tired to follow up on their "thens." We have all been there and have fallen into this trap. Just remember, though, that Discipline Without Desperation relies on consistency. And the more consistent you are, the more you will conserve your energy in the long run because you'll be putting a stop to the misbehavior.

Your Consequences Should Come on the Heels of Misbehavior

The "wait till your father gets home!" school of discipline is a bad approach with all children, but the emotional volatility of defiant children makes this approach a disaster for them. Delayed consequences just give defiant children time to rev up and become more likely to deny taking responsibility for their actions and to become even angrier about the situation. Given defiant children's tendency to challenge their parents, they are very likely to associate the delayed consequence with the parent who's giving it rather than with their earlier misbehavior. Immediate responses that occur soon after misbehavior are much more effective.

Valerie, the mother of nine-year-old Sam, learned the hard way why delayed consequences don't work. She told me, "Before I started working with you, I used to think I would *really* get Sam's attention and make him reflect all day on what he did wrong if I told him he would be punished later. But I realize now that this just got him all worried and angry." I asked Valerie to help me understand the complications that would come with Sam's increasing anger in waiting for the delayed consequence. She said, "He would just get more difficult with me as the day wore on and then by the time I took away the TV or whatever I was taking away that night, he would have done five other things out of spite. I get it now and won't be doing things that way anymore. I now use consequences as a last resort and I feel better when I act quickly."

Be Willing to Negotiate

Defiant children often feel that no one should be able to "boss them around." Their need for power can get them into trouble. Here's a good example of this. Some time ago I counseled Eliot, the dad of nine-year-old Peter, to be calm, firm, and noncontrolling when dealing with Peter's defiant behavior and after a few weeks, Peter's defiance had really lessened. But one night, when Eliot announced that he was taking Peter and his younger brother to the mall for dinner, Peter threw a fit. "You always go where he wants and never care about what I want," he said. Peter felt that he should have the power to decide where the family would have dinner. Eliot used his calm and firm approach, but Peter continued to gripe and then he threw his brother's video game down and smashed it with his feet, cracking the plastic casing.

Eliot decided that Peter needed some consequences. He stayed calm, firm, and noncontrolling as he told Peter that breaking his brother's game was unacceptable. Eliot informed Peter that he would lose his video game privilege for a week. When Peter protested, Eliot asked him if he was willing to take some other actions to help reduce the time of lost video game time. Peter agreed to apologize to his brother, pay for his brother's broken game to be replaced, and empty the garbage in the house for a week in addition to his usual chore of emptying the dishwasher. Eliot was still making Peter pay the consequences for his actions, but by being flexible and negotiating the consequences, Eliot taught Peter some important social skills. Remember that discipline is about teaching.

Seven More Discipline Without Desperation Tips

In addition to the components of Discipline Without Desperation you've just read, here are some more tips to help you administer it to the best of your ability.

Set a good example. You are a role model for your child. For example, if you want to teach your child that being inflexible won't help resolve conflicts or problems, then don't be rigid.

Set limits, but be careful not to impose too many rules. Before making a rule, ask yourself: Is this necessary? Does the rule protect my child's health and safety? Does it protect the rights or property of others? Too many rules are hard, if not impossible, to enforce.

Involve children as much as possible in making family rules. Children are less likely to break rules that they have helped establish. I have seen children surprisingly willing to reduce cell phone use, video game time, and computer time when they feel included in the rules around their use.

Help your child understand rules and what happens when they are broken. If you and your seven-year-old have agreed that he shouldn't be wandering down the street alone and he breaks this rule, be ready to enforce the consequences.

Respond in private. Embarrassing a child in front of others creates unnecessary anger and undermines her dignity and self-esteem.

Tell your children how much you love them. When they misbehave let them know it is their behavior that you dislike, not them!

Remember to reinforce positive behaviors and choices, as discussed in Day 5. Cody, mentioned earlier, opened up to his parents about his Internet relationship with Scarlet. While his parents had concerns about Cody's struggles with managing his time, they praised him for having the courage to share how confused and lost he felt with female relationships. When Cody's Internet relationship with Scarlet eventually fizzled out, he felt less alone because he was closer and more open with his parents. This shows again how Discipline Without Desperation is about coaching and supporting your child to learn from mistakes rather than just imposing rigid consequences that usually only create backlash and drama.

I hope you feel really good about how much you have learned about Discipline Without Desperation so far. Now that you know what Discipline Without Desperation is, I want to help you be clear on what it is not.

Discipline Without Desperation is not an
isolated set of parenting techniques.

There's a scene in a movie called *The Karate Kid* that I really enjoyed. The main character, Daniel, moves to California, where he is harassed and beaten up by a group of teen karate bullies. He turns to the Japanese maintenance man at his apartment complex, Mr. Miyagi, from whom he learns karate. In true Hollywood fashion, Daniel also learns lessons about life in the process. Now to the scene I really loved. . . .

After several weeks of waxing the car, sanding the deck, and painting the fence for Mr. Miyagi, Daniel was pretty upset. He thought his teacher was taking advantage of him instead of teaching him karate. When Daniel expressed his anger, his karate master took him out back and told him to make the motions of polishing his car, painting the fence, and sanding the deck. Mr. Miyagi then threw a series of punches and kicks at Daniel and, lo and behold, those movements turned out to be highly effective karate maneuvers. Daniel was astonished to realize that all along he had been learning a lot about karate from the master's unconventional teachings.

So what's my point? My point is that you have actually been learning discipline with me from the day you started reading this book. In a more recent remake of this classic movie, the setting of the story and "bad guys" were altered, but the central message about the importance of "practice and patience while learning" remains intact. As I keep saying, discipline is teaching. Please keep in mind that a big part of teaching is also being open to continuing to learn. Just look at the valuable lessons you have learned so far.

- You have learned how to understand your child much better.
- You have learned that yelling has no value in helping your child reduce his defiant behavior.
- You have learned how to avoid power struggles by being calm, firm, and noncontrolling, and by picking your battles wisely.
- You have learned how to praise, encourage, and reward positive behaviors in a powerful way.

These are huge breakthroughs in managing your defiant child and increasing your connection with him. You are teaching him a new way of relating. You are modeling how to contain your emotions more effectively. The more you have used (and keep using) the strategies from previous days, the less defiant your child will be. So the bonus here is that you are well on the way to using Discipline Without Desperation because you have been using pieces of it all along.

It's Not About Proving You Are in Control

I'm sure you're well aware of my emphasis on being noncontrolling with defiant children. Many parents get carried away and caught up in the power of being "the disciplinarian." I can't tell you how many parents I have heard rave about how their kids know better than to do this or that. Often, these parents end up feeling quite humbled when their children surprise them with behavior problems.

Years ago, at one of my children's sports functions, a parent named Alice was bragging to her friend about how she didn't take any "garbage" from her kids. She said her children were "well aware" of when she was not in the mood to hear them complain. Sadly, Alice called me a few months later and was very tearful on the phone. She wanted my advice as she explained how her oldest child, her fourteen-year-old daughter, had decided to live with her father because she felt Alice "punished too much." Alice admitted to me that she was overly strict with her daughter. To use her own words, Alice was a "parenting power freak." I recommended that Alice and her daughter go see a counselor to work on their mother–daughter relationship. Things ended up improving between Alice and her daughter. Suffice it to say, however, Alice changed her tune and no longer prided herself on her overbearing, controlling style of parenting.

Alice had what we commonly refer to as an authoritarian parenting style. She was great at setting consequences for her children's misbehavior, but she was not very good at talking to and understanding them. Alice's oldest daughter, like most children of authoritarian parents, felt the lack of a close, warm parental relationship. As I mentioned on Day 4, the more you try to control your defiant child, the more she will try to control you. As parents we must sometimes fight a natural instinct to be controlling with our children. But when you're overly preoccupied with taking control, your child does not see you as someone she can turn to for empathy and help in problem solving.

It's Not the Same as Punishment

Many parents have come to me seeking ways to better manage their defiant children. As I mentioned in the beginning of this chapter, often when parents first sit down and start talking, they confuse punishment with discipline. Punishment is punitive in nature, and it breaks down the connection and trust between a parent and child. If you have been a parent who tends to punish your child, then you probably viewed it as making him "pay" for his mistakes. By now, you have realized that your child's problem behaviors stem from emotional immaturity and a limited ability to cope. So making your child "pay" for acting out and wrongdoings is not really fair. Remember, your child did not choose to be born with emotional immaturity and inflexibility.

I find that some punishment-oriented, consequence-ravenous parents want to use an elephant gun and can be quite unreasonable. Consider the following statements:

"I grounded her for three weeks because I got sick of her being so rude."

"I told him he would not go on the family vacation with us because there is no way I could bring him with the hurt he is causing this family."

"He never listens to me so I end up taking everything away but then it backfires because he throws a fit."

"If you don't finish your dinner you can't go to your cousin's house for a month!"

"That's it! You took the car without my permission. Now you can't drive the car for a year!"

When parents take an overly punitive approach to disciplining their defiant kids, it creates even more complications. If they follow through with their threats, then they are overreacting to their children's misbehavior. Defiant children already pay too high a price in emotional turmoil, strained family relationships, lost friendships, lost time, and lost joy. Though parents of defiant children often feel very hurt by their children, it's my job to help these parents learn to see discipline in a different way and leave the punishment mentality behind. Parents need to understand what is going on with their kids and not be so hung up on trying to control them. Is grounding your child for three weeks going to help you get to the root of why she was acting so moody? Is excluding your child from the family vacation really addressing the underlying problem? Taking away things from your child when you are frustrated may feel good at the time, but after he throws a fit, then what?

A Special Note About Physical Punishment

When I was twelve I had a friend named Allen who was a bit clumsy and heavy-handed. He also was hyper before "hyper" was the household word it is today. One day I was over at his house and Allen threw a beanbag, aiming at his sister. Unfortunately, Allen missed his mark and the beanbag broke a window. Allen's mother screamed at him and told him that his stepfather would "discipline him" when he got home. I watched Allen literally shake with fear at the mention of his stepfather. Allen's stepfather, Burt, was a burly, tough-guy type who was not a fan of the warm and fuzzy school of parenting. When Burt came home, I remember him asking who broke the window. Allen, to his credit, looked at his stepfather and told him that he did it. Burt sternly told Allen to go upstairs and get "the belt." When Allen returned he and I sat there in the family room for the next three hours, waiting for the punishment to happen, while his stepfather went about his business. Burt thought if the consequences were postponed until later in the day, the children would be more likely to see them as punitive. It was as if the exchange between Allen and his stepfather had never taken place—until Burt turned to him, said, "Let's go," and marched Allen upstairs to his room. A minute later, Allen's screams echoed through the entire house. I recall shaking inside, and probably on the outside, too.

Studies have shown that physical punishment, such as hitting and slapping, and verbal abuse are not effective at changing behavior. And administering physical punishment with defiant children just leads to disaster. While physical punishment may seem to get fast results, in the long term it's more harmful than helpful. Children will do what they are told to avoid getting spanked, but they will do what they want when no one is around to spank them. That's because they haven't learned the difference between appropriate and inappropriate behavior. Physical punishment can humiliate and discourage children and can cause them to think of themselves as "bad."

Showing children that violence is acceptable will tear down their self-esteem and can even promote physical aggression in children. If you have hit your kids in the past, don't beat yourself up. We all make mistakes. Ralph, my good friend whom I have known since kindergarten, often reminds me that the only perfect people are in the cemetery. In other words, no living person is perfect. I strongly encourage you at this point to stop using physical punishment with your child. Instead, use the strategies in my program, including what I have shared today, as your alternative.

Don't Be Overly Permissive

If parents are too soft and they fail to respond to problematic behaviors by their defiant child, they lose credibility and respect. Overly permissive parents have few rules and no consistent limits. I have seen defiant children with parents who are overly permissive just as often as I have seen defiant children with controlling and authoritarian parents. If you are a permissive parent, you lack the necessary rules and structure for your kids. If you do make a rule, you fail to enforce it. By being a permissive parent, you are putting your child in charge. Permissive parents say things such as:

"He'll go to bed when he is tired." (While ignoring that it is 11:00 p.m. on a school night!)

"It's fine with me if she likes to eat ice cream for breakfast."

"Why should I be the one to caution and discuss with him to lay off the video games? He will just have to fail in school and figure this out on his own."

"She can be rude to me because I know it is just a stage."

Since children who grow up with permissive parents are used to doing whatever they want, they have trouble getting along with others. They can be spoiled, selfish, and yes, quite defiant! If you chose this laissez-faire method of parenting, don't beat yourself up about it now. You may have become overly permissive for several reasons. Maybe you grew up with strict, authoritarian parents, and consequently you decided to use very little discipline. If this is the case, then your permissiveness is probably a reaction to your harsh, punitive upbringing. Or maybe you chose this lenient style because you felt you were under stress and didn't have the energy to make rules and enforce them. Parents who are struggling with addictions to alcohol or drugs may also become compromised in the discipline department and fail to set consistent limits.

If you have erred on the side of being overly permissive with your child, make an effort to recognize how and where you are too permissive and make a commitment to change. Maybe you don't like conflict and you have become an emotional hostage to your defiant child for fear of experiencing more drama and chaos. If so, keep using my calm, firm, and noncontrolling approach to communicate with your child. Even if your child initially reacts negatively, keep your cool and speak with integrity. Encourage your child to talk to you in the same way. Point out that he will get more of your positive attention as well as more privileges if he can walk the calm, firm, and noncontrolling road with you. Remember that this "firming up" of your parenting style may be challenging and may take some time. Your child, however, will be less defiant and will respect you more in the long run if you avoid being overly passive and burying your head in the sand.

DAY 6 — SUMMING IT UP

Today you learned about the power of effective discipline. Discipline Without Desperation will help you keep your cool while helping your child learn from his mistakes and make better choices in the future. Keep the following keys to Discipline Without Desperation in mind as you move forward:

- Discipline does not have to be a confusing, overemotional ordeal.
- Not yelling, and being calm, firm, and noncontrolling are fundamentals of Discipline Without Desperation. Having a good relationship with your child is the best way to help him make positive changes.
- Careful consideration of consequences and using them sparingly is important in helping defiant children.
- Discipline Without Desperation embraces love and caring.

GETTING READY FOR DAY 7

- Keep in mind that having the self-discipline to manage your own emotions is key in helping your child to manage his feelings, as well.
- Remember that your child's challenging behaviors often reflect deeper conflicts and struggles he is experiencing.
- When you do give consequences, don't yell. Instead, discuss the issue in a calm, supportive, collaborative way. Keep a log of the successful ways you give consequences so you can track their effectiveness.
- Remember to reinforce your child's good decisions. Guiding your child by "catching him" making better choices will help him choose to follow your consequences when the time comes to give them.
- Don't be overly permissive. Remember that even though when you overreact it usually does not turn out too well, it may be better than not responding at all.

DAY 7

Rallying Family Support

I want your child's progress to keep moving in the right direction. Obviously, you want this, too. With this in mind, today you will learn how family support plays an important role in engendering and maintaining positive changes in your defiant child. The calm, firm, and noncontrolling approach and your emotional coaching skills that you've been learning and applying throughout this program will be represented in the strategies presented today. You will discover the powerful influence of siblings and how to optimize it to further lower defiance in your child. I am also going to show you how best to work with your spouse to support your defiant child's progress. If you are a single parent, you will learn ways to marshal family support for your defiant child. You will also discover how to gain the support of your extended family. From all possible angles, I am going to give you lots of tips and strategies to help you get your family involved in and supportive of your defiant child's continued progress. Let's start with siblings.

The Power of Siblings

There is a school of psychology called family systems theory that shows how family members profoundly affect each other—for better or worse. A family is essentially a partnership of parents and children with different personalities and needs who are all doing a dance together. And as you know all too well, in the family dance, each family member has his or her own ways of behaving and expecting others to behave. If one family member changes his steps during the dance, everyone else's steps will change, too. In other words, every time your child is defiant he disrupts the dance, and the rest of the family feels (and also may even unwittingly encourage) it. Until you began this program, your defiant child's moods and reactivity most likely dominated the emotional climate of your home, and all the while, your other children have been observing his demands and manipulative ploys.

If everyone in a family gets accustomed to one another's dance moves, then it makes sense that any changes in the family will leave members feeling different and possibly awkward. After all, most of us are creatures of habit. As your defiant child's behavior begins to improve, you may find that it causes anxiety and resistance in his siblings. Siblings often don't want to support the defiant child's positive changes because they've gotten used to the way things were, even if things were not so great.

So, now what? One of your biggest challenges will be getting your other children to help support your defiant child's progress, because the new dance of less defiance in your house will be strange and unwelcome to them. Not only are your other children accustomed to your defiant child's behavior problems, they get the chance to shine when your defiant child is acting up. Your other kids may fear that they will fall from grace if the defiant child improves. It sounds crazy, doesn't it? Yet, as much as siblings are victimized by a defiant child's teasing and hitting and the disproportional amount of parental attention he gets, they often feel threatened by his progress, and that's a big hurdle to clear.

The first thing you need to do is be empathetic to your other children's reactions to your defiant child's positive changes. As I shared in my first book, *Why Can't You Read My Mind?*, empathy is the emotional glue that holds relationships together. The more you understand your other children's feelings, the more you can help them to support the positive changes in your defiant child. Take a few minutes to complete the following activity so that you can get a better sense of how your defiant child's past behaviors have affected his siblings.

A SIBLING INVENTORY

Below is a series of questions to help you better understand how your child's defiant behaviors affected your other children.

- What did your other children do when your defiant child misbehaved?
- What feelings did the other children express in relation to their sibling's defiance?
- In what ways did your other children protect themselves or cope with your defiant child?
- Which siblings were most negatively affected by your child's defiance and how?

As you think about your responses to these questions, try to stay mindful of the impact your defiant child had on your other children. The next section contains suggestions to help you keep all siblings working together and supporting one another.

Don't Compare Your Children

Your defiant child has likely been typecast in your family as the "problem child." It's essential that you don't make unfavorable comparisons between your children. I have worked with many adults who had a past family label of "problem child" who reported that such comparisons with their siblings as they were growing up left them emotionally injured.

To help siblings cope with and support the changes going on, it's crucial for them to understand that they hold the same value as your defiant child. Siblings need to see and believe that they will still "look good" in the family even if their defiant sibling's problematic behaviors improve.

Many parents are unaware that they've made comparisons that influenced their other children to treat the defiant child as the family scapegoat. In the midst of their challenges and frustrations, many well-intended parents unwittingly make verbal or nonverbal communications that are taken as comparisons.

Here are some verbal examples:

- "She's just too demanding."
- "We will have to send her away."
- "She is sucking the life out of this family."
- "No one else has kids this difficult."
- "I really don't see a future for her."
- "She doesn't care about what anybody thinks of her."

And here are some nonverbal examples:

- Eye rolls
- Sighs
- Grunts
- Gasps
- Shrugs
- Hands thrown up in the air

If you have sent or continue to send these messages, it can lead the other children in your family to see your defiant child as:

- Less loved
- More work to raise
- Less enjoyable
- Less rewarding to raise
- More upsetting
- Less valued than other family members

You must be careful not to make unfavorable or negative comparisons between your defiant child and his siblings. If other children in your family pick up on these sentiments, you'll have some major repair work to do.

One family I worked with serendipitously discovered that their seven-year-old defiant daughter Natalie believed she was being compared unfavorably to her ten-year-old sister Phyllis. Natalie's mother, Gussie, was cleaning up Natalie's room one day when Natalie was at summer camp. Gussie was shocked to find a piece of paper with a picture that Natalie drew of herself as disproportionately smaller in stature than Phyllis. Natalie also had written the word "loser" next to herself in the drawing. Gussie quickly realized that Natalie had internalized an unfavorable comparison of herself as a "loser" to Phyllis.

Natalie and I had a few sessions together, and she began feeling better about herself after making some positive behavior changes, as you will see below. I encouraged Gussie to speak to Phyllis and ask for support. She explained to Phyllis that for Natalie's progress to continue, it was important that Phyllis discuss Natalie's positive changes with me. In a session with Gussie and Phyllis, Gussie and I helped Phyllis realize that it takes a "really cool" sister to support her younger sister's changes. I then had Phyllis step out into the waiting room while I modeled to Gussie how to use empathy to let Phyllis know that she understood Phyllis's struggles with Natalie. Once Phyllis rejoined our session, she acknowledged how difficult it had been for her to see Natalie get so much of Gussie's attention—even though it was often negative. Gussie assured Phyllis that positive changes in Natalie would help Natalie feel better about herself and that Gussie would consequently be able to give Phyllis more of her time and attention. In the next session, Gussie and Phyllis sat down with Natalie and together they reviewed a list of seven positive behavior changes that Natalie had made. They were:

- No longer picking up the phone when Phyllis or Gussie was using it
- Getting ready for school on time
- Being demanding less often in wanting new dolls and toys
- Saying please and thank you much more often
- Letting Phyllis play with her
- No longer teasing Phyllis when asked to stop
- Being less fussy and more accepting about dinner choices

Gussie reported that "Natalie was beaming" when she and Phyllis gave Natalie this recognition. Phyllis was able to see firsthand that her support as a sister meant a lot to Natalie. Phyllis's role in supporting her sister left her feeling fulfilled instead of threatened by Natalie's changes.

SIBLING POWER TOOLS

Take a few minutes to brainstorm with your other children about what you and they can do to support your defiant child. Help them realize that by creating and sharing in good times with your defiant child, he will feel more included and less alienated, and will feel much less need to act out in defiant ways to get attention. You can choose items from the list I've provided or add to this list using the blank lines below:

Take a walk	Bake or cook	Walk the dog
Play a video game	Praise positive	Shoot baskets
Explore a video game	changes	Pass a soccer ball
tutorial together	Play cards	back and forth
Watch TV	Draw a picture or	Play a board game
Go skateboarding	design together	Use makeup

_____   _____   _____

_____   _____   _____

_____   _____   _____

_____   _____   _____

_____   _____   _____

Have Fun with Operation Cooperation

Defiant children, as family behavioral outcasts, have isolated themselves from their siblings. As a result, the siblings may feel competitive and do what they can to keep the defiant child down. Competitiveness among siblings is not helpful to any of your children, especially your defiant child who is struggling to make positive progress. The more she feels her siblings are competing with her, the more she may feel compelled to use her defiant behaviors to reestablish her best means for getting your attention.

If competitiveness is the overarching sibling dynamic in your family, you must reboot the sibling system with an infusion of cooperation. The more you encourage cooperation among siblings, the better they will live and thrive together. I have coached many parents to start a mission in their home called Operation Cooperation.

Parents set up as many cooperative tasks as possible so they can be-gin to teach their kids to cooperate rather than compete with one another. Instituting Operation Cooperation in a lighthearted and spontaneous manner is really important for its success. Winning co-operative activities that you can try with your kids include:

- Having them race against the clock to pick up toys, instead of racing each other
- Putting together a jigsaw puzzle
- Digging and planting a garden together
- Cooking together from a new recipe
- Developing and presenting a shared pantomime
- Creating a collaborative picture or design
- Exploring safe, interesting Web sites on topics of mutual interest
- Eating a meal together without an argument

Emphasize That Fair May Not Be Equal

Your children need to learn that you will do your best to meet each of their unique needs, but this does not mean that everything will be equal between them. Even if you were actually able to treat your chil-dren equally, which is absolutely impossible, your children will still feel as if they're not getting their fair share of attention, discipline, or responsiveness from you. "It's not fair" is the mantra of all children, not just defiant ones.

It's imperative that siblings understand that your defiant child has some major emotional limitations that you are helping him work through. If siblings have a hard time grasping this, and you are still accused of being unfair or unequal, try diffusing tensions by being nondefensive and empathetic.

Here's how Maxine, mother of Betsy, Eileen, and Lorraine, dealt with the "inequality" issue. Lorraine, the defiant child, needed a dif-ferent set of rules from Betsy and Eileen, and they felt frustrated be-cause they perceived this as unfair. Maxine acknowledged how Betsy and Eileen felt and stayed open to hearing suggestions from them about how to make the playing field more even. For example, Betsy and Eileen were frustrated that Lorraine was allowed to sleep fifteen minutes later than they were each morning. This rule had been put in place for Loraine because she was taking medicine for her ADHD that left her more tired in the mornings. Betsy and Eileen asked if they could have some extra phone time in the afternoon to help offset Lorraine's extended sleeping privilege. Maxine agreed to this request as long as it did not interfere with their completing their homework. Maxine explained how this negotiation was a victory to her. "In the past I would get angry at the other two girls and tell them that they were not being understanding. In this case I tried to be sensitive to their feelings and it really worked. They also stopped complaining that Lorraine got to sleep later." Maxine was amazed to find that her daughters lost their fairness obsession when she lost her defensiveness about it. I have found that most siblings have less anger over time when they feel heard and accommodated, where possible, with other allowances. What is most important is that you stay calm, firm, and noncontrolling with all of your children when trying to sort out issues related to fairness.

Stay On, But Be Willing to Take a Break from the Clock

Pay attention to the time of day and other patterns when sibling conflicts occur. Perhaps a change in routine, an earlier meal or snack, or a well-planned activity when the kids are at loose ends could help avert some conflicts.

Sheila, the mother of three children, had decided that she would be more flexible in offering snacks prior to dinner. She had noted that the tensions between siblings increased significantly when they were hungry and on the way to becoming "hangry" (as mentioned in Day 1, "hangry" is when your lack of food causes you to become angry, frustrated, or both). By offering snacks more freely, there were fewer conflicts and less of a tendency for her defiant child to get his back up.

Create New Rituals

Kids tend to enjoy family rituals, even if they don't admit it. Rituals provide a sense of security and can be very soothing. A family ritual is anything your family does together deliberately. Whatever the activity is, it's important that your entire family give it a heightened sense of attention. The routine of whatever you do is what counts. It can be anything from eating bagels on Sunday mornings to having a game of darts (use plastic tips if you are concerned about safety) every Sunday night. Just make sure you do it consistently.

Rituals are spiritually and emotionally enriching. Shane, a single father, found that his three children bonded with great fervor while making chili every Sunday. Each child added his own spice off the spice rack. Lucy began a ritual in which each of her children read from a book of jokes at dinner. All the kids laughed and gained a renewed sense of one another. Some defiant children may resist being involved in such rituals. But if rituals are presented in a non-controlling manner and you manage your expectations, your defiant child may get on board much more readily than you thought.

RITUALS ARE GOOD FOR YOUR CHILDREN

Rituals will help all your kids, not just the defiant child, by:

- Creating a climate of support and emotional healing
- Providing comfort and security
- Engendering a sense of family togetherness
- Creating a structure for shared time
- Passing on ethnic or religious heritage
- Developing a sense of shared joys and positive memories
- Bringing humor

Take Plenty of Strolls Down Sibling Memory Lane

Most brothers and sisters enjoy reminiscing about good times. Talking about the fun times that your kids had together in the past can be a great way to help them reconnect. This worked well for Francine, mother of Robby, age fifteen, and Seth, age sixteen. Seth had struggled at home and at school for many years and Robby felt "cheated" because Seth took up so much of his parent's time and attention. One night Francine told both her sons the story of when she took them camping and Seth got his hair caught in the zipper of the tent. They laughed as they recalled how the whole tent moved up and down as they worked to get Seth's hair out of the tent zipper. Seth had been very scared during that experience and Robby had consoled him. Looking back at this image was very amusing and calming for both boys. Good memories like these can help eclipse the upsetting ones.

Pull out old family pictures and movies and look at them. Search and explore your digitally stored photos together and make a cool video or slide show. Once you do, you'll be surprised at some of the fun memories they spark. It's also a soothing experience for both you and your children to review these pictures and movies together, sharing your reactions to past joys.

Allow Your Children to Get Lost in Time and Space

Make sure each of your children has enough time and space of their own. Kids need chances to do their own thing and play with their own friends without their siblings, and they need to have their space and property protected. Twelve-year-old Jessica felt much more supportive of her brother, ten-year-old Christopher, when her parents allowed her to have more private time with her friends. Her parents were calm, firm, and noncontrolling with Christopher as they helped guide him to accept Jessica's increasing need for privacy. Christopher was given plenty of praise for being able to comply with boundaries to protect Jessica's space. This meant that Christopher would now knock before entering Jessica's room and that she had the right not to let him in. I coached Jessica to tell Christopher how his willingness to respect her boundaries and personal space meant very much to her. Jessica said it best when she told me later, "Now that Christopher has shown me more respect, it makes me want to be more understanding and nicer to him. I really liked that Mom and Dad realized that I need more privacy now, and they helped Christopher realize that I was not trying to be rude."

Provide All the One-on-One Time You Can

Make sure you spend individual time with each of your children. Ask them to make a list of things they would like to do with you, and then note how much the activities will cost and about how long each will take. Rank activities based on affordability, interest, or feasibility, then choose something, schedule it, and do it. The rewards to you and your child will be well worth the effort. Fifteen-year-old Brittany had felt left out when her nine-year-old brother, Eugene, went through a period of defiance during the past year. Brittany told me that as much as she likes the clothes and other material things she gets from her parents, what she really enjoys is positive attention. "My parents have given me everything I want but the thing that means most is the time they spend with me."

All children need one-on-one time and caring from their parents. They need positive affirmation, emotional support, nurturing, and, above all, their parents' time. This means giving your child your undivided attention—whether you're talking to each other, playing a game, or doing a project together. For children and adults alike, nothing is more important than receiving focused attention and love.

Consider this emotionally fulfilling story of Harry, father of three children. One day his twelve-year-old son, Tyler, stood next to him and waited while he was on his cell phone. Tyler did not interrupt but he stood there with a distinct presence. Harry turned to Tyler and asked what he needed. Tyler asked Harry if he would throw the football with him outside. Harry's first instinct was to say he was busy, since he was under some work pressure. Harry, teary eyed, recounted this memory in a counseling session with me. "I had this huge epiphany that Tyler would be busy with his friends and going places a few years from now. I realized it really is now or never. I set down my phone, and we had a blast throwing the ball and running pass patterns."

Reward Anger Control

Remind your other children that your defiant child will need ongoing support to manage her anger. Encourage them to use healthy anger management skills to help model "doing the right thing." Show them how they can cope with their own anger by the way you control your own. It's important that your children see you deal successfully with your anger. In the spirit of your family being "in this together," remind your kids that *you* still need to work on controlling your anger, too. Tamara, a client of mine, coached her other children to model counting to ten when angry. "Now," she says, "I'll see Bart (the defiant child) do what his brother and sister do. We used to be a 'fire at will' house when it came to anger. Now we all try for a 'ready, aim, fire' approach. I praise my kids left and right for learning to think before they react, and they have been flaring up much less than they used to." The more you work on teaching these skills to your other children, the more support there will be for your defiant child when he is angry. And once all of your children have learned to deal with their anger, they will be far less apt to provoke your defiant child.

THE NEW FAMILY DANCE OF ANGER MANAGEMENT

If everyone in the family does their part to control their anger, everyone—not just your defiant child—will benefit. Here are some suggestions for you, your spouse, and all your children when you start to feel angry.

- Acknowledge your anger to help diffuse it.
- Ask yourself why you are angry so you can understand it.
- Talk to a friend you can trust.
- Take three deep breaths.
- Remind yourself that conflicts and problems don't last forever.
- Avoid toxic thoughts and words (e.g., hate, should, must, never, always).
- Talk to your parents.
- Go for a walk.
- Draw an angry picture.
- Count to ten.
- Hug your pet.
- To cool down, picture yourself rolling in the snow (in this case, dogs can be great emotion coaches, too!).
- Watch a funny movie scene or whole movie.
- Punch a pillow.
- Draw a picture of your anger.
- Play a video game.
- Exercise.
- Play a song and sing along with it.
- Write an angry letter or e-mail but do not send it.

- Think of great memories (maybe about a fun vacation or your favorite sport).
- Take a bike ride or go in-line skating.
- Work on a hobby or play with a favorite toy.

The suggestions above are aimed at helping siblings, as well as you and your spouse, support the growth of your defiant child. Now it's time to look at the role your marriage can play in supporting your defiant child.

The Stronger the Marriage, the Less Defiant the Child

You've probably been told that it's not wise to put your children before your spouse. But let's face it, that can be easier said than done. Sadly, I have had many couples on the brink of divorce come to my office for counseling because they neglected their marriage while meeting the needs of their children. When you have a defiant child, it can be even more challenging to stay connected as a couple because of the emotional demands this creates. Your mission to help your defiant child can prevent you from taking proper care of your marriage. In most cases, defiant children tend to act up with Mom more than Dad. But no matter which parent the defiant child directs her anger at, both parents end up feeling depleted, and this can damage your connection as a couple. Defiant children are demanding, and meeting those onerous needs makes marriages more likely to revolve around the children. The following activity will help you assess to what degree your defiant child has affected your marriage.

MARRIAGE INVENTORY

Below is a series of questions to help you better understand how your child's defiance has affected your marriage.

- How do you react to your spouse when your child misbehaves?
- How does your spouse react to you when your child misbehaves?

- When you and your spouse are working together to manage your defiant child, what kinds of things work?
- What kinds of things don't work?
- To what extent have you and your spouse blamed one another for your child's misbehavior?
- What do you and your spouse do as a couple to comfort each other and cope with your child's stressful moments?

THE SACRIFICIAL LAMB

In some cases, a defiant child may become the "sacrificial lamb" if the marriage is troubled to begin with. I once counseled a couple named Lenore and Ivan, who had a very rocky marriage. Their biggest issue was Lenore's fifteen-year-old, highly defiant teenage son, Ryan, from her previous marriage. Ryan would test Lenore and Ivan in every way possible. This included leaving messes, destroying property, and sneaking out at night. Lenore and Ivan had tried to outmaneuver Ryan, had come down hard on him with consequences, and had made many threats. Matters just got worse.

Once I began working with Ryan and coaching the couple with the strategies in this book, he started to improve his attitude and behaviors. But once Ryan was no longer a problem, Lenore and Ivan realized they had little in common. I have repeatedly seen couples like Lenore and Ivan who have been so consumed with their defiant child that they had not taken care of their relationship. Fortunately, I was able to help Lenore and Ivan rediscover themselves as a couple, and this helped support Ryan's progress even further. Ryan confided to me privately, "I was bad sometimes just because I felt that Mom and Ivan then would at least talk to each other."

Cultivate Non-Child-Related, Shared Interests

One helpful way to reconnect as a couple is to develop new interests together. Doing new things provides an infusion of excitement and gives you and your spouse wonderful things to talk about that are not related to your defiant child. Here are a few suggestions that several of the couples I have worked with have tried.

- Go to church together.
- Cook a dinner together.
- Get massages together.
- Go away for the weekend.
- Play cards or go bowling.
- Take a class together.
- Work on home projects.
- Join a wine-tasting club.
- Play a board game like Trivial Pursuit or Scrabble.
- Get dirty together by gardening or fixing up the house.
- Try rock climbing.
- Go bike riding.
- Take long walks around the neighborhood or go hiking.
- Join the gym together (one couple I know works out with a private trainer).
- Take a stress management class.
- Take day trips to historic sites or museums.
- Attend a lecture.
- Go out for dinner or dancing.
- Join a book group for couples.
- Volunteer together.

More on Making Your Marriage Stronger

Your marriage is the fundamental relationship in your family, remaining long after your children are grown and gone. Even the best marriages need lots of support and nurturing. Below are three more tips to strengthen your marriage and further help your defiant child in the process.

Tip #1: Stay united as parents.

Your defiant child may try to use a divide-and-conquer strategy to get around you as a couple. Make sure you communicate with each other so you're on the same page. Eric, a fifteen-year-old client of mine, was a master at dividing and conquering his parents until they wised up and learned to communicate with one another first before responding to Eric. A classic example of Eric's strategy was to tell his father that his mother said Eric could have a very expensive guitar. Of course, Eric had not yet spoken to his mother, and later confessed to me, "Well, when I talked to my dad all I could see in my head was that guitar, so I just kind of thought I'd do anything I could to get it. I thought I would tell my dad later that I really had not talked to my mom yet, but first I wanted to see if Dad would say yes." In this case, Eric's father stayed calm, firm, and noncontrolling and told Eric that he had to discuss this with Eric's mother. In the past, Eric's father would get upset and immediately accuse his wife of giving in to Eric's manipulative ploys, and they would wind up arguing. Eric's parents learned to support each other. This reduced family tensions and lessened Eric's chances of relapsing into more manipulative and defiant behaviors.

Tip # 2: Catch each other using the strategies in this book.

Trish and Shauna had come to me seeking support for their relationship. They were a lesbian couple raising their eight-year-old adopted child, Naomi, who was defiant. I felt a surge of compassion for Trish when she told me that her uncle had told her, "Sure you're having problems with that kid. You two have screwed up her life." I worked with Shauna and Trish to help them use the ten-day program you're following now. I later learned that Naomi would occasionally still test both Shauna and Trish. Trish added that it was helpful when she and Shauna praised each other for using the strategies we had discussed. Shauna agreed, saying, "We now really give each other credit for when we handle Naomi in a good way. In the past we would just get upset and blame each other for Naomi's being difficult. Now there are far fewer challenges with Naomi. The other day Trish told me I was doing Discipline Without Desperation the way you taught us and that really made me feel good."

Praise each other when you "catch" each other being calm, firm, and noncontrolling with your child or using any of the other strategies in this book. When you and your spouse disagree, don't turn on your spouse or withdraw to handle it alone. Remember how important it is to keep your relationship a safe place in which to express your opinions and needs for meeting parenting challenges. Praising each other as parenting partners can help keep you open to talking about your differences and frustrations. You must be a solid parental team to be able to comfort each other and overcome setbacks as your child's defiant behavior lessens.

TIPS FOR TALKING TO YOUR PARTNER ABOUT YOUR DEFIANT CHILD

It's not always easy to talk to your partner about his methods of parenting your defiant child. The last thing you want is to be accusatory and get your head bitten off. The good news is that by using effective communication skills, you can maximize the chances of having fruitful discussions with your partner. When approaching your partner about your defiant child's behavior or needs, follow these do's and don'ts:

Do:
- Approach the subject at a good time. The second your partner walks through the door from work is not a good time to bring up your child's concerns.
- Be clear on the need to share certain things with your partner. Do you really need to tell him that your child needs an occasional reminder to clean up his dishes? Or are you just venting?
- Focus on what you need from your partner to help your child. Don't just whine. For example, don't say, "You need to change your hours at work next week so I can get a break." Instead, be fair and specific, saying, "I know we have made progress but I still get tired and stressed with the kids. Can you and I please sit down and figure out how I can get a few breaks of time for myself each week?"
- Mention the positives. You and your partner will benefit from sharing your child's successes rather than excessively focusing on his problem behavior. This is a huge omission many couples make in working together as parents. Try framing the issues positively. For example, you could say, "I've noticed that Ralph is going to bed as soon as we ask him to, and that's great to see. I'm hoping we can work

together to get him to work more independently on his homework."

- Give your partner a chance to explain or offer feedback on managing your children. This is a two-way process.

Don't:
- Offer any scary preambles like, "Okay, this situation is really bad. Joey is a creating a huge problem for this family, and I'm moving out unless he gets it together."
- Act before you think. Going for the short release of reacting before you first think about what you want to say or do can cause you deep regret later on. The same principle of responding instead of reacting, discussed in Day 4, applies to your relationship with your partner as well.
- Play amateur psychologist. Giving your partner your unsolicited analysis of why he did not parent the way you wanted him to can shut down communication about your children—even if your interpretation is accurate. For example, Linda told her husband, Glen, "I think you have a harder time being calm with the kids than I do because you are an obsessive-compulsive person." Linda later acknowledged that this was said when she felt angry and that it was both inaccurate and damaging to Glen.
- Make comparisons. Statements such as the following are damaging: "You are just like your father because he and your mother did not work together to manage the kids." This can influence your partner to feel unfairly leveraged by the negative qualities of a third party.
- Make "you" statements. If you say, "*You* are impossible to talk to about anything regarding the kids and *you* just don't listen," your partner will feel justifiably defensive. "I sometimes find it difficult to bring up how the kids are doing with you" is a much less threatening way to broach the subject.
- Be sarcastic or unkind with your criticism. You will shut your partner down instead of opening him up to your suggestions.

GETTING YOUR PARTNER TO TALK TO YOU ABOUT YOUR DEFIANT CHILD

You may see yourself as generally easy to talk to, but hearing your partner's concerns about how you manage your defiant child may not be so easy. Keep the following tips in mind so that you don't feel defensive when your partner talks to you about your defiant child:

Do:
- Listen with an open mind. One of the biggest things holding us back from personal growth is an unwillingness to see our own faults. Your entire character is not on trial.
- Go with a "ready, aim, fire" instead of "fire at will" philosophy. Too often we react instantly instead of reflecting on what we hear.
- Ask for specifics so you know which of your parenting behaviors concerns your partner.
- Ask for clarification if needed. Often, partners on the receiving end of criticism avoid such probing. What you may not realize, however, is that getting to the deeper issues will more likely diffuse rather than intensify the negative feelings because your partner will feel understood.
- Understand the parenting issue(s) in the context of the other person—be empathetic.
- Offer solutions. Set up specific ways to monitor the progress of your parenting efforts. Show your partner that you are willing to do what needs to be done.
- Thank your partner for being open and taking the risk to give you the feedback.

Don't:
- Interrupt. You can't listen if you're talking. Hear your partner out.
- Yell or otherwise act out in response to what your partner says.
- Make excuses or get defensive.

- Deny. Think how frustrating it is when someone negates what you have to say.
- Go blow for blow. I have seen this happen when couples are locked into trading volleys of spoken toxic thoughts, particularly all-or-nothing thoughts, such as, "You always give him everything." "Oh yeah, well you never have given that kid one compliment." Avoid these countercriticism wars—nobody wins.
- Address more than one concern at a time.
- Shut down. Instead, be a grown-up. Don't withdraw and pout—it's very unattractive. Try to figure out why you feel emotionally unsafe with your spouse and address it.
- Get passive-aggressive. Clanging the plates loudly after you hear the feedback is not going to help.

Tip # 3: Laugh together.

Humor is one of the most powerful bridges between people. Sharing a joke can be a fun and intimate experience. Laughing makes us feel good. Laugh with your partner as often as you can.

Reminiscing about funny, goofy times as a couple and with your children can make you feel really good. The following exercise will help you connect or reconnect through laughter. Get together and each of you write down some of the funniest things that have happened throughout your history as a couple. Choose the one or two most humorous ones and share your memories.

Diane and Ethan did this exercise and here's what they came up with.

Diane: "I remember when you and I went to Europe on that trip years ago, and how crazy it was when we rented that car and we put the wrong type of gas in it. Remember what happened? The fuel pump got all fouled up and the car had to be towed. You were so mad and I was laughing at how funny the whole situation was. It was not fun paying a thousand bucks to get the car fixed, but the look on your face when they told you how you put the wrong gas in was priceless.

Ethan: "How about the time when we did not secure the rooftop luggage carrier down very well when we went on vacation a few years ago. We thought it was fine and then we got a half mile down the road and the thing fell off the car."

When Your Spouse Is Not Supportive

Many times, one parent (usually the mom) finds herself trying to deal with a child's defiance by herself. If you are married, then it's important to work together as a team when dealing with your defiant child. I have seen many not-so-involved partners become engaged in helping when they are approached in a calm, firm, and noncontrolling manner. Bonnie recently did this very successfully with Aaron, her previously uninvolved husband. Bonnie was mentally and emotionally drained from single-handedly managing her *two* defiant children, Dante and Roberto, ages eight and ten, respectively. Bonnie and I rehearsed how she would discuss this concern with Aaron. Speaking from her heart, Bonnie told Aaron that she needed him to take the two boys on Saturdays to give her a break. She also asked Aaron to come in alone to speak with me to learn more about their children's defiance. Aaron was surprisingly open, telling me that he had stayed on the periphery because he thought it was a way to avoid being an ineffective father. I thanked Aaron for his openness and he saw me for a few sessions alone to productively work through these parenting fears.

At the same time, some spouses may not come around in such a supportive manner. Obviously, you did not get married or become a parent to be ignored, neglected, or abandoned by your partner. If your partner is not supportive, it's certainly your prerogative to shoulder the needs of your defiant child without support from your partner. Should your concerns persist about your spouse's unwillingness to adequately support you as you manage your defiant child, you may find it helpful to consider couples counseling. If your partner will not cooperate with counseling, you need to face the fact that your partner may not change and that you will likely be the only one dealing with your child's concerns.

Single Parent Support

If you are on your own, or you are married but your spouse is not supportive, you can still effectively reduce your child's defiance. Sometimes it's even easier to be a single parent because you don't have to compete with the other parent's attempts to undermine your efforts. Whether you are leading the parenting efforts as a single mother, father, or a grandparent, you know that raising children alone, especially defiant ones, is an enormous task. But you can do it. I know you can! Below are some tips especially for single parents or parents whose spouses are not supportive.

Take a positive view.

Parents and children do better when the single parent or the involved parent perceives the situation as a benefit and not as a loss. Start with a positive attitude and focus on the benefits of doing this yourself. You will have autonomy in making parenting decisions. This can help you to feel hopeful about the future.

Expect to be overwhelmed at times.

I have worked with many single parents or solely involved parents who make the mistake of forgetting that they are parenting alone. No matter how loving and competent you are, you are still only one person and you are doing a job that most agree is meant for two people. Do not allow your children to manipulate you by making you feel guilty about the situation. You will frequently feel overwhelmed by the responsibility, tasks, and emotional overload associated with your defiant child. Give yourself credit for all you have accomplished. Pat yourself on the back for reading this book and for trying to learn new parenting skills.

On a logistical level, it's important to manage time wisely and ask for help when necessary. Stay calm, firm, and noncontrolling and remember to ask your children to help with appropriate chores and tasks. Remind your children that you are a team and have to work together.

Arrange carpools when possible, and ask other parents for help when you can. You may have to wait until your kids are grown before you get any credit from them. Around the time I wrote this chapter, I attended a friend's fiftieth birthday party. In a heartwarming speech, her three adult children got up and sang praises about how their mother raised them as a single parent. The room became very quiet when her twenty-year-old son, who had been very defiant as a teenager, became teary and thanked his mother for all of her patience during his past difficulties. His mother winked at him and said, "Honey, you were a piece of cake." A sense of humor definitely comes in handy!

Establish schedules and predictable routines.

Part of creating stability and security in the home involves establishing predictable schedules and routines for your children. Don't be rigid and inflexible, since defiant children tend to rebel against these stances. Simply try to find a healthy balance that works for everyone.

Develop a reliable support system.

Develop a wide network of people who can provide you with emotional support, companionship, help in emergencies, child care, and reality checks. Be selective: choose caring, reliable, and trustworthy people. There are also some online forums for single parents that can be found and researched though Internet searches. While it is best that you are cautious about what you share, having support from others facing similar challenges can help you feel less alone and overwhelmed.

Extending Yourself to Your Extended Family

Your defiant child may have become the subject of family gossip; this happens often. My recommendation is to create boundaries between your family issues and your extended family. This isn't easy, as some extended families do attempt to meddle. Nevertheless, it's helpful to plan a strategy and stick with it if your extended family tries to intrude or interfere. You don't have to cut off all contact, but you may need to have an open discussion with your extended family about what type of influence you'll allow them to be in your lives.

Defiant children are often great salespeople, convincing your extended family that you are evil and that your rules are insane. Of course, what your defiant child tells your extended family and what is really going on may be two very different things.

Be assertive. If you don't feel comfortable when your slightly tipsy older cousin tells you how your child needs a good slap in the face, you should respond with your opinion. Be calm, firm, and noncontrolling, but speak from your heart. Tell your cousin that you appreciate her views but that you see things differently.

Similarly, if your father suggests that your eleven-year-old son should be able to stay up till midnight on school nights and you disagree, simply say, "I'm sorry, Dad, that's not acceptable to me." Then continue to set your boundaries with your son in a calm, firm, and noncontrolling way. When dealing with your own parents, it's easy to fall into the trap of wanting to please them—or just not wanting to hurt their feelings. But remember that you're a parent now, too, and are quite capable of making your own family and parenting decisions.

Be flexible. You may never be able to change your father's controlling ways, but you can change the way you deal with them. Laugh about it with friends while quietly continuing to do things your own way, or react with humor instead of impatience when he starts to dictate the best ways to raise children. Similarly, you may hate the fact that Aunt Sylvia always gives candy to the kids. But try to remember . . . didn't you love the doughnuts your grandmother used to set out at her house? You might think it's unhealthy now, but remember that you can always ask your kids to brush their teeth, and you can remind yourself that they're not being neglected at your house. There are issues about which you might be able to give your relatives a bit more leeway, as long as health, safety, or your family's basic values aren't endangered.

Enlist Your Defiant Child to Support the Effort

Encourage your defiant child to be aware of and monitor his own challenging behaviors. Let him know that he plays a valuable role in supporting not only his own progress—but yours, too. Ask him for help, within reason, to reinforce your improvement as a parent by giving you both positive and negative feedback. As discussed in Day 5, praise can feel really good and motivate positive changes. Offer your child an opportunity to give you praise for being patient and less reactive with him. He will likely feel supported in seeing that his encouragement and praise feels good to you.

Give your child the "green light" to call you out if you yell or are slipping back to acting in an abrupt, controlling manner. Remember, we are all human! Even though you have come a long way in this program, you and your child will still have setbacks (I will address dealing with setbacks further on Day 10). Having your child give you both positive and constructive feedback, in a respectful manner, is good role modeling and coaching on your part. This helps to encourage him to receive feedback as well.

Let your defiant child know that you appreciate it when he shows patience with siblings and other family members who may become demanding and difficult. The more you can reframe your child from the "difficult, challenging one" to him as increasingly aware and supportive of his own progress, the less your child will feel typecast as defiant. This will spur him to show you and those around him that he can be a more compliant, patient, and flexible member of your family.

DAY
(7) SUMMING IT UP

Today you have learned many important things about rallying family support for the positive changes in your defiant child. Keep in mind the following key points as you move forward.

- Remember that you are not alone in helping your defiant child.
- Families have their own ways of relating to one another, and changes in your defiant child will best be maintained by gaining the support of other family members.
- Siblings, when seeing the benefits to themselves, are very likely to support changes in your defiant child.

- It will be very helpful for you and your spouse or partner to strengthen how you work together as a team to manage your defiant child.
- It is important for both you and your defiant child not to let your extended family's perceptions and input determine how you deal with your child.

GETTING READY FOR DAY 8

- Empathize with siblings who feel a lack of fairness.
- Remind siblings that fair may not be equal. Accommodate them, where possible, with any flexibility that you can extend to them.
- Spend time with all of your children on a one-to-one basis, even if this is for only brief time periods.
- Do fun, invigorating, and connecting activities with your spouse to keep your marriage strong.
- If you are a single parent, give yourself credit and rewards for your efforts and successes with your child.
- Keep your boundaries clear, while being understanding with extended family.

DAY 8

Lessening Defiance
at School

There is no quicker ticket back to Stress City for a parent than receiving a letter or an e-mail from your child's school saying that he is acting out. Some defiant children have problems with schoolwork demands and getting along with teachers and peers. Today you will learn how to manage and reduce your child's defiant behavior at school.

You have made powerful changes at home by understanding your defiant child in a new, enlightened way. You are now using a calm, firm, and noncontrolling approach, you're choosing your battles more wisely, you're mindful of coaching and guiding your child to keep his cool (while retaining your own), you're rewarding appropriate behaviors, and you're using Discipline Without Desperation. All of these program elements can be implemented to varying degrees at your child's school.

Defiance at School May Not Be a Problem—Yet

Some defiant children are able to hold it together at school and don't have major problems. Your child may fall into that category. However, I do recommend that you read today's plan, because even if your defiant child has no problems at school now, he very well may in the future.

Defiant behaviors at school can take many different forms; arguments with teachers and other students, fighting, and cutting class are just a few. Sometimes, defiant behavior can manifest itself in less noticeable ways, such as refusing to do homework, participate in class, or even attend school. This more passive form of defiant behavior in the school setting can also be manifested as a child feigning illness to be excused from class, or otherwise acting tired even if he really is not.

Today is about empowering you to work smarter with your child's teacher and others to help reduce your child's defiance at school. Obviously, you are not the teacher's supervisor and you can't oversee teaching practices and school policies, nor would you want to. However, you can position yourself as a helpful consultant rather than an intrusive parent and help advocate for your child's best interests at school. Teaming with the school will improve your child's chances of success. The vast majority of the school personnel I have worked with are very open to collaborating with parents to meet the needs of their students.

Teachers Are a Powerful Influence

Teachers wield a considerable amount of power and influence over their students. I have warm memories of teachers whose support, concern, efforts, and wit have touched me. This includes teachers who gave me advice on personal matters as well as those who helped me understand challenging academic material. I'm sure if you think back to your own school experience you'll be able to name a teacher or two who did the same for you.

I also have some not-so-fond memories of some teachers. As a fourth grader, I used to take a forty-minute bus ride to the middle school once a week for a clarinet lesson. It was intimidating for me to get on that bus with all of those older kids. Even more intimidating, however, was Mr. Jones, my music teacher. Mr. Jones used to yell at us a lot. One day he asked me to play "Mary Had a Little Lamb" and then he yelled at me because I messed up. I tried again and messed up again, and he asked me if I had practiced. I was honest and said "no." He grabbed me by the arm and marched me over to the "doghouse" affixed to the wall and told me to stand underneath it. This was literally a flat, painted woodcarving of a doghouse. It was only about six inches wide and eight inches high. In reality, I only had to stand under it for five minutes. Yet, as a very self-conscious fourth grader, I wished I could magically shrink myself and crawl up the wall into that doghouse for good. Fighting back tears, I stood under that doghouse feeling humiliated. I remember that day very clearly. Suffice it to say, I stopped studying the clarinet after that day with Mr. Jones.

A teacher's impact on how his students feel about themselves is immeasurable. For defiant students who have difficulties fitting in and are trying to manage their frustration and other emotions, a teacher's influence—both positive and negative—is even more powerful. Defiant children don't want to have conflicts and be misunderstood by their teachers and peers, but this is often the case. The approach I describe today will help you boost your child's self-esteem and manage her emotions in school.

Lashing Out at School

Your defiant child's teachers may find that he has a low frustration threshold when it comes to completing assignments, as well as problems getting along with his peers. Teachers witness your child having temper tantrums. They may also see him lashing out at others or being passive-aggressive by subtly inciting or provoking others. Your child may have difficulty managing his feelings and solving his own problems due to his lack of emotional intelligence. More often than not, defiant children lash out at teachers and peers whom they feel threatened by and disconnected from. Some typical threatening events at school that kids have described to me include:

- Being questioned in front of the class about why you didn't complete your homework assignment
- A teacher making a face if you walk in late
- Being told by a teacher that you are getting "chunky"
- Being rejected by a girlfriend or boyfriend
- Being told by peers at school about offensive, nasty rumors about you or about a peer on social media
- Being excluded from a group of friends at a lunch table

To be fair, often the "spin" you get from your child on what happened at school may not be what actually happened. For example, your child may be confrontational with a teacher because "that teacher is never fair to me." In reality, your child may not know how to ask for help on a difficult assignment or for more time to turn in an assignment that is late. Or she may claim that all the kids in seventh grade are losers because of an exaggerated belief that resulted from her inability to address a peer and work though a conflict. I have seen defiant children so good at "spinning" stories that they even believe their own fabrications. Defiant kids who repeatedly tell themselves and others that their teacher is unfair tend to overlook exceptions to this perception. Their emotional immaturity hinders them from seeing others in a balanced and objective way. The payoff for spinning stories is getting their parents and teachers to lower the bar so they can avoid engaging in classwork or homework.

Do you remember seeing or have you ever heard of the 1985 movie *The Breakfast Club*? It depicts five very different students spending a morning together in the library for Saturday detention. There is a scene where one of the teens acts defiantly toward the assistant principal and ends up receiving a slew of additional detentions for mouthing off. This is a great example of the way many defiant kids shoot themselves in the foot in dealing with school.

I find it fascinating that Hollywood knows that audiences will watch a scene like this and root for the defiant child, even think of him as a hero. We want to see the defiant child test an educator who comes off as coercive and rigid. *Ferris Bueller's Day Off* is another classic movie in which the slick, manipulative student outwits the "evil educator." Weren't we all cheering for Ferris, who was defiant yet suave? Defiant children seek the audience of their peers in classrooms all over the world. Yet they tend not to challenge warm, supportive teachers as much as they do rigid, coercive ones. As you will see in other parts of today's discussion, I will give some real life examples of defiant students, and ways in which teachers can successfully support them. Hollywood's version of handling the defiant child is far different from the strategies I recommend. My goal is to support the dignity of your child, the educators, and you.

Consider the following interaction between fourteen-year-old Jake and his teacher after Jake yawns obnoxiously in the middle of class.

Teacher: "Jake, that's enough out of you."

Jake: "Can't anybody yawn around here?"

Silence, class giggles, and then Jake coughs loudly.

Teacher: "You obviously don't know how to show respect for this class."

Jake: "You're the one being disrespectful."

Teacher: "You keep it up and you're going down to the main office!"

In this situation, Jake disrupted the class and his teacher publicly reprimanded him. Teachers who directly and derisively confront a defiant student are taking a huge risk that he may lash out at them. This teacher did not feel empowered when he challenged Jake. He had backed himself into a corner with his response to Jake's inappropriate behavior and had to make a decision about whether or not to send Jake to the office. Unfortunately, in this case, the decision caused Jake to act out even more. The teacher got caught up in a distracting conflict and lost class time. Jake may think he won this round, but the class material that he missed and lingering tensions with his teacher will likely surface as learning obstacles on his return to this teacher's class. In this instance, Jake challenged his teacher and his teacher obviously did not have the right tools or the right training to handle the situation effectively.

The above example does not depict a character flaw in the teacher. Rather, it shows that he needs to be armed with a particular set of skills to deal with defiant children in his classroom. Many teachers have not undergone the appropriate training for handling defiance in the classroom. In general, colleges do not prepare their graduating teachers to use discipline in the classroom effectively despite the fact that they will frequently need to use it. A skilled teacher would have managed Jake by using the strategies that I will cover in this chapter, and would have dealt with Jake in a nonpublic venue so he was not put on the defensive.

In cases such as Jake's, the teacher often ends up kicking the student out of the class. As the student departs, he may take a verbally abusive shot at the teacher and slam the door. Now Jake will miss valuable class material and the other students have lost class time while this scene unfolded. Most troubling is that unless the teacher learns an effective way to manage Jake's behavior, he will surely continue to repeat his defiant pattern. Jake's actions stem from having a low frustration tolerance and problems controlling his impulses— these are the hallmarks of a defiant child. Given these deficits in Jake's emotional maturity, it's important that his teachers know how to handle them properly.

Defiance in Preschool and the Early Grades

Defiance at school can surface at any age. I had been working with Dana to help reduce her four-year-old son Tim's defiance at home, and he had come a long way. School, however, was a different story. Tim's preschool teacher called Dana in for a conference because Tim had hit a child who wanted to share a toy with him. Tim had yelled, "I hate you, I hate this place, I hate it!" Tim's main problem seemed to be sharing toys with his peers. His teacher put him in the time-out chair at least once a day as a result of these conflicts.

I coached Dana to meet with Tim's teacher and come up with a plan. Dana realized that she had to collaborate effectively with the teacher first before they, working together, could manage Tim. The teacher was a rookie and she had a tendency to raise her voice and to rush to put Tim in the time-out chair.

Dana worked closely with Tim's teacher to come up with a plan that addressed his needs within the confines of the classroom. As his teacher began to use a calm, firm, and noncontrolling approach with Tim, his behavior improved dramatically. This is a good example of a parent giving a teacher useful information that she can add to her educational toolbox. The key to the process is the quality of the parent–teacher collaboration.

The plan that worked for Tim at preschool included the following:

- Tim's teacher agreed to approach Tim in a calm, firm, and non-controlling manner with requests to share.
- Tim's teacher used the time-out chair less frequently.
- Tim's teacher used praise to reward specific incidents when he did not protest against requests to share.

- Tim's parents got a daily report card from the teacher and rewarded him with praise and occasional candy treats at home for his improved school behaviors.
- Tim's parents and teacher had two follow-up meetings to review his progress.

This plan brought about very positive results. At the follow-up meeting at the end of the first week, Tim's teacher reported that he had been willing to share each day. In one instance, when Tim went to grab a toy out of another child's hand, the teacher gently put her hand on Tim's shoulder and he stopped his behavior. Dana and the teacher scheduled a second follow-up meeting for three weeks later, since the changes had been so immediate and positive. Tim's progress remained positive for the remainder of the year.

Some Teachers Bring Out Defiance in Kids

I have found that most of the defiant children who rebel at school do so against teachers who don't understand them and who are overly controlling and coercive. Defiant students will also walk all over weak teachers in much the same way that they rebel against controlling ones. Most of the defiant children I've worked with have had some teachers that were overreactive and tried to control them.

Teachers who are overly rigid and controlling, and who react too emotionally may gain compliance from most kids, but defiant kids are likely to strike back. Defiant kids quickly learn how to push these teachers' buttons. The defiant student is armed with manipulation techniques (distracting gestures, behaviors, and reactions) that really wind these teachers up. And remember, defiant kids are able to fool lots of folks by making false or embellished claims. I have seen defiant students pull the wool over the eyes of professionals who are supposed to assess them and help them, because they have mastered the art of manipulation.

Some teachers try to justify their overly coercive methods, claiming that this is "the only thing the child understands." On Day 3, when I talked about yelling, I explained how easy it was for parents to adhere to this same line of reasoning. Teachers who are overly controlling and reactive tend to stir up negative feelings in defiant kids. Teachers who are stern but not emotionally reactive are less likely to be perceived in this negative way.

The way in which a teacher reacts to a student has a profound impact on the student's self-esteem. If a defiant child feels belittled, he will likely become even more defiant to compensate for his feelings of inferiority.

One night, during the time I was writing this chapter, I spoke to a thirteen-year-old client named Vince about defiance at school. Vince had a lion's share of previous defiance-related problems at school and had made very impressive progress. I asked Vince to give me his thoughts on how teachers can have an impact on a student's self-esteem. Vince's response was "They thought I was a head case because I would say things and get in trouble. But no one really understood that I hated myself for getting into trouble and I never knew how to avoid it." He acknowledged that his past year's defiance at school reflected poor choices on his behalf.

I helped support Vince and his new teachers by attending a teacher's team meeting during this current year. We shared strategies similar to those in this chapter and in the Guide to Handling Defiant Students in Appendix 3, which helped Vince's teachers manage his defiance issues. This effort seemed successful as Vince now believed that the majority of his teachers were sensitive to his problems. He had actually confided in me that he felt more accepted now by his teachers. This was certainly a shot in the arm for Vince's self-esteem.

A few months later, Vince returned to see me for a counseling session, and I realized that we were not quite out of the woods yet. He shared his feelings about one teacher with whom he had recently had a conflict. He said, "I don't think Mr. Edwards should have told me to shut up and get smart with me. I got really mad when he did that." I had spoken to Mr. Edwards personally when I was at the above-mentioned teacher meeting, and he seemed like an understanding teacher at the time. As we spoke again, this time by phone, however, Mr. Edwards told me that he had taken Vince's defiance too personally and had overreacted to him. He felt he had learned a lot from his dealings with Vince and reasserted his resolve to react more calmly with students who appeared defiant.

TEACHING STYLES AFFECT
YOUR CHILD'S SELF-ESTEEM

As a concerned parent, I encourage you to stay mindful of how teachers affect their students' self-esteem. If they are positive and supportive, they can help students feel good about themselves for the rest of their lives. Defiant children need teachers who are supportive of them in this way. The following points speak to the critical impact that teachers can have on the self-esteem of defiant students:

- Self-esteem in the classroom is associated with increased motivation and learning.
- Teachers boost self-esteem by being supportive in their tone of voice, by giving praise, and by listening with concern and understanding.
- Boosting self-esteem in class can be part of teaching academic skills.
- Boosting self-esteem can create a more exciting, satisfying teaching environment for both the students and the teacher if every student's self-esteem is boosted, including that of the defiant student.
- Promoting self-esteem in students helps them feel accepted. It provides them with responsibilities through which they perceive themselves as contributing and making a difference.

As your child's best school advocate, you should keep in mind that children prone to defiance or those with learning difficulties are especially vulnerable to feeling demeaned or belittled when struggling to understand what is being taught in the classroom. They may be told (overtly or subtly) that they are lazy and unmotivated or that they should pay closer attention so that they won't have to ask so many questions. Teachers can help ward off conflicts by emphasizing that mistakes are part of the learning process and that no student should ever feel embarrassed to ask questions if he does not understand something.

Problematic Teachers Use Problematic Methods

Jacqui was the mother of Brooke, age twelve. Brooke had been defiant toward her math teacher, Mrs. Brown. Jacqui was at her wits' end listening to Brooke complain about her teacher. Jacqui knew that her daughter was by no means an easy, low-maintenance kid. She had dealt with Brooke's defiance at home for years before I started working with them.

Even though Jacqui and I knew that Brooke was more than capable of embellishing stories, we also had a very strong sense that Mrs. Brown had some difficulties managing defiant students. I had heard reports of Mrs. Brown's harsh methods from other parents and kids. I also spoke to the principal about this teacher, and he conceded that while Mrs. Brown had been given feedback about her rigid teaching style and had made some improvements, she had reverted to her old ways. During a parent–teacher meeting, I had the opportunity to meet Mrs. Brown in my role as consultant to Jacqui. It turned out that Mrs. Brown was prone to doing the following:

Using interrogation. Mrs. Brown often fired "why" and "how come" questions at Brooke, such as, "Why didn't you complete the assignment?" or "How come you did not ask me for extra help?" Brooke found it very difficult to feel emotionally safe while she was being interrogated. The less safe Brooke felt, the more belligerent she was.

Using blame and shame. "You" statements and nonverbal demeaning gestures (eye rolls, sighs, headshaking) were a large part of Mrs. Brown's teaching style. Her way of blaming while communicating with students made them feel ashamed. One day Mrs. Brown said to Brooke, "You just don't seem to want to really try." Brooke then became highly defensive.

Using labels. Negative labels are just as destructive in the classroom as they are at home. Mrs. Brown's label for Brooke was "not caring," and this was very upsetting to Brooke. Brooke later wondered aloud to me, "If Mrs. Brown doesn't think I care, then why should I even bother to try?"

Failing to acknowledge positives. Brooke, like many defiant children, was highly sensitive to Mrs. Brown's failure to give her a chance. She told me, "Mrs. Brown doesn't seem to notice when I raise my hand and try."

A lot of questions are probably running through your head right now, such as:

- Is the teacher being overly critical?
- Is my child really being treated fairly?
- Is the school doing enough to help prevent my child from having these difficulties?
- Has my child been given a negative label by her teacher or by the school?
- Have I failed as a parent because my child is having problems at school?

All of these concerns are perfectly normal. Most parents of defiant children tell me they have these types of thoughts. The key is not to let yourself be thrown into emotional turmoil. You don't want to misjudge or take out any negative feelings on the school. Your goal is to educate the school about your defiant child's needs and get the school to work with you.

I have seen many parents of defiant children fly off the handle when they visit their child's school. Try not to let yourself feel intimidated by the school personnel and policies. Don't compensate for this feeling by being overly aggressive and demanding when dealing with school officials. This will be a major obstacle to your ability to collaborate with them.

I have also seen some parents fail to advocate enough for their child's needs at school, thinking that they have little to offer the school experts. You have a responsibility to advocate for your child's educational and emotional needs if you feel that the school is not doing enough. But you must work together with the educational personnel involved.

In the above situation with Brooke, Jacqui met with Brooke and Mrs. Brown and they were able to work out their differences. Mrs.

Brown agreed, with the principal's encouragement, to soften her approach to Brooke. They agreed to a few biweekly follow-up meetings so that all parties could be accountable and acknowledge progress. Brooke became less defiant rather quickly once she realized that she was working together with her mother and her teacher.

Let's say your child's teacher or other school personnel contacts you to report that your child has a discipline problem, such as acting out in the classroom. It's important for you to approach this just as you have learned to do at home with my program:

Be calm, firm, and noncontrolling. Your child has the right to get the most out of his education whether it is in a public or a private school. At the same time, you don't have the right to be emotionally reactive, accusatory, or difficult with your child's school personnel.

Be proactive. Learn everything you can about your child's school and current class situation. The more you know, the easier your job will be. Ask if the school has a Web site and, if so, get the address. School Web sites can provide you with all kinds of information— schedules of events, names of people to contact, rules and regulations, and so forth.

Stay involved. Make sure you keep on top of what is happening in school. Stay current with upcoming school projects and homework assignments. Contact your child's teacher or teachers at the beginning of the year or as soon as you can and talk with them often. Get acquainted and show your interest.

Consult others who are knowledgeable. Get in touch with your pediatrician, psychologist, social worker, mental health center, or other parties or agencies. I also encourage you to talk informally with school personnel who might be willing to tell you their opinions on or off the record (teachers, guidance counselors, therapists). Be careful not to misuse whatever opinions you get in an inflammatory way when you deal with the school. Roberta realized she had made a mistake when she yelled at her child's teacher, claiming that I thought the teacher was "bad." What I had said to Roberta prior to this outburst was that her daughter seemed to have a conflict with the teacher and Roberta might want to explore it. Talk about whisper down the lane!

Be clear about what you want. The school needs you to be specific about your concerns and requests. You need to explain what you'd like to see happen differently with your child's educational needs. It's not enough to say that the school is messing things up for your child. You must know what you want changed. If you aren't sure, consult people who can advise you. Get independent evaluations if necessary. (The school district might be required to pay for this.)

Tell the teacher what she needs to know about your child. If you notice a change in your child's behavior, school performance, or attitude during the school year, contact the teacher immediately. Talk often with the teacher and others about your child's tendency to be defiant. Keep informed throughout the school year. If your schedule permits, attend PTA or PTO meetings. If you are unable to attend, ask that the minutes of the meetings be sent to you. Or check the school's Web site to see if these minutes are available online.

Give praise to the teacher. Between daily teaching responsibilities, voice mails, e-mails, and internal school pressures, teachers often feel depleted and unappreciated. Write a kind note, send an e-mail, or make a phone call and say thank you when your child's teacher reaches out to your child in a positive manner.

Advocate but don't irritate. You may have a child like Brooke who's had to deal with a difficult teacher like Mrs. Brown. Maybe your child is no angel, but her teacher is also not exactly giving your child any support. If your child is having problems, the first thing you must do is to get the correct information from the school. Don't indict your child's teacher based on secondhand reports.

Report Cards

Parents (and hence students) become overly focused on report cards. Report cards are only one indication of how well your child is doing

in school. You also need to know how things are going between report cards. Don't wait for the school to keep you informed about
your child's performance and behavior. As the parent of a defiant
child, you need to be highly vigilant and proactive. If you are, you
won't be taken by surprise if your child's report card shows that he is
having difficulties. For example, if your son is having trouble getting
along with his English teacher, contact the teacher to get her views
on your child's behavior and academic performance. Most schools
have online access for parents to check on the status of grades and
assignments to help stay on top of any emerging academic concerns.
With defiant children, the chances of things quickly mushrooming
are pretty high, so it's best to get involved as early as possible.

Try coaching your child to talk to his teacher if he doesn't understand an assignment or if he needs extra help to complete it. Children need to learn how to deal with others and tackle problems that
come their way in life. Many defiant children have a very hard time
doing this, so I encourage you to make contact with the teacher as
well. As I mentioned in the example with Brooke, having all of you
working on the same page—you, your child, and the teacher—is the
ideal way to go. Another good way to stay in the loop is to find out if
your child's teachers use e-mail to communicate with parents. Using
e-mail will allow you to send and receive messages at times that are
most convenient for you and the teacher.

MAKE THE MOST OF
PARENT–TEACHER CONFERENCES

- Think ahead. Before you go, come up with two or three
  issues that you want to discuss with the teacher. It helps
  to write out questions and comments in advance.
- Take a notepad to the conference so that you can jot
  down important information the teacher gives you about
  your child's test scores, homework, class participation and
  attitude, social adjustment, and curriculum.
- Ask the teacher how you can help your child achieve the
  goals for his grade level.
- If the teacher doesn't offer specific details about your
  child's behavior and academic performance, ask for them.

- If your child's teacher seems difficult or rigid, don't go to the principal right away, as this can burn bridges with the teacher or lead to misunderstandings. Be calm, firm, and noncontrolling in voicing your concerns to the teacher.
- Talk about your child's talents, skills, hobbies, study habits, defiance issues, and any other concerns such as learning challenges.
- Be sure to remember the positive things the teacher says about your child to report to her when you get home.
- Where possible, consider making an appointment to see the teacher with your child. As was noted earlier, defiant children sometimes do not recount situations entirely accurately. A meeting with all three of you is a good opportunity to set the record straight.
- If by the end of your child's teacher conference the teacher does not express a willingness to work with you and your defiant child in light of his emotional limitations and acting-out behaviors, you should talk to an assistant principal. If you're still dissatisfied, talk to the principal. If you continue to be dissatisfied, you can talk to the superintendent. Following the chain of command is important and it gives you multiple opportunities to advocate for your child.

Ben's Struggles in Elementary School

Ben was an eleven-year-old fifth grader who was prone to seeking attention at school. One day he brought a "little jackknife" (Ben's words) to school. Ben had been showing the knife to friends on the playground at recess when a teacher took notice and confiscated it. As a result of this, Ben was suspended for three days and only allowed back on the condition that I write a note. Ben also had his fair share of conflicts on the bus and with peers at school.

I worked with Ben, and he made some strong progress in controlling himself. What helped immensely was Ben's understanding and supportive teacher. In the beginning of the school year, Ben had publicly humiliated another student, flipped a chair, swore at his art teacher, and refused to do most of the things he was asked to do. What sparked these incidents seemed so trivial. For example, when Ben was told he would have to wait to go to the bathroom, he flipped his desk. When his art teacher told him to stop tapping his colored pencils, he swore at her.

It was especially difficult for Ben to keep it together during recess. Like many children with defiant behavior patterns, Ben claimed to have many friends. Yet kids avoided him on the playground at recess. Several kids had initially been kind to Ben, but he drove them away with his bossy and aggressive behavior.

To tackle this problem, Ben's parents, main teacher, guidance counselor, and I spoke a few times and we agreed to have a few meetings with the assistant principal. Ben's teacher persuaded him to volunteer to be a mentor to a younger child at school. She lavished praise on him for positive social behaviors, which included avoiding peer conflicts. Ben also had weekly meetings with his guidance counselor to help him reduce his anger. It was accountability and understanding that helped Ben become less defiant.

Watch Your Step, but Step Up

You are in a difficult position, as you can't tell your child's teachers how to do their jobs. But you can teach the teachers about your child. Your job is to help teachers understand that you want them to help support your child without enabling her defiance. Your child's teacher has the difficult challenge of not only trying to educate your child, but also twenty or more others at the same time. Schools are ranked based on the students' test scores, and many teachers feel considerable pressure as a result. Adding to the stress are the even higher demands placed on their time now that parents can communicate with them through voice mail and e-mail.

Don't discount the possibility that you have insights about your child's problems that the teacher doesn't have. Contact the teacher as soon as you suspect that your child has a problem with his behavior or staying afloat academically. By alerting the teacher, you can work together to solve a problem in its early stages. When meeting to discuss problems, let the teacher know that you appreciate her time.

Tell her briefly why you want to meet. You might say, "Stephanie is having trouble with her social studies homework. I worry when she can't finish the assignments, and I'd like to figure out what we might do to help her."

If you have concerns about your child's behavior at school, knowing whom to contact can make a big difference in getting the situation resolved. If your teacher's explanation doesn't satisfy you, move up the chain of command until you are satisfied. Do not feel intimidated by titles or personalities. An educator's primary responsibility is to ensure the success of each and every student in his classroom, school, or district. As long as you are calm, firm, and noncontrolling and you advocate but don't irritate, you have every right to support your defiant child at school. If you feel stuck or overwhelmed, seek out a reputable educational advocate to help you support your child's educational needs and rights.

Give the School Support to Get Support

Defiant behaviors at school can lead to considerable educational challenges. Because of their emotional immaturity and poor coping skills, defiant children often bite the hands that feed them the knowledge they need.

Defiant children need clear rules and consistent enforcement to guide their behavior. In school, as at home, the most effective rules are those decided upon jointly by students, teachers, administrators, and parents, and enforced by all the adults. Do your best to have a positive working relationship with your child's teachers. Guidance counselors can be helpful as supports as well. I recall as a middle school student many years ago feeling calmer and more confident at school just knowing my guidance counselor was there for me. Supportive personnel in the school who can offer a soothing presence for your child will help her feel more positively about walking in the door each day.

Educational planning for defiant children with problems at school can feel like an overwhelming task. Keep hanging in there. Try to keep an attitude of openness and cooperation, and an expectation of accountability. You will see that the same basic approach that helps you get the best results in dealing with your defiant child at home

will also help you get the best results in dealing with school personnel and others. That approach includes being calm and consistent,
avoiding threats, and thinking carefully before you speak or act. This
is also the same approach that an effective teacher uses to bring out
the best in his students, whether or not they are defiant.

Make it clear that you want channels of communication kept
open so that you can get feedback from the school about how things
are going. Keep giving the school feedback from your perspective.
More often than not, I have seen teachers and staff make accommodations for the educational needs of challenging students. If you have
disagreements with the school, address them directly with the school
and avoid disparaging the school in front of your child.

In some cases, a teacher or other school personnel may refer your
child for an assessment. The purpose of an assessment is to determine
whether your child's defiance grows out of a disability that may qualify your child to receive special education and related services.

Understanding Student Assessments

Under federal and state law, school authorities are required to identify and assess students who may suffer from a disability that interferes
with their ability to benefit from education; these disabilities often
require custom-designed educational plans tailored to meet the student's unique learning challenges and needs. The disabilities that are
recognized by federal law include serious emotional disturbance and
"other health impairments," which may include ADHD and learning
disabilities. I discuss ADHD and learning disabilities further on Day 9.

As part of the evaluation, a school psychologist will test your
child to get a better idea of her strengths and weaknesses in natural ability and academic achievement. The evaluation is intended
to be comprehensive. The law requires that a variety of assessment
tools and procedures be used in determining whether your child has
a qualifying disability and would benefit from special education and
related services. As the parent, you are a member of the evaluation
team. Other members of the team may include your child's teachers,
her counselor, and a representative of the Special Education Department. In carrying out the evaluation, the team is required to consider
the information that you provide about your child.

If the team finds that your child has a covered disability and is in need of special education and related services, the school will convene a team to develop an individualized education plan (IEP). The IEP team usually consists of the same individuals who developed the evaluation, including, of course, you as the parent.

The IEP is essentially a contract between you and the school that sets out all of the important elements of your child's program of special education and related services. It describes the specialized instruction that will be provided to your child and the setting in which that instruction will be delivered. Educational modifications that will best benefit your child based on his disability will be considered. These modifications may include extended time on tests and homework, having test questions read to him, spelling exemptions, one-on-one aides, and resource room support. Counseling may be included as part of your child's IEP and may be tailored to her disability. Defiant children can benefit greatly from an intensive counseling regime that is made a part of their IEP.

A major goal of the federal law governing students with disabilities is to ensure that they receive a "free and appropriate public education" within the least restrictive environment possible. Children with disabilities learn and develop best when able to participate in school classes and other activities with nondisabled peers whenever appropriate. If you are participating in an IEP meeting, listen, take notes, and sensitively make this meeting a discussion about your child's unique needs in the midst of reviewing the paperwork. Don't be afraid to ask questions! Connect with the special education teacher as your main point of contact for your child's academic needs and possible interventions.

Examples of IEP accommodations can include:

- Twice the allotted time compared to regular education peers to complete a test or quiz
- Use of study guides given prior to a class
- Access to a computer for extended writing assignments
- An extra set of textbooks to keep at home
- Preferential seating close to the source of instruction

It is also important that your child learns self-advocacy skills. As your child's coach and parent, you need to guide him how to help himself in the school setting. The following is a sampling of self-advocacy skills that can be included in an IEP or encouraged for any child who can benefit from them:

- Raising her hand twice during the class period
- Self-monitoring of grades
- Asking for clarification or extra help from the teacher
- Going to the teacher and having her sign an assignment book

Each situation is based on the child's history. Defiant children, depending on their level of defiance, may be placed in residential settings when other modalities have been unsuccessful. Since the goal is to keep your child receiving as much of a standard education as possible, placement in a residential facility is something that you want to avoid if you can.

Rejection Led to Gabe's Defiance

Several teachers and peers of sixteen-year-old Gabe increasingly had conflicts with him. He lost his temper most days and exhibited a negative attitude to most of his teachers. The bottom fell out one day when Gabe swore at one of his teachers and was sent to the principal's office. Gabe's parents met with his school personnel and found that Gabe was very distraught over a girl who had rejected him. Gabe had a decent relationship with his health teacher, who agreed to serve as a mentor for Gabe as he dealt with relationship problems.

Gabe's health teacher clued in his other teachers that Gabe was in a difficult emotional place, feeling sad and distraught about being rejected. Once the school personnel saw Gabe as a sad and hurt young man instead of a defiant one, a significant positive shift occurred at school. His teachers showed him understanding and Gabe showed them more courtesy and respect. Gabe was no longer defensive and he stopped expressing his sadness and hurts as defiance. After three months, Gabe was more centered and appeared much happier.

Make Time to Be Involved
with Your Child's School

Staying in touch with your child's teachers is the most important thing you can do at school, but sometimes it can be hard to find a good time to talk. One mother I know called her son's teacher and asked that her parent–teacher conference be changed to a better time for her. Another mother asked the teacher to call her at work when the teacher needed to talk to the mother about her child. If it's hard for you to come to classroom open houses at night, ask if they also can be held in the mornings before school. E-mail also provides a means for parents and teachers to keep in touch regarding a child's progress a school.

Make Sure You Are
Doing Your Part at Home

Guiding your child for success at school is more challenging than ever. Children's focus is being pulled in many directions by TV screens, computer screens, and other, ever evolving and increasingly alluring mobile devices of many varieties. Insisting that the school provide academic accommodations to assist your child at school does not make sense if you bypass teaching your child to take responsibility for making his schoolwork a greater priority amid all the digital-age influences that compete for his attention. See Day 4 and Appendix 2 for a discussion on managing your child's use of screen technology.

As mentioned earlier, most schools also have Internet portals where parents can check on their child's grades and see if they are up-to-date on assignments. Stay calm, firm, and noncontrolling with your child when discussing their academic assignments and grades. Avoid having an "Aha, caught you!" mentality.

Leading with a supportive discussion by sharing your concern versus interrogating with a "Why didn't you complete that assignment!" will guide and influence your child to be more open about academic struggles with you. Tamika effectively used the calm, firm, and noncontrolling approach with her fourteen-year-old son, Jayden. She said, "Jayden, I am frustrated and want to yell, but it won't help us. I am seeing some missed assignments on the school Web site. How about we start looking at the Web site together to help you get in the habit of doing this on your own?"

Alternative Educational Options

Some children, for a variety of reasons, including learning style, personality style, emotional limitations, challenges connecting with peers, and perhaps personal preferences do not perform as well in conventional, public school settings. Often these students will less likely be successful if they remain in the public school setting. Fortunately, there are options for children who do not fit well in public schools. Every child's educational needs are different based on his individual strengths and limitations.

I have seen children benefit greatly who have followed these alternative educational paths. Some alternative school settings have smaller class sizes or more hands-on learning experiences. Other settings have more or less structured learning environments, depending on the particular school.

I am certainly also mindful of situations where these options outside the public school did not turn out to be helpful for some children. It is important that you and your child discuss options and do your due diligence when checking out alternative school settings. I encourage you to be resourceful and seek out parents with students who attend or recently attended educational options outside your local public school. If you have the resources, it may also be helpful to seek out reputable educational consultants who can assist you. A brief representative but not exhaustive listing of alternative, nonpublic school options appears below:

Private schools, also known as independent schools, are not administered by local, state, or national governments. They have the right to select their students and are funded in whole or in part by charging their students tuition, rather than relying on mandatory government taxes. In some cases there are scholarships for funding at some private schools, which lowers the cost, depending on a talent the student may have—for example, sports, art, or academic scholarship.

Parochial Schools are private primary or secondary schools affiliated with a religious organization and whose curriculum includes general religious education in addition to secular subjects, such as science, mathematics, and language arts. They are usually associated with the educational wing of a local parish church.

In addition to schools run by Christian organizations, there are also Jewish (Hebrew), Muslim, and other schools. These, however, are not usually called "parochial" because of the term's historical association with Christian parishes.

Charter Schools receive public funding but operate independently. They are elementary or secondary schools that have been freed from some of the rules, regulations, and statutes that apply to other public schools, in exchange for some type of accountability for producing certain results, which are set forth in each charter school's charter.

Cyber schools are institutions that teach courses entirely or primarily through online methods. These virtual schools are online learning platforms offered by an educational organization whereby individuals can earn credits in the particular area of interest, which can be counted toward graduation or advancement to the next grade. One teen client of mine, Larissa, age fifteen, who attended a cyber school commented to me, "I get my schoolwork done on my computer but I still go to dance lessons and yeah I also hang out and have fun with my friends from my old public school." Most states offer some type of online public school courses to resident students. Some states offer full online high school diploma programs, while others offer a limited number of virtual courses.

Homeschooling is an approach to learning outside the public or private school environment. For most families, their "schooling" involves being out and about each day, learning from the rich resources available in their community and environment, and through interactions with other families who homeschool. One mother in my practice, Cynthia, had shared with a neighbor, a recently retired public school teacher, that her son performed very well on the SATs. Her friend's response was, "Couldn't you be holding him back by homeschooling him?" The teacher apparently went on a long soliloquy about Cynthia's son being a bright, high performer and that he was missing out on many opportunities offered in public school. When I asked Cynthia how she responded to this unsolicited advice, she said, "I kept my cool and asked her if she had considered that my son is performing so well *because* he is being homeschooled."

Therapeutic boarding schools are boarding schools based on the therapeutic community model that offer an educational program together with specialized structure and supervision for students with emotional and behavioral problems, substance abuse problems, or learning difficulties.

Therapeutic boarding schools are different from conventional residential treatment programs, which are more clinically focused and primarily provide therapy and treatment for adolescents with serious mental health issues. The focus of a therapeutic boarding school is toward emotional and academic recovery involving structure and supervision for physical, emotional, behavioral, family, social, intellectual, and academic development.

Adolescent partial hospital programs are less restrictive environments for adolescents with psychiatric problems or a combination of psychiatric and substance abuse problems that impair functioning at home and school. Adolescents live at home and attend a day program (typically six hours, for example 9:00 a.m. to 3:00 p.m.) five days per week. Transportation is available within defined areas. Another variant of this option is after-school treatment programs. These are also designed for adolescents with less sever psychiatric or substance abuse problems that still impair their functioning at school or at home. In this shortened form of treatment, adolescents attend the three-hour program a few days per week after attending school.

DAY
(8)   SUMMING IT UP

Today you learned how to manage your child's defiance at school. Consistent with the approach of my ten-day plan, the emphasis is for you to be calm, firm, and noncontrolling with the school personnel and to coach them to use this approach with your child. You also learned:

- How the emotional immaturity of defiant children leads them to have problems at school
- How teachers' styles and methods can provoke or alleviate your child's defiance at school
- That your defiant child's level of self-esteem is largely determined by how he fares at school
- That if you advocate and don't irritate, teachers are generally open to working with you to help your defiant child
- That there are laws to protect the educational rights of your child

GETTING READY FOR DAY 9

- Stay mindful that your child may need your support with managing challenges at school.
- Stay calm, firm, and noncontrolling with your child when discussing his academic status and any related issues.
- Establish rapport and seek the advice of academic support personnel if your child is struggling at school.
- Keep informed of evolving education laws and how these may bear upon your child's possible academic support needs and available interventions.
- If your child continues to struggle in public school, consider exploring alternative educational settings. Make sure you think through the advantages and disadvantages and do so in an informed manner.

DAY
9

Overcoming
Stubborn Obstacles

Congratulations—you have come a long way in a short time. Think of all the strategies you've learned to help your child to be less defiant! If you remember back to Day 1, I mentioned that there can be other causes of defiant behavior above and beyond parenting approaches, genetics, and environmental factors. Now that you are on Day 9, it's time to learn about some mental health conditions that can cause or exacerbate defiant behavior in children. The good news is that no matter what other condition exists in your child, the strategies I have provided for you in this book will still help reduce his defiance. As you have discovered by now, the heart of my approach involves:

- Harnessing the power of understanding your child
- Avoiding yelling and being your child's emotion coach as well as his parent
- Sidestepping power struggles by being calm, firm, and non-controlling, and by picking battles wisely
- Reinforcing the positive changes in your child
- Using my Discipline Without Desperation strategies
- Rallying family support for your defiant child
- Addressing and reducing defiance at school

While these strategies and tools are very effective, there are some mental health conditions that make defiance in children more persistent and stubborn. If you're not seeing results, it's possible that your child suffers from one or more of these conditions. Today you're going to learn about these as "stubborn obstacles" to reducing defiance. Understanding these stubborn obstacles and how to deal with them means you're leaving no stone unturned on the path to reducing your child's defiance.

Please Note:

As with all the information in my ten-day program, the knowledge provided to you today is educational in nature. Please bear in mind that the formal diagnosis and treatment of any mental health conditions, including those described in this section, should be made by a qualified mental health professional.

Identifying Stubborn Obstacles

Here is a list of the most common stubborn obstacles to reducing defiance. It is representative of the types of conditions and related problems that I have seen engender defiance in children. The severity of all the conditions listed below can vary. Some kids can have several symptoms from more than one condition mixed in with their defiant behavior. Also, remember that these are only conceptual classifications. In the same way that each defiant child has his own individual strengths and weaknesses, each of these conditions affects children uniquely. Don't get discouraged if you discover that your defiant child has one or more of these problems. They can usually be managed effectively.

- Attention-deficit/hyperactivity disorder (ADHD)
- Learning disabilities
- Depression or bipolar disorder
- Anxiety
- Drug and alcohol abuse
- Health problems such as allergies, gastrointestinal problems, migraine headaches, obesity, and sleep disorders
- Autism spectrum disorder (ASD)

- Tourette's syndrome
- Other stresses, such as arrival of a new sibling, school pressures, peer conflicts, divorce, and relocation

ADHD Aggravates Defiance

Of all the conditions that can overlap with and fuel a child's defiant behaviors, attention-deficit/hyperactivity disorder (ADHD) is the most common. It's estimated that ADHD affects 3 to 5 percent of school-age children nationwide. While the severity of ADHD symptoms may vary in children, ADHD-related concerns include any combination of hyperactivity, distractibility, poor concentration, and impulsivity. One colorful example of ADHD was relayed to me by Paul, a stay-at-home dad of a very impulsive nine-year-old girl. When his daughter was four years old, she moved a chair to climb on it and reach the car keys on top of a cabinet. This adventurous and very determined four-year-old then proceeded outside and started up her parents' car—all because she wanted to listen to the radio! ADHD usually affects performance in school, social relationships with other children, and behavior at home. These concerns can make life quite difficult for all children, but especially for defiant ones. Defiant children with ADHD are more likely to be disrespectful and lash out at authority figures such as parents and teachers than are other children with ADHD.

A PRIMER FOR UNDERSTANDING ADHD

The following information is based on the diagnostic criteria for ADHD listed in the American Psychiatric Association's *Diagnostic and Statistical Manual of Mental Disorders, Fifth Edition* (DSM-5). Symptoms of ADHD need to be evident for at least six months to a degree that they create problems that are inconsistent with your child's developmental level. Some of the symptoms causing the impairment need to have been present before age seven. For a child to be formally diagnosed with ADHD, some impairment from the symptoms needs to be present in two or more settings (e.g., at school and at home). And there must be clear evidence of significant impairment in school and social functioning.

It is interesting to note that in contrast to earlier editions of the *DSM*, ADHD is now included in the section under neurodevelopmental disorders, rather than being grouped with the disruptive behavior disorders, that is, oppositional defiant disorder and conduct disorder. Below is a description of the actual diagnostic criteria for ADHD.

Children diagnosed with ADHD must have at least six symptoms from either (or both) the inattention group of criteria and the hyperactivity and impulsivity criteria, while older adolescents and adults (over age seventeen years) must present with five. *DSM-5* includes no exclusion criteria for children and adults with autism spectrum disorder, since symptoms of both disorders co-occur. However, ADHD symptoms must not occur exclusively during the course of schizophrenia or another psychotic disorder and must not be better explained by any other mental disorder, such as depression or bipolar disorder, anxiety disorder, dissociative disorder, personality disorder, or substance intoxication or withdrawal.

A child with ADHD who has symptoms of inattention often:

- does not seem to listen when spoken to directly.
- does not reliably finish his chores or homework.
- finds it hard to keep his mind on what he's doing for very long unless he finds it interesting or stimulating.
- makes a lot of careless mistakes due to poor attention. Note: Extended video game use (a few hours) can lead many parents to think, "See, he really can pay attention if he wants to." But video games are an exception because they have multimodal input (visual, auditory, and tactile) and give immediate feedback—this makes them exciting, fun, and attention grabbing/sustaining.
- is really disorganized. Kids with poor attention may take hours to finally finish homework, then "lose" it at school (but the whole time it's in their backpack), or forget to turn it in.
- tries to avoid doing homework or chores.
- gets distracted easily, or pays attention to other things.
- is forgetful and needs frequent reminders.

A child with ADHD who has symptoms of hyperactivity and impulsivity often:

- blurts out answers in class.
- has difficulty waiting his turn when playing games or at school.
- interrupts others.
- does things without thinking about them first.
- does not consider the consequences of his actions.
- moves his hands and feet and squirms.
- can't stay in his seat for very long when he's supposed to at school or the dinner table.
- runs around too much, or climbs on things he's not supposed to.
- is too loud.
- acts like he is constantly "on the go," as if he is "driven by a motor."
- talks too much.

Defiant children have a low tolerance for frustration to begin with, and once ADHD is thrown into the mix, the added chaos can exacerbate defiant tendencies. Think about it. Not being able to sit still or stop your mind from drifting all over the place can be very upsetting and frustrating. Some kids have inattention as the main problem, while others have hyperactivity/impulsivity as the bigger challenge, and some must contend with both issues.

As I was writing this chapter, I heard from a former client named Leah who wanted to let me know that her fourteen-year-old son, Glen, was currently managing his life well. A few months earlier, Leah had brought Glen in after he stole twelve hundred dollars from her checking account and went on a skateboard and music shopping spree. Glen's impulsive behaviors were very consistent with ADHD-related problems. He had been diagnosed with ADHD at age seven.

When he was brought to see me, Glen had a surge of impulsive behaviors. These were in response to being very upset about his parents' recent divorce and his academic and social problems adjusting to a new school. Largely due to his ADHD, Glen's historic pattern of behavior had been to become more impulsive and defiant when he was anxious. I discovered by talking to Glen that he had also been "forgetting" to take his ADHD medication around the time he stole the money. I encouraged Glen to begin taking his medication again, and he agreed, "as long as mom stops nagging me." In addition to nagging less, Leah used the Discipline Without Desperation strategies you learned on Day 6. Glen became much less defiant after we all agreed on the following:

- Glen would take his medication.
- Glen would return the merchandise to the stores.
- Leah would praise Glen's willingness to come back to see me to discuss the concerns bothering him about the divorce and school.
- Glen would do additional chores for a month to earn a new skateboard.

The kicker with children with ADHD is that they are often perceived in a pejorative way. Parents sometimes view kids with ADHD as *choosing not* to listen, stay focused, control their impulses, or be quiet. What these parents forget is that children with ADHD often *cannot* control themselves in these ways.

Kids with ADHD can't regulate themselves because ADHD is a neurological problem. The brain of an ADHD child cannot control impulses and facilitate attention as well as the brain of a child without ADHD. It has been heart wrenching for me to see hyperactive and impulsive ADHD children lumped into the category of "disciplinary problem" without their challenges being understood. Similarly, children with ADHD who are inattentive, disengaged, and internally preoccupied are viewed as unmotivated, or worse yet, "lazy." Yet both groups have different types of ADHD and typically cannot (as opposed to choosing not to) stop these problems on their own. Complicating things even further, the symptoms vary widely across settings, making ADHD difficult to diagnose. This is even more the case when inattentiveness is the primary symptom, since these types of children are usually quiet and blend in more than hyperactive children.

Heather, age eleven, turned out to be a child with a classic combination of defiant behavior and ADHD. Heather's mother, Mary

Beth, brought Heather in to see me after her teachers expressed continuing concerns about her concentration and attention problems. I did a screening for ADHD, which resulted in overwhelmingly positive ADHD ratings (mainly around inattention) from Heather's teachers and her parents. In addition to her focusing and attention problems, Heather also had problems making and keeping friends. Heather's peer problems were likely due to her inability to sustain focus and listen and respond to peer conversations. Homework battles continued to be a problem even though Mary Beth used many of the suggestions I shared with you on Day 3.

Like many parents of defiant children, Mary Beth was quite frustrated and had been yelling a lot. I was pleased to see that Heather's defiance began to decrease considerably once her mother began using my calm, firm, and noncontrolling approach. Heather's pediatrician prescribed a medication to further help her improve her ability to focus. Once the school had a confirmed diagnosis of ADHD, they made special provisions for Heather so she could better meet the academic challenges.

If you recall, on Day 8 I discussed school issues related to defiant behavior. Schools often will agree to make reasonable accommodations to help a child with ADHD to focus, learn, and behave better in the classroom. They usually recognize that it is in everyone's interest to help the child improve. Schools may agree to change a child's seat location, provide you with a copy of his homework assignments, or assist the child in other ways. In seeking the school's agreement to make such changes, you should be prepared to explain why the changes are necessary. It may also be helpful to produce a letter from your child's psychologist or counselor of the requested changes. Or you could ask this individual to contact the school directly to advocate for the needed accommodations. In many cases, the school will offer additional ideas on changes and accommodations that can be made.

You should be aware, however, that under current school laws, a diagnosis of ADHD alone does not necessarily qualify a student for any special help, instruction, or accommodations. As described on Day 8, a child with ADHD or other disability will need to be screened and determined by the school to have a disability in order to qualify for special education and related services. This is a legal determination that can occur only after an evaluation is performed that conforms to federal and state law. If this requirement is satisfied, the child may then be eligible for an individualized education plan (IEP) that specifies the accommodations and other services for which he is eligible.

In other cases, a child may not qualify for an IEP, but may qualify for a "504 plan," named after a separate federal law that is designed to prevent unlawful discrimination against children or others with a disability. To be eligible under this federal law, a child must be evaluated and found to have a physical or mental impairment that "substantially limits" performance in at least one "major life activity." The ability to learn is one such activity. If your child is found to be eligible for a 504 plan, she may be legally entitled to accommodations that are not available to nondisabled children.

ENSURING THAT YOUR ADHD CHILD'S NEEDS ARE BEING MET AT SCHOOL

It's important for you to be aware of the possible types of classroom accommodations that can be offered to your child at school. The more specific the strategies you suggest to your child's teacher to use with your child, or encourage her to keep using, the more effective you will be in advocating for your child at school. Feel free to discuss with your child's teacher or educational support team how such strategies as those below may be helpful for your child's educational needs. Several of these ideas are based on Edward Hallowell's book *Driven to Distraction*. In addition, my book *10 Days to a Less Distracted Child* presents a comprehensive yet easy to apply ten-day program to lessen distractibility in children. While your goal is clearly not to take over the teacher's job or become her boss, you will be supporting your child by determining if and how his teacher is doing any of the following:

- breaking down large tasks into small tasks so that children avoid becoming overwhelmed.
- being sure to give positive feedback when appropriate
  This is so important because children with ADHD often hear so much negative feedback.

- providing additional time for homework, classwork, tests, and projects to compensate for the difficulties with attention common to many students with ADHD.
- using tutors in school.
- using preferential seating close to the source of instruction.
- allowing your child to check his notes against a peer's to ensure accuracy of recorded information.
- using private, quiet rooms for test taking, if possible.
- supporting oral directions with written ones, and vice versa.
- empathizing with your child's feelings.
- clarifying and repeating directions.
- making frequent eye contact. You can "cue back" an ADHD child with eye contact. Do it often. A glance can retrieve a child from a daydream, give permission to ask a question, or just give him silent reassurance.
- setting limits and boundaries but not in a punitive way. Doing it consistently, predictably, promptly, and plainly.

The best treatment for ADHD is to be a supportive, caring parent, which I'm sure you are if you're reading this book. I encourage you to refer to the Resources section on page 296 to get more information on this topic. One organization that can be very helpful is CHADD, the contact information for which is listed in the Resources section.

Learning Disabilities Can Also Cause Defiance

Defiant children can also have underlying learning disabilities, which can exist alone or with the other conditions discussed today. Educators estimate that between 5 and 10 percent of children between the ages of six and seventeen have learning disabilities. More than half of the children receiving special education in the United States have learning disabilities. Dyslexia is the most common learning disability. Eighty percent of students with learning disabilities have dyslexia. Learning disabilities, like ADHD, have a neurological basis and are disorders that affect the ability to understand or use spoken or written language, do mathematical calculations, coordinate movements, or direct attention. Again, similar to the issues with ADHD, defiant children can be easily frustrated and act out in response to the challenges of their learning disability. Here is a list of common learning disabilities:

Dyslexia. This is a language-based disability. Children with dyslexia have trouble reading and understanding words, sentences, or paragraphs.

Dyscalculia. This is a mathematical disability in which a child has a very difficult time solving arithmetic problems and grasping math concepts.

Dysgraphia. This is a writing disability in which a child finds it hard to form letters correctly or write within a defined space.

Nonverbal learning disabilities. These include any learning disability that is not language related, such as difficulty in recognizing, reading, and interpreting nonverbal communication and with problem solving. Other problems involve controlling one's actions, restraining and delaying responses, focusing one's attention, organizing information, and setting goals.

Auditory and visual processing disabilities. These are sensory disabilities in which a child has difficulty understanding language despite normal hearing and vision.

Children with learning disabilities often require the services available through the special education system. Special education is instruction specially designed to meet a child's unique needs. This instruction may include intensive remediation in reading, math, or other areas of need. It also may include services such as psychological counseling, physical and occupational therapy, speech and language services, transportation, and medical diagnosis. A high percentage of all children receiving special education are considered to have some form of learning disability.

Phillip was a ten-year-old defiant child who had been diagnosed with dyslexia. He had considerable anger at not being able to read as easily as his peers, let alone his eight-year-old sister. At my suggestion, Phillip's mother, Jeanette, worked closely with the school to support and collaborate on an IEP developed for Phillip to help him learn despite his learning challenges. In addition, Jeanette privately sought out a very effective reading specialist who had extensive experience working with children with dyslexia. Once the dyslexia was addressed, Phillip's defiance was considerably lessened. He and I worked on helping him to see his unique talents and on how to compete less with his sister.

Learning disabilities can be a lifelong challenge. In some children, several overlapping learning disabilities may be present. Other children may have a single, isolated learning problem that has little impact on their lives. The good news is that there are many educational recommendations and resources to help address them. Turn to the Resources section for more information.

Depression Drives Defiance

Depression can also be a complicating problem for defiant children. Its origin can be genetic and physiological. Depression can also occur in response to events such as divorce, relocation, social problems, death of a loved one, or breaking up with a boyfriend or girlfriend. While only 2 percent of preteen children and 3 to 5 percent of teenagers have clinical depression, next to anxiety disorders, depression is the most common diagnosis of children who have mental health problems. While depression can be similar between adults and children, there are a few differences. Adults more often experience an enduring sense of sadness, while some children and adolescents can display a more irritable than depressed mood. Adults may tend to lose weight, while children may not gain the expected amount of weight for their age.

I have met with many children with depression who feel chronically sad and discouraged. I have found that defiant children who are depressed tend to "act out" their depression with negative behaviors such as being disrespectful, provoking peers, or sabotaging their school efforts. The anger is often huge in defiant children who are depressed. In mental health circles we believe that "anger is depression turned inward." This certainly seems to be the case for defiant children struggling with depression. Depression can occur in a vicious cycle. If a child has negative feelings about herself and the world around her, it leads to problems at home and at school, which leads to more depression, which in turn can lead to defiance. Depression sucks a defiant child's self-esteem dry, which is another reason it's so crucial to address.

DISCERNING THE SIGNS OF
DEPRESSION IN CHILDREN

Following are common symptoms of depression in children. If at least three of the following symptoms persist for more than two weeks, you should seek out a thorough professional evaluation of your child. Not all children with depression experience each of these symptoms. The severity of the symptoms also varies from child to child. The diagnosis of depression should be made only by a trained medical or mental health professional.

Children who struggle with depression may:

- feel sad or cry a lot.
- feel guilty for no reason.
- have low self-esteem.
- view life as meaningless, or feel that nothing good is ever going to happen again.
- withdraw from doing the things they used to like—music, sports, being with friends, going out—and want to be left alone most of the time.
- have trouble concentrating and making decisions.
- get irritated often and overreact.
- have sleep pattern changes, including sleeping more or having trouble falling asleep at night.
- have either a marked loss or gain of appetite.
- feel restless and tired most of the time.
- think about death, or feel like they're dying, or have thoughts about committing suicide.

In the words of an insightful speaker, Kevin Breel, speaking about depression on social media, "There's this pretty popular misconception that depression is just being sad when something in your life goes wrong, when you break up with your girlfriend, when you lose a loved one, when you don't get the job you wanted. But that's sadness. That's a natural thing. That's a natural human emotion. Real depression isn't being sad when something in your life goes wrong. Real depression is being sad when everything in your life is going right." As Breel further shared, children, teens, and adults feel shame about depression and our society largely ignores the magnitude of this mental health problem. He gave the compelling example contrasting how people post pictures of their casts for broken bones on social media but they don't announce to the world that they are feeling so depressed that they don't want to get out of bed.

If you have any suspicion that your child is depressed, you must have her evaluated and treated. Self-injury or even suicide attempts are a possibility if depression is not addressed. Depression can be managed, and it's common for oppositional and defiant behaviors to lessen as the depression is treated. Sometimes antidepressant medication helps. I have personally seen that if depression and defiant behavior are not managed, they will both get worse.

Elise was fourteen years old and increasingly spent time listening to music and writing dark poetry. Her mother and father tried to ask Elise why she felt sad. Her answer was, "Nothing makes me happy and no one likes me." Elise's grades were deteriorating, and when she made a few cuts on her arm and leg in response to her emotional pain, her parents brought her in to see me. (Self-mutilation is usually more about using physical pain to offset and release inner, emotional pain than it is about intent of suicide.)

Elise had always been defiant, but not to the extremes she had recently reached. Elise was quite physically mature (she looked sixteen or seventeen), but she didn't have the emotional maturity of a girl that age. Handling the changes, expectations, and pressures of her physical maturation was very stressful to Elise.

Elise had become extremely difficult to live with. As her depression had increased, so had her defiance. She would fight her parents or anyone else for no reason at all. She seldom seemed happy—her baseline moods were sadness and anger.

Elise worked with me in counseling and she also received antidepressant medication from a psychiatrist. Elise told me that she felt she disappointed her parents because she could not meet their expectations. She had very low self-esteem, and to a large extent this came from being objectified for her physical attractiveness by boys and being rejected by female peers who were jealous of her. She described, "loving and hating a huge amount of 'likes'" on social media. As I spoke further with Elise, I realized that her parents were actually far more supportive than she thought. At the same time, her parents did not communicate this support to Elise very effectively. After a few emotional family counseling sessions and my coaching her parents to listen in ways they never had before, Elise began to feel better. We all worked together to validate Elise's peer concerns and supportively guided her to seek more supportive friends. Her defiance lessened as a result of relieving her depression.

What Your Child Thinks Will Shape How He Feels

In helping defiant children who suffer from depression, I find it very useful to learn how they think about themselves. My immediate goal, however, is to build trust with children by being empathetic and supportive, and, where appropriate, using humor. I also incorporate activities including counseling-oriented card decks and board games to develop trust and to foster more effective coping skills. Throughout the counseling process I also have children draw to express feelings, along with using other child-friendly counseling techniques.

In trying to help children learn how to think in more rational and helpful ways, I use tools from cognitive therapy. Cognitive counseling strategies can be very helpful for children with depression and anxiety, and this includes defiant children. The basic assumption of the cognitive counseling model is that there is a strong relationship between thinking, feeling, and behavior. In other words, feelings and behavior are influenced by our thoughts. This means that our feelings can be controlled by changing our distorted thinking patterns. Examples of these patterns are:

Black-and-white thinking—"I'm either a good person or a bad one."
Catastrophizing—"Nothing will go my way, ever."
Overgeneralization—"No one can be trusted."
Personalization—"It must have been my fault."
"Should" statements—"He should invite me over to his house."

Such negative thinking can be changed to more healthy, helpful thoughts as shown in the box on the next page.

Negative Thinking Pattern	Negative Thought	Alternative Helpful Thought
Black-and-white thinking	"I'm either a good person or a bad one."	"I can still like myself even if there are parts of me I want to change."
Catastrophizing	"Nothing will go my way, ever."	"I'd like more things to go well for me, and many have already."
Overgeneralization	"I can't keep any friends."	"My friendships have not gone as well as I would like, but I can explore why they have not worked and learn from this."
Personalization	"It must be my fault."	"I can learn good things from this mistake."
"Should" statements	"He should invite me to his house."	"I would like him to invite me over, but if he doesn't, I will do something else instead."

Contrary to the popular belief about defiant children, I have found that using cognitive therapy methods with them is very effective. When working with depressed, defiant children, my goal is to help them:

- Understand the relationship between thoughts, feelings, and behavior
- Recognize their own distorted thoughts
- Examine the evidence for and against their irrational thoughts
- Identify alternatives to distorted thinking
- Adopt more realistic thoughts that will lead to more stable and positive emotions

Geoff was an eleven-year-old depressed and defiant child. His parents brought him to see me after he threatened to stab his father with a knife during an argument. Once Geoff sat down with me, I drew a picture of two sticks of dynamite, one with a short fuse and one with a long fuse (I have found this visual modality helpful for children who are not as self-aware of their emotions). Next, I asked Geoff to pick which stick of dynamite represented a better way to handle his anger—he picked the long fuse over the short fuse. I explained to Geoff how controlling his thoughts can make the fuse either shorter or longer.

With my prompting, he identified the following distorted thoughts:

- "I can't do anything right."
- "Everyone thinks I am stupid."
- "I suck at basketball."

These negative thoughts were quite easy to disprove. Geoff and I made lists of successes in his life that showed him that these thoughts were just not true. We agreed that he did many things well, that he was by no means stupid, and that his basketball abilities were average, not horrible.

Then I helped Geoff come up with these alternative healthier thoughts:

- "I do many things well, and I am still okay if I make some mistakes."
- "I'm not stupid, but I do have to work harder in math than some other students."
- "I'm not a basketball star, but I can get stronger skills by practicing more and going to a basketball camp this summer."

As a result of our work together, Geoff had far fewer self-deprecating thoughts and comments. This shift in thinking helped chip away at Geoff's depression.

My point is that cognitive counseling (and medication, when deemed necessary) can help most depressed children start to feel better in just a few weeks. A critical consideration in helping defiant children with depression is to get them to see that they are not alone. Being supportive and trying to understand what is troubling your defiant child makes a huge difference.

Bipolar Disorder

Bipolar disorder, formerly termed manic-depressive disorder, can occur in children and adolescents as well as adults. Bipolar disorder affects an estimated 1 to 2 percent of adults worldwide. The numbers have not been firmly established in children. In kids, symptoms of bipolar disorder may initially be mistaken for normal emotions and behaviors. In addition, bipolar disorder in children and adolescents can be hard to tell apart from other problems that may occur in these age groups. For example, while irritability and aggressiveness can indicate bipolar disorder, they also can be symptoms of attention-deficit/hyperactivity disorder, conduct disorder, oppositional defiant disorder, or other types of mental disorders more common among adults, such as major depression or even schizophrenia. Drug abuse also may lead to such symptoms.

Many parents may get a chuckle or two out of their children's moodiness. Unlike normal mood changes, however, bipolar disorder is no laughing matter. It significantly impairs functioning in school, with peers, and at home with family. Bipolar children may show no clear-cut mood cycles but rather sustained or rapidly fluctuating periods of high energy, volatility, defiance, grandiosity, irritability, anxiety, and explosiveness. In many ways, children with bipolar disorder can appear like other defiant kids. When a child is defiant and has bipolar disorder, things can be even more challenging. It's important to stay optimistic if your child does have bipolar disorder. Most people with bipolar disorder—even those with the most severe forms—can stabilize their mood swings and related symptoms with the proper treatment.

DEMYSTIFYING BIPOLAR DISORDER

Children with bipolar disorder will have some symptoms from the list of signs of depresssion (see page 222) and at least three from the following list of manic behaviors persisting for one week:

- Severe changes in mood, either extremely irritable or overly silly and elated

- Overly inflated self-esteem
- Increased energy
- Decreased need for sleep, ability to go with very little or no sleep for days without tiring
- Increased talking, talks too much, too fast; changes topics too quickly; cannot be interrupted
- Distractibility, attention moves constantly from one thing to the next
- Hypersexuality; increased sexual thoughts, feelings, or behaviors; use of explicit sexual language
- Increased goal-directed activity or physical agitation
- Disregard of risk; excessive involvement in risky behaviors or activities

I worked with a fifteen-year-old defiant child named Charles who also had bipolar disorder. When Charles first came in to see me, he was very negative in his outlook and was quite depressed. Charles had a long history (since age six) of emotional volatility and verbal outbursts.

Over the course of a few short weeks he became more and more cheerful. I thought I was doing a wonderful job of helping him work through his depression. What I soon realized, however, was that Charles was in the midst of a manic episode. He had no desire to sleep and stayed up all hours of the night surfing the Internet to watch porn and voraciously explore Wikipedia as well. He talked a mile a minute and, according to him as well as his parents, had abundant surges of energy. A referral to a psychiatrist colleague confirmed my suspicions that Charles had bipolar disorder. Charles was put on a mood stabilizer and some other medications that were successful in reducing his mood cycling.

Anxiety Amplifies Defiance

Approximately 10 percent of all youth experience anxiety disorders, and most go untreated. Sadly, as in the case of depression, there is also often denial of anxiety. This is because of the concern that anxiety is perceived as weak, particularly among defiant children. As mentioned previously, defiant children tend to have lower emotional self-awareness, and so for many of them with anxiety, their "go to" emotion tends to instead be anger. I have often seen that underneath the bravado of a defiant child lurks significant anxiety. Anxiety-related problems in defiant children can interfere with school attendance, create problems with peer relationships, lower self-esteem, and drive negative self-perceptions. Children with anxiety have a subjective sense of worry, apprehension, and fear. Most kids have these feelings on occasion, so it's important to distinguish between normal and unhealthy levels of anxiety.

While there are different forms of anxiety problems, which I describe in the next few pages, kids who struggle with anxiety tend to have these types of symptoms:

- Intense worry
- Headaches
- Nausea
- Sweating
- Stomach pain
- Shortness of breath
- Poor decision-making ability
- Distorted views of others
- Problems concentrating
- Negative perceptions of their environment

Defiant children who struggle with anxiety feel a lot of shame and frustration. The diagnosis of normal versus abnormal anxiety depends largely upon the degree of distress and its effect on a child's functioning. The degree of problems is best viewed in the context of the child's age and developmental level. Defiant children I have counseled have shared a wide range of fears with me. These include:

- Fear of the dark
- Fear of being rejected by peers
- Fear of doing poorly in sports and activities
- Fear of doing poorly at school

Eight-year-old Corey was brought to see me because he took a key and scraped it against his father's car. Corey's father had threatened that he would have to sleep with his light off—something Corey was very afraid of. Corey dealt with his fear by becoming more defiant. I helped Corey's dad learn that Corey's way of coping with his fear was to become defiant. In counseling with me, Corey learned to verbalize and work through his night fears instead of suppressing them and acting out angrily with poor behavior choices.

Various patterns of anxiety can plague children. I've detailed some of the more common ones below.

Generalized Anxiety Disorder

Generalized anxiety disorder appears to be the most common form of anxiety in children. Children with generalized anxiety anticipate the worst and often complain of fatigue, tension, headaches, and nausea. Defiant kids with generalized anxiety have excessive worry, apprehension, and anxiety occurring most days for a period of six months or more. They tend to feel restless, keyed up, or on edge; are easily fatigued; have difficulty concentrating or their minds go blank; are irritable; have muscle tension; and have difficulty falling or staying asleep or have restless sleep.

Darryl was a seven-year-old boy who had symptoms of generalized anxiety disorder. His defiance (mostly evidenced by loud banging and by bullying his younger sister when his parents tried to talk to one another) was amplified in response to his worrying episodes, which were quite frequent. I showed Darryl how to "breathe away" his worries with deep-breathing exercises. His mother and father also learned to give Darryl praise any time he distracted himself from his worries. For example, Darryl was keyed up one day, and at his mother's supportive urging he agreed to try to forget about his worries by helping her make cookies. These efforts, combined with individual and family counseling, helped reduce Darryl's generalized anxiety. Over the course of a few months, Darryl's anxiety diminished and his defiance followed the same course.

Panic Disorder

Panic disorder is characterized by panic attacks and results in sudden feelings of intense fear. These seem to come out of the blue. The most difficult aspect of panic is the panic over being panicked. Like depression and all forms of anxiety, the thoughts and feelings can become a vicious cycle. Anna, thirteen, had made a lot of progress in lowering her defiance in response to her father making the changes suggested in this ten-day program. Anna was raised primarily by her father, and she told me that she was deeply scared because she had begun to question her sexual orientation.

Not long after we finished about three months of counseling, Anna began to develop classic symptoms of panic-related problems. Panic disorder can include chest pain, heart palpitations, shortness of breath, dizziness, nausea or abdominal distress, lightheadedness, abdominal discomfort, feelings of unreality, intense desire to escape, feelings of doom or dread and impending danger, and fear of dying. Anna had most of these symptoms. Like most children with this disorder, Anna had considerable worry, self-consciousness, and tension. I used cognitive therapy and relaxation training as the main ways to help her reduce her panic. I also employed a visualization tool I had learned years ago at an anxiety-reduction seminar. I asked Anna to imagine slowly wrapping a ball of string made of warm, soothing white light all around her to feel safe and secure. Once she was able to control her panic symptoms, I worked with Anna to help her explore her issues with her sexual orientation. While Anna was aware that she was genetically predisposed to panic since her mother also had anxiety issues, she realized that her questions about her sexual orientation had been fueling her panic. By giving Anna "permission" to continue to explore her sexual orientation without feeling pressured to figure it out immediately, she found that her panic was greatly reduced.

WHAT YOU CAN DO IF YOUR CHILD HAS A PANIC ATTACK

Panic attacks include shortness of breath, heart palpitations, dizziness, dry mouth, nausea or diarrhea, high levels of muscle tension, and possibly an irrational fear of death. If your child has a panic attack, the following may be helpful:

- Use my approach of being calm, firm, and noncontrolling. In addition, be sure to speak in a supportive, soothing, and accepting manner. The calmer you remain, the greater the likelihood your child will calm down as well.

- Maintain eye contact, listen, and reassure your child that she will be fine.
- Gently encourage slow deep breaths, while being reassuring and nonjudgmental. Sit with your child. Seek medical attention if the situation worsens.
- Listen for irrational thoughts (e.g., "I have no future," "No one will ever like me," "No one ever takes me seriously," "I suck at everything I do," "Everyone in the school is going to say bad things about me for the next ten years.").
- Once your child starts to calm down, help her to see that irrational self-talk can provoke anxiety. Work to show the lack of evidence for irrational (unhelpful) thoughts and help your child find evidence for more rational (helpful) thoughts. So, for example, give fact-based reasons why your child is not a total failure or total loser or totally unpopular. Pointing out such exceptions to the rule is very helpful. For younger children age four to six who have fears that drive their panic, you can use puppets, drawings, and stories to help them see scary things differently. Vernon was a five-year-old boy I helped break free of panic by helping him "believe" that the imaginary monster under his bed was actually his personal bodyguard.
- To help prevent future panic, have your child ask himself, "What is the worst that can happen?" when he begins to feel panicked. This may help him calm down and see that panic is not warranted.

Obsessive-Compulsive Disorder

Some defiant kids may also have obsessions (intrusive, unwanted thoughts or urges) and compulsions (intense uncontrollable repetitive behaviors related to the obsessions) that are unreasonable and excessive. These obsessions and compulsions wreak havoc on a child's ability to feel good about himself. They cause considerable distress and impairment and can be time-consuming (they often eat up more than one hour a day). The most common obsessions involve germs, dirt, and contamination; repeated doubts; the need to have things arranged in a specific way; fear of aggressive or harmful impulses; and disturbing sexual imagery. The most frequent compulsions involve repetitive washing of hands or using a tissue to touch things; checking drawers, locks, windows, and doors; counting rituals; repeating actions; and requesting reassurance.

Katie, age nine, had temper outbursts. While reviewing her family history, I noted that obsessive-compulsive disorder had apparently been suspected in her maternal grandmother. With the help of counseling and a referral to a psychiatrist who prescribed medication, Katie's excessive needs to check to see if the doors were locked, to make sure the refrigerator handle was clean, and to tap her fingers all decreased along with her defiant temper outbursts.

Post-Traumatic Stress Disorder

I've worked with some defiant children who experienced a trauma such as sexual or physical abuse, natural disasters, or extreme violence. They developed post-traumatic stress disorder symptoms, including nightmares, flashbacks, the numbing of emotions, depression, anger, irritability, and being easily distracted and startled. Nine-year-old Roberto was referred to me after he was attacked by a neighbor's dog. Roberto had been defiant prior to the attack and he became more defiant because of his post-traumatic symptoms. Part of the plan to help Roberto involved cognitive therapy as described above. In addition, his parents got him a small puppy, which helped him work though his post-traumatic stress.

Phobias

A phobia is a disabling and irrational fear of something that actually poses little or no real danger. The fear leads to avoidance of objects or situations and can cause extreme feelings of terror, dread, and panic, which can substantially restrict one's life. Specific phobias center around particular objects (e.g., certain animals) or situations (e.g., heights or enclosed spaces).

Jacque was an eight-year-old boy who was scared of vampires. He would chase his younger brother and try to scare him in an effort to displace his own fears. My review of the family tree revealed that his mother and relatives on her side had different forms of anxiety disorders. In Jacque's case, however, his anxiety was very localized around his fear of vampires. I played a movie for him that showed the antics of a blundering, inept vampire, and this helped me challenge Jacque's negative image of vampires. He also became less defiant with his brother. Jacque returned to see me as a teenager, this time because he felt hurt at being rejected by a girl he liked. We laughed together about how dealing with vampires was a lot easier than dealing with relationships!

Social Phobia

Social phobia is a stubborn and persistent fear of one or more social situations in which a child is exposed to unfamiliar people or to possible scrutiny by others. Kurt was an eleven-year-old boy who had some of the classic symptoms of social phobia. He was anxious about showing anxiety symptoms (notice the cyclical nature of this) that his peers could view as embarrassing. As a result, Kurt was a loner when he really didn't want to be.

Children with social phobia have poor social skills. For most of the nondefiant and defiant children I have seen with social phobia, the avoidance, anxious anticipation, or distress in the feared social or performance situation(s) interferes significantly with their lives.

Common symptoms of social phobias are:

- Hypersensitivity to criticism
- Difficulty being assertive and low self-esteem
- Fear of reading aloud in front of class
- Fear of musical or athletic performances
- Fear of joining in on a conversation
- Fear of speaking to adults
- Fear of starting a conversation
- Fear of giving a class presentation
- Fear of attending dances or birthday parties

- Fear of answering questions in class
- Fear of asking the teacher for help

I have helped defiant children like Kurt manage their social pho-bia by teaching them how to relax and how to use appropriate social skills. I have also found that children tend to respond well to learning to identify and change anxious thoughts that serve to increase their feelings of anxiety in social situations. By thinking more positive, ra-tional thoughts, children are typically able to enter social situations more easily. Again, I rely on cognitive therapy techniques to help children reduce distortions in their thinking. I also help children de-velop lists of successful social situations they have been in. We work together to try to "spread this around" to future social situations. I also guide children to develop lists of situations that are challenging for them, such as going to a party, talking on the phone, or talking to a friend. Then they are taught to use their coping skills while grad-ually facing each of these situations. Children's successes are highly praised by me and by their parents. I also stress that expectations are best kept realistic and that the goal of counseling is not to transform the child into a social butterfly.

Health Problems Heighten Defiance

There are many health problems that defiant children can have. While there are too many to mention all of them here, some repre-sentative medical problems of children include:

- Asthma
- Allergies
- Bone diseases
- Cancer
- Constipation or encopresis
- Cystic fibrosis
- Gastrointestinal problems
- Headache/migraine
- Heart disease
- Irritable bowel syndrome

- Juvenile diabetes
- Lyme disease
- Mental retardation
- Obesity
- Sleep disorders
- Seizure disorder
- Physical or sexual abuse

Thirteen-year-old Jerome, recently diagnosed with diabetes, was referred to me because of his newfound habit of "knocking over" smaller children. Jerome worked with me after he became defiant and refused to follow his parents' rules in response to the challenges with his diabetes. As Jerome grew to accept his diabetes, his bullying behaviors ended. Another client, fifteen-year-old Sylvia, was brought in to see me as she struggled to deal with her lupus-related health complications. Sylvia had broken picture frames and stolen money from her parents when her fears and frustrations about her condition got the best of her. Fortunately, her condition stabilized after she was given some newer forms of treatment.

These are just a few examples of the health conditions that can exacerbate defiance. I should also mention that some children may also be affected by anxiety or depression as a result of their struggle to deal with health conditions and challenges. In all of these situations, I empower parents to join support groups and keep addressing the physical aspects of what is going on.

A big challenge for children with chronic illnesses is they get burned out from managing their condition. These children want to be like everyone else and not have to visit the specialists or take the medicine or follow a strict diet.

Drugs Can Drive Defiance

Defiant kids may also have problems with alcohol or other drugs. Children experiment with drugs to experience the "high" they have heard about. They also use drugs because of peer pressure to "fit in" with their friends. Some children use drugs as a way to avoid or forget their problems. Getting "stoned" offers a temporary escape from life's harsh realities. Parents and other adults often set a poor example with their own use or abuse of alcohol or other drugs. Some parents may not understand what addiction is. There are more ways today than ever before to obtain chemicals as well as misinformation on drugs via the Internet. The exposure to and availability of addictive chemicals in most communities surprises most parents.

Barry, age fourteen, was brought in to see me for his increasingly defiant behavior. He was surprisingly open about smoking marijuana once he decided to trust me. Barry spoke to his mother in the most derogatory manner I had ever heard. I told Barry that as much as I liked him, I could not accept the cruel way he spoke to his mother. While Barry's treatment of his mother improved, his marijuana use became more of a problem. He denied smoking marijuana to feel better and instead pridefully claimed that he smoked it to feel "even better." He started a pattern of coming home smelling like "weed" and skipping school. I referred him to an after-school drug treatment program and worked with him throughout the time of his rehab. It was only after he participated in this more intense drug treatment that Barry finally gave up his marijuana use and his behavior improved.

Unfortunately, in many cases a child will use drugs and alcohol for quite some time before parents notice the signs of a problem. Often, by the time a parent sees the obvious signs, the child has a problem that goes beyond occasional use of these substances. The child may have developed an abusive pattern of use and may be addicted to the substance. The best solution for kids in this situation is to get them out of the immediate environment and away from the peer influences that are enabling their abuse of drugs or alcohol.

Drug or alcohol rehab may be necessary to give your child a chance to get back on her feet and begin a program of recovery from addiction. And sometimes you can't tell which came first, the defiance or the drug use. The bottom line is that *your child has both of these problems, and the sooner you get her into treatment, the better.* Either problem can make the other worse and lead to bigger trouble, like addiction or increased defiance and flunking school. Denying that your child has a problem will only make things worse when it comes to drug problems. You really need to be honest about both problems—first with yourself and then with someone who can help you get your child into treatment. It's the only way to help your child get better and *stay* better.

WARNING SIGNS OF DRUG USE

It's crucial for you to be aware of the signals that may suggest your child is using drugs. The more you are aware of what to look for, the more likely you will be able to determine if your child has a drug problem.

- Increased moodiness—anger, sadness, excessively energetic episodes
- Alcohol or prescription medicine missing from your cabinet
- Glassy eyes, low eye contact, pasty skin
- Sick more often, coughs in morning
- Money or valuables missing, iPods or cell phones "lost"
- Child "disappears" for long periods
- Change in sleep patterns or increased fatigue
- Running away
- Secretive text messaging and dramatic increase in cell use
- Unusual containers, wrappers, tin foil
- Reports of intoxication at school
- Dramatic drop in grades, skipping classes
- Desperation, withdrawal from family
- Switching friends
- Drug-seeking behavior—for example, researching drugs on the Internet
- Seeming mentally preoccupied, easily distracted
- Lost interest in healthy outlets such as sports, church, and family contact

The important thing to keep in mind when dealing with drug and alcohol problems in your defiant child is that she's not a bad kid trying to become good, she has a disease that she is trying to recover from. Many parents think that drug use is "just a phase" or that everybody's got to get their "drinking legs." However, the issue is much more serious than that. The development of the adolescent brain and the risk of damage in these formative years is a very serious matter.

For example, neurologists can show that where marijuana sits in the frontal cortex of the brain affects development, encoding memory, and even hand-eye coordination. The earlier the appropriate intervention stops the progression of an adolescent addiction, the less strain there is on family relationships and community functioning.

It's also vital that parents watch what they do. If you drink excessively or condone drug use, your child will use that against you. A colleague of mine recently shared with me the following powerful quote:

"A parent is a thousand schoolteachers" (author unknown).

Autism Spectrum Disorder Adds to Defiance

Autism spectrum disorder (ASD) is a *DSM-5* term that includes four previously separate disorders that are actually a single condition with different levels of symptom severity in two core domains. ASD is characterized by (1) deficits in social communication and social interaction and (2) restricted repetitive behaviors, interests, and activities (RRBs). Because both components are required for diagnosis of ASD, social communication disorder is diagnosed if no RRBs are present.

Higher functioning children with ASD often have solid or even strong vocabularies that seem advanced compared to other children their age. Despite their large vocabularies, these children are quite literal in their understanding of what others are saying.

In addition to their problems with social interactions, children with ASD often have an obsessive interest in a particular subject and very little interest in much else. They may obsessively seek information about maps or clocks or some other topic. They may also be very inflexible in their habits and rigidly adhere to certain routines or rituals. Children with ASD may show strange mannerisms such as hand flapping or peculiar postures that make them appear clumsy. Children with ASD are considered to have a higher intellectual capacity while suffering from a lower social capacity.

The typical symptoms of ASD include:

- Being locked into one or more stereotyped and restricted patterns of interest that is abnormal in either intensity or focus

- Having an apparently inflexible adherence to specific nonfunctional routines or rituals
- Showing stereotyped and repetitive motor mannerisms (e.g., hand or finger flapping or twisting, or complex whole-body movement)
- Having persistent preoccupation with parts of objects

Joel was an eleven-year-old boy who was diagnosed with ASD. He had a preoccupation with imaginary stick fighting in his backyard with an invisible opponent. Joel was also obsessed with feeding the family dog in a ritualized manner by pouring out the food into a smaller bowl and then back into the larger one. Joel tended to make a flapping motion with his left hand, particularly when he felt anxious. He also had a preoccupation with tightening the screws on the toilet seats in his house. Things got difficult for Joel and his family when he began an increasing pattern of ritualized regurgitation. When his parents confronted him about this, Joel broke a vase and attempted to set fire to a toilet seat.

The optimum treatment for children with ASD involves educational and social interventions to give them the support and skills they need to be successful in life. Educational interventions that focus on making the environment more predictable are particularly helpful. Graphic organizers and other similar strategies that capitalize on a visual learning style are also beneficial. Because some individuals with ASD have IQs in the gifted range, they need to have learning opportunities commensurate with their skill levels. Enrichment activities are therefore usually a part of the curriculum for these children.

Tourette's Syndrome Triggers Defiance

I have worked with some defiant children who also had Tourette's syndrome. This is a neurological disorder characterized by involuntary body movements and vocal outbursts (tics) that last for at least twelve months. Tourette's syndrome occurs in about one in every two thousand children. It is more likely to occur in boys.

Tics are involuntary and usually sudden, rapid, and repetitive. Children with vocal tics may make compulsive barking and grunting noises, have frequent throat clearing, coughing or sniffling, blinking, echolalia (vocal tics characterized by repeating words that a child hears), or coprolalia (vocal tics characterized by repeating or shouting obscene words), although coprolalia is rare.

Julian, eleven, had been diagnosed with Tourette's syndrome by his pediatrician and was brought to see me by his parents. Like many children with sniffling and eye movement tics, Julian had been relentlessly teased by classmates. He had poor self-esteem and had convinced himself that he was "freaky," "stupid," and "was going to have a horrible life." Julian had begun dealing with these negative feelings by physically lashing out at his peers.

I saw Julian for individual counseling to address his self-esteem issues. I also worked closely with his school. Julian's teacher agreed to speak to his classmates about Tourette's at a time when Julian was not in the classroom. Julian's peers became supportive—the teasing stopped and so did Julian's aggressive behaviors.

Tourette's syndrome currently has no cure, but symptoms can usually be managed with counseling, accommodations at school, and medications. Julian's mother came in to see me a few years later for some supportive counseling when her father died. As we became reacquainted, she told me that Julian's tics had decreased appreciably since I had last seen him.

Stress Speeds Up Defiance

Children can face many stressors that can increase their defiant behavior. These include:

- Arrival of a new sibling
- School pressure
- Conflict with a teacher
- Conflict with a peer
- Being bullied
- Being overloaded or overscheduled with too many activities
- Relocating
- Parents' divorce
- Health problems of a parent

- Financial strain/unemployment of parent
- Death of a loved one
- Domestic violence

Defiant kids tend to act out, often in an uncontrolled manner if they are experiencing stress. Life in contemporary society is a competitive, complex, and constantly changing experience. We all have to adapt to the new, the unexpected, and the unknown, which can produce many kinds of pressures. For some people, facing uncertainties and pressures may simply add pleasure and vigor to their lives. For defiant children, however, often the variety of stresses can aggravate and overwhelm them. They have real difficulty adjusting to change.

Seven-year-old Dillon was brought to see me literally kicking and screaming. Once he stopped his tantrum (listening to the ocean through a few of my sea shells helped make this happen), we discussed what was bothering him. It became clear that Dillon was very upset about the recent death of his paternal grandmother, to whom he had been very close. Dillon also struggled with the fact that his new stepbrother had just moved into his house and was sharing his room. Individual and family counseling helped Dillon significantly lessen his tantrums. This, along with Dillon's mother and stepfather's use of the strategies in this ten-day plan, helped Dillon make very solid progress in reducing his defiance.

DAY 9 SUMMING IT UP

Today you have learned a lot about what I refer to as the stubborn obstacles to reducing your child's defiance. Please keep the following points in mind as you move forward:

- Some defiant children may have one or more mental health issues that drive their defiant behavior.
- It's important for you to educate yourself about any of these mental health concerns if you suspect that they occur in your child.
- As long as you are patient and persistent, brighter days are ahead in helping your child deal with these other stubborn obstacles.

- There may also be medical issues that exacerbate your child's defiant behavior.
- Please consult a qualified mental health professional for any persistent problems or to gain further information.

GETTING READY FOR DAY 10

- If your child is persistently struggling emotionally or socially, stay mindful of any underlying mental health issues that may be influencing his continued problematic behaviors.
- If your child is determined to have underlying mental health issues, help your child to see them as an explanation but not an excuse for defiant behavior.
- Be open and educate your child about any challenges he faces and always present resources and strategies for him to cope with them.
- In addition to seeking out qualified mental health treatment for your child and you, consider joining in-person support groups or online forums to provide you with support but don't be easily influenced by questionable advice.

DAY
10

Reducing Defiance
for the Long Run

You're in the home stretch, and by now you have seen impressive
changes in your child and yourself. The principles of this program are timeless, and I encourage you to use them throughout your
life as a parent. As long as you continue to work at them, my strategies and tools keep on working, too. What follows today are some
key strategies and suggestions aimed to help ensure that your child's
improvements (and yours) remain strong over time.

Sail Beyond Those Setbacks

If you have applied what I have shared with you, you've likely seen
a vast improvement in your child over the last ten days. Perhaps you
have paced yourself to work through each chapter by allotting more
time, over a few or even several days. That's okay, too. The most
important thing is that you have made it through this program. I am
pleased to share that many readers have revealed to me that the progress they have made with their defiant child has remained intact and
often grows over the test of time.

Keep in mind, however, that as you go forward, your defiant child
may have some setbacks. There will still be times when he will challenge you. Doors may occasionally still get slammed, and increased
argumentativeness may rear its ugly head again. Please don't get

discouraged when your child tests limits in these ways. It's normal for children who have been defiant to have recurrences of their problematic behaviors. Keep the faith going forward and you will not go backward.

You may also run into setbacks of your own when dealing with your feelings and behaviors. You may get stressed out, "lose it," and do something you regret. You may resent having to work with your child to improve her behavior and feel frustrated because you think other parents appear to have it easier. It's so easy to lose your patience or just get bogged down in life's demands and stop using the skills you've learned in this ten-day program.

It's important to remember that whether it is you or your child that is having a setback, these backslides are only natural. When either one of you is facing disappointment, think about all the hard work you put into this ten-day program and how very far you both have come. Your caring and hard work shouldn't be forgotten. Please keep the following in mind if you hit any setbacks while going forward.

You have overcome setbacks before.

Like everyone, I'm sure you've had your fair share of setbacks throughout your life. You've probably weathered disappointments in school, on jobs, in activities, and in other relationships. The secret to successfully handling setbacks is to get right back in the saddle again.

One of the parents I worked with came in to see me recently for a follow-up session. Carolyn's husband had complimented her on how she handled a setback with their eleven-year-old daughter, Rachel. Rachel had pushed her younger brother, Austin, out of a room and slammed the door. Austin's hand got caught in the door and, while he was not severely injured, Rachel showed no remorse for what she had done. Carolyn began yelling at Rachel and demanded that Rachel open the door so she could speak to her. Rachel refused. To her credit, Carolyn realized that this door had become a window—a window of opportunity. Carolyn took a few quick deep breaths and said, "Rachel, I realize you did not intentionally try to hurt Austin. I would like you to please open the door so I can talk to you." After a minute of silence,

Rachel complied. The reason Rachel became cooperative was because Carolyn was—you guessed it—calm, firm, and noncontrolling.

So if your child has slipped back into being overly reactive or you have stopped being calm, firm, and noncontrolling and are not picking your battles wisely, don't throw in the towel. Reread this ten-day program and re-empower yourself with the strategies and tools I have provided for you. Keep in mind that a setback is only temporary, and positive things lie ahead.

There are ways you can keep yourself prepared for those times when you get shaken by your own setbacks. Justine, the mother of a defiant child I worked with, had a friend who taught her to keep a "mop and bucket," metaphorically speaking, under her chin when she overreacted. For those times when Justine would lose it, she would meditate on the image of taking out her mop and bucket and cleaning up her emotional mess. Other ideas to help you recover after a setback include:

- Reminding yourself of all of the positive changes you have made so far
- Remembering that you are working hard and continuing to make a strong parenting effort
- Apologizing to your child for "losing it"
- Talking to a friend or trained mental health professional, if necessary, to sort out what is pushing you into some problematic, counterproductive parenting behaviors or decisions

More on Preparing for Setbacks

The more prepared you are to handle the times that your child does backslide into defiant behaviors, the easier they'll be to handle. As a good friend of mine has often said to me, "Strive for progress, not perfection."

Here are some strategies to keep in mind when you have hit a setback in managing your child.

Don't Panic

If your child acts up and you overreact in response, don't panic. This is essential to handling all setbacks and crises. No matter what your child does to rattle your chains, or what you wish you had done differently, resist hitting the panic button. Don't start saying to yourself things like, "Great, nothing changed after all," or "I knew these positive changes were going to come to an end sooner or later." These are globalized distortions that pop in your mind when you feel overwhelmed. To get past them, just slow down and clear your head. Remind yourself of how much progress has been made.

Meditate on Your Parental Strengths

Reminding yourself of your progress not only lowers your anxiety but it also inspires you to feel more positively about your relationship with your child as you go forward amid the challenges. Many of the parents I counsel have found value in meditating to help them find peace, acceptance, and continued resilience for the parenting challenges that they continue to face. Here is a mediation exercise for you to gain clarity about your parenting strengths.

Recall the deep breathing exercise I introduced you to back on Day 1. Sit in a quiet, peaceful setting, with your hands resting on your knees. Close your eyes and breathe slowly and deeply, focusing on your breath filling and returning from your abdomen.

Think about a positive interaction you had with your child, recent or past. While imagining this positive interaction, actually lift your right thumb up while keeping your hand resting on your knee. Next, while continuing to breathe deeply, think about another positive interaction between you and your child and lift your index finger to acknowledge it. Continue with this exercise until you have lifted all five fingers on your hand or all ten fingers on both hands. Once you have completed lifting as many fingers as possible, open your eyes and you will literally see your parenting strength in hand!

If you are having a bad day or for any reason are having a hard time starting this exercise and are drawing a blank to begin your finger lifting, don't be discouraged. If this is the case, start with lifting your right thumb to give yourself credit for reading this book. Feeding your child and driving him places counts, too. You certainly could not do these things without raising a finger, so raise at least one now. You get the idea. Once you start lifting one finger, you will likely be moved to continue through the exercise. Even if you can only lift a few fingers and not all ten, celebrate your willingness to lift your parenting spirit by identifying and valuing what you do for your child.

Stay the Course

Your child's setback (or yours) is just a blip on the radar screen. Remember that you are helping to prepare your child for his life's journey. Think long term and not short term. Staying the course means remembering that you and your child will keep learning as you continue to make mistakes going forward. Step back and look at the situation. Take responsibility when necessary, but don't place blame on yourself or your child. Parenting in challenging situations is not about deciding where to affix blame. Remember, you and your child don't have to be perfect. After all, nobody else is. You and your child are both learning and growing together on your parenting journey.

Own Your Part

Whether you realize you mistakenly failed to take action or you had a strong overreaction to your child, reflect on what you did and think about how you can work beyond it. Tanya was the mother of eight-year-old Betsy, whose tantrums and outbursts had become very infrequent as Tanya used the skills in this ten-day program. Tanya, who had been staying at home to take care of Betsy, decided to go back to work a few months after Betsy's defiant behaviors began to diminish. Betsy, frustrated that her mother had to shoulder new employment responsibilities, had a setback. She told Tanya that she was a "bad mother." Upon hearing this, Tanya temporarily reverted to her old explosive and commanding ways and screamed at Betsy, called her "impossible," and told her to stay away from her. Tanya winced as she heard what she said to her daughter. She forced herself to slow down with a few deep breaths, and she realized that she had taken Betsy's comment too personally. Tanya had lost sight of the fact that Betsy was struggling, too.

Once she was calm, Tanya discussed the incident with Betsy. Betsy told her mother that she felt scared because she felt her mother didn't have as much time for her and didn't want her around. Tanya smiled at Betsy and said, "Honey, I reacted too strongly. I understand that I have less free time now. But I still ask that when something bothers you, you be respectful when telling me what it is." Predictably, Betsy said, "Yeah, Mom, but you weren't nice to me either." Tanya, owning her part, agreed. This admission enabled Tanya and Betsy to move beyond this setback in a productive manner.

Stay Out of the Negative Questioning Trap

It's important to stay positive in the face of setbacks. Questioning yourself in self-destructive ways will suck the positive energy out of you and leave you filled with negativity. Try to avoid dwelling on thoughts such as:

- "What if I had? . . ."
- "If only I'd . . . "
- "I should not be so . . . "

Don't get hung up on all the "right things" you *should* have done or *should* have said. Remember that hindsight is always twenty-twenty. Marsha, the mother of seven-year-old Liza, remembered the value of staying positive and focusing on solutions. Marsha was complaining to me one day about how upset she was at herself for "biting Liza's head off." Marsha was referring to an incident where she screamed at Liza for deliberately interrupting her phone call to a friend.

I helped Marsha step back and focus on Liza's considerable progress over the past year. By refocusing on her own positive mind-set and behavior changes, Marsha felt less threatened by Liza's setback. Marsha also had a very important insight—she was using her phone a lot to make calls and check e-mails. Had Marsha continued to beat herself up about what happened, she would not have been able to see that her excessive phone usage was a problem for her daughter. I coached Marsha on how to help Liza learn more appropriate ways (including a nonintrusive hand signal) to get her attention when necessary. Marsha also decided to scale back her phone usage.

The fact is that things may not always go as smoothly as you wish, but this does not have to get you down in the dumps. There's nothing you can do to change what has already occurred. And yes, maybe if you had acted differently, things would have turned out differently, but what is the point of dwelling on this? Focus on staying positive and remember that once the dust settles, you will find a way to get back on track.

Keep Disputing Negative Thoughts

In the section on page 249 I discussed how to deal with nagging negative questions. Now let's talk about dealing with your nagging negative statements. I have mentioned at different points in this book how the power of your thoughts plays a huge role in how you approach situations in your life, including parenting. It's easy when you feel tired or stressed to have negative thoughts such as:

- "I can't manage my child."
- "I'm just not cut out to be a good parent."
- "My children will never respect me."
- "No one else has the type of parenting challenges that I do."

If you have these thoughts, you are not alone. Most every parent at some point or other experiences doubts about their ability to parent. Perhaps you are having a bad day, and your child's bad behavior is the icing on the cake. Just reassure yourself that everyone has days when things don't go as well they'd like. Try to remove yourself mentally from that negative thought by reminding yourself of a better day when you felt less pressure, everything went smoothly, or you laughed with your child. You will be surprised at how effective that can be. For more on how to overcome your negative and toxic thinking patterns, check out my book, *Liking the Child You Love*.

Stay Loose

As I cautioned you on Day 3, being too attached to results can work against any positive strategies you use to lessen your child's defiance. You may have heard the expression "a watched pot never boils." There will be times when your child may not respond positively as quickly as you'd like, even when you are calm, firm, and noncontrolling and pick your battles wisely. This is okay. Keep in mind that every time you follow the approaches I have provided in this book, you are planting more and more antidefiance seeds. Some of them may take longer than these ten days to germinate. During your interactions with your child, don't get yourself worked up if she is not immediately less argumentative or less difficult. Remind yourself that you have already been successful in handling your child effectively by not becoming more upset yourself. If you stay the course and continue to be calm, firm, and noncontrolling, you will see the positive changes in your child become stronger and stronger over time.

I suggest keeping that "watched pot" metaphor handy when you are using any of the strategies I have suggested in this ten-day program. It'll help you see the bigger picture. Remember that the reason most positive change efforts, including parenting ones, are unsuccessful is because people give up too early.

Stay Joined

Everything you have read in this book can work—quite powerfully—to lower your child's defiance. To help support all that you have learned, I encourage you to envision yourself as joining with your child instead of being his adversary.

What I mean is, don't try to emerge the winner. When it comes to parenting your child, whether you win or lose is not important. The key is to treat your defiant child with respect and as fairly as possible.

Think about other parents you may have seen get hooked by the antics of their defiant children. I have seen parents have temper tantrums in amusement parks, supermarkets, roller rinks, and my office. Remember that you are there to support your child.

The key to avoiding becoming your child's adversary is to avoid becoming defensive or creating defensiveness in your child. When you and your child discuss concerns, stick to the issues. Discuss all concerns in a calm, unaggressive, concrete, and specific way. Avoid using words such as "always," "never," and "should," which tend to create defensiveness. Remember that staying calm, firm, and noncontrolling will yield the best results.

Along these lines, remember that none of the strategies in this book are meant to "manipulate" your child into being less defiant. Yolanda, the mother of seven-year-old Danielle, perfectly illustrates this confusion about my program. In our first counseling session

Yolanda told me she had heard that I can "make defiant kids less defiant." I smiled and assured Yolanda that I felt my strategies could help her and her daughter. At the same time, I made it clear that it was not my intention to *make* her daughter less defiant. My program is not about mandating positive changes in your child, it's about facilitating them. Remember, you can lead a horse to water, but you can't make him drink. When I share this saying with clients, I like to add that once the horse realizes he is thirsty, he will drink plenty. My program builds your relationship with your child by helping you parent more effectively. As long as you are supportive and patient with your child, he will eventually not only follow your lead but grow a thirst for making positive changes on his own. Yolanda quickly realized that the mind-set of joining with her child to encourage less defiance would be far more productive than trying to make her be less defiant.

BE A JOINER, NOT AN ADVERSARY

Once I encourage them to think about it, many parents are shocked to realize the extent to which they have become a challenging foe instead of loving supporter of their defiant child. Keep the following in mind and you will keep channeling your love and energy in the right places with your child.

Parents who act as joiners:
- Empathize with (but don't enable) their child's problem behaviors
- "Catch" their child's positive behaviors
- Listen to their child's frustrations and understand them
- Stay optimistic in the face of setbacks
- Act in a loving and respectful manner

Parents who act as adversaries:
- Make rigid, controlling comments
- Give ultimatums
- Act in a threatening manner
- Use shame to try to influence change
- Show anger

Don't Neglect the Rest of Your Life

Balance, balance, balance. I can't stress enough the importance of having a full life apart from your parenting responsibilities. The more you keep yourself vibrant and learn new things, the better you will feel. This will only enhance your parenting efforts. Think about doing any of the following to keep your emotional batteries charged:

- Take up gardening.
- Do fun things with your friends.
- Keep nourishing your marriage.
- Try rock climbing.
- Play pool.
- Go bowling.
- Play cards.
- Take up quilting.
- Go bike riding.
- Take long walks around the neighborhood or go hiking.
- Join a local gym.
- Take a yoga class.
- Take day trips to historic sites or museums.
- Attend a lecture on a topic you are interested in.

Make a "Positives" List

Magic occurs when you put pencil to paper. Writing things down helps you see concretely and appreciate efforts you have made and steps you have taken. In this spirit, I encourage you to review all the positive changes you and your child have made so far. In the introduction to this program, I suggested that you keep a running log of successes. If you did this, keep it going. If you did not, consider starting one now. By listing examples of your child exhibiting less defiant behavior, you will continue to feel inspired. A single-father client of mine kept a log that he found helpful. A three-day sample of that log looked something like this:

Monday: Josh started to yell, and he stopped when I calmly asked him to.

Tuesday: Josh was pushed by his little brother. He made a fist and was about to hit his brother but complied when I calmly and firmly asked him not to.

Wednesday: I started to raise my voice when Josh kept asking me who I was dating. I remained calm, firm, and noncontrolling, and he stopped hounding me.

As a variation of keeping a log, you can create and use a Positive Changes Jar. Any functional or decorative glass jar will do. Just make and affix a label to it such as "Positive Changes Jar," "Positive Cooperation Jar," or "No More Yelling Jar." Each time you "catch" yourself or your child choosing not to do undesirable behaviors and instead doing desirable ones, write it on a small piece of paper and put in the jar. You can purchase blocks of small colored square papers at a craft or office supply store, or online, and use one color for you and one for your child. Seeing the papers noting positive behaviors and interactions pile up inside the jar can feel very gratifying—to both you and your child.

Respect Your Child's Unique Personality

Accepting that you and your child have different ways of approaching the world can be very liberating. Some parents get frustrated because they try to convince their children to do things the way they do. You may well have discovered by now that if you try to turn your child into someone just like you, you will encounter a lot of conflict.

I once had a thirteen-year-old client named Abbey who insisted on keeping her hair in a ponytail and did not want to be a cheerleader, much to the chagrin of her more fashion- and social-oriented mother, Belinda. It took Belinda some time to accept Abbey for who she was, but once she did, they developed a much closer relationship.

I also counseled a man named Fred who had to accept the fact that his nine-year-old son Shane had a very different personality from his. Shane liked time to calm down before trying to resolve matters, but Fred felt a need for an immediate resolution to issues. After I worked with the two of them for a few sessions, I was pleased to see that Fred and Shane had learned the art of compromise. Interestingly, the more willing Fred became to compromise, the less he seemed to need to resolve issues right on the spot. And not surprisingly, the less pushy for solutions Fred was, the fewer problems Shane felt there were to be resolved.

Differences make the world go around. It's not the end of the world if your child does not see things your way or respond in the way that you think she *should*. In fact, that's what makes life interesting, isn't it? You and your child will work through conflicts much better if you respect and work with your child's style.

Draw Support from Friends

Parenting is difficult and keeping yourself positive is not always easy. One strategy is to keep positive people around you. Turn to your friends and talk about your successes in working with your defiant child. Allow your friends to give you support and don't feel that you have to keep up with their family relationship successes or their parenting victories. Be open to their praise when they offer it.

Looking to the Future

No one is born a good parent. Parenting is a learning experience as you get to know your children while they grow and develop. As with everything in life, there are challenges. *10 Days to a Less Defiant Child* is meant to help you meet the challenges that your children will bring. It's about helping you understand that while each defiant child is different, they all have the basic need for understanding, love, and boundaries.

Continuing to Write the Story of Your Relationship with Your Child

Back in Day 1, I suggested an exercise to help you restore your positive memories with your child. Recent research has shown that writing, and rewriting, about your personal experiences can improve your emotional health and help to create more desired outcomes in your life. A group of college students who struggled academically, for example, were asked to write about their experiences after they watched videos of upper classman who shared how their own grades had improved as they adjusted to college. The younger college students were then asked to rewrite their story, which helped them shift from self-defeating beliefs such as, "I'm too dumb to succeed in college," to more empowering thoughts such as, "College is hard for everyone but I can succeed." Incredibly, the college students who edited their stories in this positive manner improved their grade point averages and were less likely to drop out than those students who were not exposed to the inspiring videos from upperclassmen.

I am convinced, as exemplified by this provocative research, that we are in charge of creating the relationship story with our children going forward. A very powerful example of this from my own practice involved a mother, Pauline, of a defiant child. Pauline had struggled with pervasive self-doubt. Her prior story was "I'm a bad parent." After coaching Pauline to recognize her successes amidst the challenges she faced with her child, her story became "My child is spirited and has strong convictions. Every mother has challenges, and even though I struggle from time to time, I continue to learn to better navigate conflicts and play a valuable role in his life."

By putting into practice the ideas and strategies presented in this book, you have already begun to change the story of your relationship with your child for the better. You now have the power to favorably write the story of your relationship with your child going forward. As you continue to implement the ideas and strategies presented in this book, reflect on how you can shape your attitude and actions to keep cultivating a cooperative, respectful, and loving relationship with your child as he matures and grows.

As a final exercise, take some time to create a vision of your ongoing and future relationship with your child. As you create this vision, you may want to write down your thoughts about the following:

- How will you support your child's beliefs that are similar and dissimilar from yours?
- How will you create the emotional safety for your child to share his inner struggles?
- What will you say or do to inspire your child to make healthy, choices?

- What self-disclosures are you comfortable and willing to share from your own past challenges to help your child overcome setbacks?
- Recognizing that your child will make her own decisions and choices in the future, what can you do to remain a respected voice for your grown child?

Ultimately, the quality of your relationship with your child in the future is more important than you "winning" day-to-day power struggles. Maintaining a calm, firm, and noncontrolling stance will not only lead her to be more compliant in the short term but will also encourage your child to make the best future choices for herself. Allowing her to also learn from her mistakes while you continue to be emotionally present will keep your relationship strong and connected in the future.

My strategies have equipped you with the proper tools, but it's your response and dedication to helping your child that will bring you results. As you watch your child now, knocking over a glass of juice, fighting with a sibling over which TV program to watch, or responding to you in a sassy manner, it's hard to imagine that one day he will be an adult. But I promise you, the day will come when your child will have her own children, and you will look back on these ten remarkable days of change. You will smile to yourself as you watch her face her own challenges as a parent. Perhaps you'll have put this book in a place of safekeeping, and when the time is right, you can ask her, "Want to read a helpful book?"

Appendix 1

Determining If
Your Child Needs
Professional Help

Parents and caregivers who read this book and earnestly complete this program report a high improvement rate for their children becoming significantly less defiant. If your child's defiance-related problems do not seem to be improving, however, then it is likely time for you, your child, and your family to think about getting professional help. Assuming that any of the following circumstances apply to your situation, consider taking the next step to consult a qualified health care professional.

- You've diligently completed this program and your child's defiant behavior (e.g., often argues with you, loses his temper, frequently refuses to comply, often blames others for his mistakes, or is spiteful or vindictive) is not getting better or is actually getting worse.
- Your child continues to show problematic behaviors in school, either academically or socially.
- Your child is having problems in your community such as troubling conflicts with other children or adults, or is breaking the law.
- Your child is struggling with any of the coexisting conditions described in Day 9, including anxiety, depression, persistent learning or attention problems, or substance abuse.
- You and your spouse/partner (or ex-spouse/ex-partner) are generally at odds about how to manage and discipline your child and this is creating significant problems or worsening existing ones.

Which Type of Health Care Professional Should You See?

If your child is having unyielding behavioral and emotional problems, it can feel very overwhelming to know which type of health care professional to turn to. The types of health providers included in the list below are meant as a guide but are by no means exhaustive. These professionals, however, represent the most common sources recommended for parents and caregivers seeking help for defiant children with persistent problems.

Primary care physician. It is important to rule out any underlying medical concerns that may be negatively influencing your child's problematic behaviors. Environmental or food allergies, gastrointestinal issues, sleep problems, diabetes, headaches, and Lyme disease, among other medical conditions, can cause or exacerbate behavioral and emotional concerns. For a considerable percentage of children, their primary care doctor is their pediatrician. Some families, however, use a family doctor to provide care to all family members, including children.

If the causes of your child's behavioral and emotional struggles appear to be related to stress, poor coping strategies, anger issues, emotional immaturity, anxiety, depression, substance abuse, or school problems, then your child's doctor can refer you to a professional who holds a degree in mental health (psychologist, social worker, licensed professional counselor, or psychiatrist). School guidance counselors, clergy, and trusted friends can also be good sources of referrals for qualified mental health professionals in your area.

Psychologists have doctoral degrees in psychology. Those working with children have been trained to help them with emotionally-based problems and to develop stronger coping skills. Psychologists holding doctoral degrees (either a PhD, PsyD, or EdD) spend an average of seven years in education and training after they receive their undergraduate degrees. Ask your pediatrician or school guidance counselor to help guide you to a qualified psychologist who has strong experience working with children, teens, and families.

Licensed professional counselors are masters-degreed mental health service providers who work with individuals and families who have or are coping with behavioral or emotional problems and disorders. They are specifically trained to diagnose and treat mental and emotional disorders.

Clinical social workers often work for social service agencies and in medical and hospital settings. They also can work as private practice therapists who diagnose and treat individuals with emotional problems and psychological disorders.

School psychologists work primarily in school settings. They use many different strategies to address individual student needs and to improve classroom and school climates and support systems. I briefly described assessments conducted by school psychologists in Day 8. If your child has persistent attention or learning issues then advocate for having your child evaluated by a school psychologist. Some parents opt to seek out private practice school psychologists to get independent opinions, separate from the school.

Psychiatrists are medical doctors who specialize in prescribing medication. A child and adolescent psychiatrist is a physician who specializes in the diagnosis and treatment of mental health disorders that affect children, adolescents, and their families. Child and adolescent psychiatrists have completed four years of medical school, at least three years of residency training in medicine, neurology, or general psychiatry with adults, and two years of additional training in psychiatric work with children, adolescents, and their families.

A Note About Psychiatric Medications for Children and Teens

Primary care physicians and psychiatrists are the two professions listed above that can prescribe psychiatric medications to children and teens. That said, if your child needs psychiatric medications for more complicated conditions such as, for example, severe anxiety, depression, or ADHD, or signs of a thought disorder such as schizophrenia, I would encourage that you see a child psychiatrist. Child psychiatrists have the most experience in prescribing medication for this population.

The topic of prescribing psychiatric medications for children and teens can be unsettling to parents and teens. I have even heard some mental health colleagues mutter, "Pills don't teach skills." This sentiment speaks to those who are concerned that children and teens need to learn how to calm themselves, manage their emotions, and solve problems without being on, or "dependent on," medications. I have also heard parents voice fears about possible deleterious side effects of psychiatric medications. These are understandable concerns about using psychiatric medications with children and teens.

My position is that medication should only be used after all other non-pharmacological interventions have been attempted. Importantly, though, I do think medications can be quite beneficial for a wide range of challenging mental health issues interfering with the lives of children and teens. For example, I have seen where medications used to treat anxiety, depression, and ADHD, among other mental health concerns, can dramatically change children's lives for the better. There are times that medications can be catalysts, making counseling efforts even more effective. With respect to ADHD, I have observed how medication helped children go from doing poorly in the classroom and frequently getting in trouble in school and at home to being very successful in both settings.

Is There a Difference Between Counseling and Therapy?

More so in the past, the term "counseling" was viewed as a short-term and very focused approach taken toward solving a client's problems. The term psychotherapy ("therapy" for short) was used to apply to a more long-term and more in-depth approach. In recent years, more often than not, these terms are used interchangeably as are similarly the terms, "therapist" and "counselor." These typically refer to psychologists, licensed professional counselors, and social workers.

Whether it is referred to as therapy or counseling, the bottom line is that parents choose to take their child to a therapist for additional support because their child is highly challenging, which may be fueled by a coexisting condition. They may also seek help because as parents it has been very difficult for them to let go of the counterproductive parenting strategies they use with their defiant child (e.g., being rigid, giving over-the-top consequences, yelling, or being overly permissive). Often, of course, the issues warranting professional help reflect both the child's and the parents' struggles. The goal of therapy is to help you, your child, and your family to get to a place of understanding one another.

Keep the School in the Loop

I encourage you to inform your child's key school personnel (e.g., teachers, guidance counselor, and nurse) if he is receiving psychiatric medication and, depending on relevance of the issue, receiving outside counseling or therapy as well. As discussed in Days 8 and 9, working with your child's school with a team-oriented, "advocate but don't irritate" mind-set, goes a long way in obtaining needed supports for your child at school.

If a child's teacher observes, for example, that your child is tired, or "out of it" while he is adjusting to a new medication for his ADHD, this can be very crucial information. Many parents are afraid that their children will get negatively labeled by their school if they get identified, for example, with ADHD, or any problem that can negatively influence their learning.

I have seen parents panic and ruminate about whether their child will be unfairly singled out if there are conflicts or that academic expectations for them will be lowered. At the same time, I am seeing more and more parents advocating to get their children appropriately diagnosed with learning and emotional concerns so they can receive valuable support at school.

In general, the benefits of alerting your school outweigh the dangers. Some children with ADHD, for example, benefit from taking tests in a quiet area, or with expanded time limits. See Day 8 for further considerations in working with your child's school to provide him with helpful educational accommodations. I have written extensively on this topic in my book, *10 Days to a Less Distracted Child*. In short, the advantage of communicating with your school, depending on the nature of the issue, about your child receiving professional help for his emotional needs is that you can ask for instructional accommodations to help your child succeed.

Alternative Treatments

I know of parents who seek alternative treatments such as herbal remedies, nutritionally-oriented routes, or biofeedback-based options for children struggling with emotional concerns. I am supportive in those cases where parents report that these alternative avenues are helpful. At the same time, I encourage that parents do their due diligence to ensure safety and true efficacy of products and services, beyond any initial hype. Living in our information age, with easy access to a myriad of data and accessible, helpful information, checking out the efficacy and evidence for all kinds of treatments, even including more conventional ones such as counseling, is essential when seeking support for your child.

Get Your Child Help Sooner Rather Than Later

Frederick Douglass said, "It is easier to build a child than to repair a man." It is sad for me to see teens and young adults who needlessly struggled because they flew under the radar. By this I mean that they had longstanding difficulties (though not formally diagnosed or treated) with anxiety, depression, ADHD or learning problems, or autistic spectrum disorder and failed to receive help.

I have seen way too many children, for example, prior to being medicated for ADHD, being unfairly labeled as "lazy" and as "choosing not" (e.g., with regard to paying attention, doing homework, or remembering to do chores at home). Once these children receive educational modifications and are treated successfully with medication, however, it becomes clear that there were "cannots" that were all along erroneously presumed to be "choose nots." Too often children and teens who do not get help in a timely manner, or never receive it at all, have low self-esteem, lack self-compassion, and do not properly learn those all-important coping strategies for being able to calm down and solve problems in their lives. The more proactive you are in helping your struggling child, the less he will emotionally suffer in his life. Responding to his struggles by seeking counseling as a preventive measure can also help your child be less vulnerable to negative influences later on.

Stay Tuned In for Warnings of Substance Abuse

In the spirt of prevention, I will share that I have seen drug and alcohol use wreak havoc on the lives of teens and their families. Children who feel demoralized and disenfranchised from experiencing themselves as unsuccessful or perceive that they do not fit in can turn to drugs as an escape from their problems. Too often, parents can fall prey to denial, holding a "Not my child!" attitude that influences them to be blind to any warning signs of drug use and addictions as discussed in Day 9. If you suspect your preteen, teen, or young adult is using drugs or alcohol, consult a qualified treatment professional. Some therapists specialize in alcohol or drug abuse. Others, while qualified to address this problem, may have far less experience. There is also a sub-specialty of certified addictions counselors who have extensive training in this area.

It is your right and duty as a parent to ensure your child's safety and well-being. Communicate with other parents, to the best degree possible, to stay informed of preteens, teens, and young adults who may be dealing drugs or are otherwise negative influences. Stay vigilant and trust your instincts.

See Therapy as a Positive Step

Most children, even the resistant ones, actually feel a sense of relief when seeing a therapist. By getting help for your child you are acknowledging and modeling that you don't have all the answers. If life at home feels out of control, you as a parent or caregiver are making a positive statement by seeking to restore the order and structure that can often be achieved by seeking professional help. The very act of bringing your child to see a therapist can make a positive difference.

Throughout this program I have presented you with the empowering message that viewing yourself as your child's coach will enhance your effectiveness as his parent. Both roles, parent and coach, involve your continuing to learn and grow and to help your child do the same. In keeping with a coaching mind-set, I recommend that you present seeking professional help as an opportunity for growth, and not as a sign of failure.

While my primary role is as a therapist when working with defiant children and their families, I work from a coaching standpoint as well. For example, when giving parents constructive therapeutic feedback in front of their children, I am mindful that this also represents a coaching opportunity. I may say something like, "Joey, your video game may have online tutorials with instructions and you probably know that there are plenty of tips, strategies, and even tutorials on the Internet of how to learn to play better. You may not think of it like this, but you did not come with an instruction manual, and your mom is trying to figure out how to be the best parent she can be. I think it is really cool that your mom just showed that she was open to learning from me when I encouraged her to respond to you differently." This kind of statement reinforces to parents and children that learning from an outside professional is a supportive, growth experience, rather than a situation where someone is "being bad" or "the one to blame."

The decision to seek support for your child, and yourself, too, is both a valuable skill and a positive step forward. That's right, by demonstrating to your child that in response to your shared struggles you are seeking outside support, you are teaching her a valuable lesson: asking for help can improve your situation.

I find that children of all ages, and especially preteens, value approaching, and do better with, counseling delivered from a "We are getting help together" versus an "I am taking you to the doctor so you can get fixed" mentality. The counseling process should also help the parents and child see their strengths. My first session usually includes a child and his parents. In that first session, we start highlighting each party's gifts and assets, and then we discuss the issues that would benefit from improvement.

Helpful Reassurances for Your Child Prior to Seeing a Therapist

Explain to young children that this type of visit to the doctor doesn't involve a physical exam (many young children are relieved to hear they won't be getting a shot). You may also want to stress that this type of doctor talks and plays with kids and families to help them calm down, solve problems, get along better, and feel better. Often kids don't want to feel like the "identified patient" so, as mentioned above, let your child know that the therapist will be helping you as parents and possibly other family members, too.

Older children and teens may be reassured to hear that anything they say to the therapist is confidential and cannot be shared with anyone else, including parents and school officials, without their permission—the exception being if they are having thoughts of hurting themselves or others.

Giving kids this kind of information before the first session can help set the tone, prevent your child from feeling shame or singled out, and provide reassurance that the family will be working together on the problem. At the same time, don't overdo it. I have seen parents, feeling their own anxiety over seeing a therapist, unwittingly hype up the anticipation of going, and that can lead to children feeling less receptive to it. As an experienced psychologist working with children and families, I have found that children and teens are more open to counseling than parents may first anticipate.

Important Considerations for You and Your Child in Selecting Your Therapist

Remember that when seeking a therapist, you and your child are not *just* clients or patients. You are also consumers of a professional service. You want to ensure, to the best degree possible, that your experience in seeking a therapist is a positive one. The best possible therapist–client match is critical, so you might need to meet with a few before you find one who clicks with both you and your child.

Bear in mind the following when considering and evaluating a potential therapist.

- Is the therapist licensed to practice in your state? (You can check with the state board for that profession or check to see if the license is displayed in the office.) I would caution against you consulting an unlicensed therapist as she may be uninformed about, or intentionally noncompliant with, state laws protecting consumers from unethical practices.
- Is the therapist covered by your health insurance plan's mental health benefits? If so, how many sessions are covered by your plan? What will your co-pay be? If the therapist does not participate in accepting insurance, what is his fee? Is he willing to give you a sense of the approximate length of treatment based on his clinical impressions from the initial session?
- What are her professional credentials? Different types of therapists were described on pages 259–260. Asking a prospective therapist about how and where she was trained is appropriate.
- Does the therapist offer an informed consent agreement? It is important that your therapist provide you with an informed consent agreement that includes information about his professional services, confidentiality, and business policies.
- What type of counseling experience does the therapist have? Just because someone has a teaching affiliation at a college (or even writes a book about defiant children) doesn't mean that he will be the best choice for every parent, child, or family who consults him. For some

individuals, it is important that therapists have worked with, or are sensitive to, certain racial, cultural, or religious issues and, as a prospective client, it is understandable and appropriate for you to inquire about this.

- How long has the therapist worked with children and adolescents? This point is very important. Therapists who have considerable experience in seeing the trajectories of how children with varying problems fare over time can provide a more informed perspective on outcomes.
- Do you find the therapist friendly and does or would your child?
- Is the therapist willing, if deemed appropriate and with proper consent, to communicate with your child's school in support of issues impacting his emotional and educational needs?
- What is the cancellation policy if you're unable to keep an appointment? It is common for therapists to charge for missed sessions without advance notice.
- Is the therapist available by phone during an emergency? If not, what provisions are in place for you to seek care in that instance? In my practice, within clearly understood professional boundaries, I allow clients to text message me for scheduling issues or more urgent concerns. Therapists vary in what they are comfortable with regarding how to contact them, but there needs to be a clear understanding of this logistical part of the counseling relationship.
- Who will be available to your child during the therapist's vacation or illness or during off-hours?
- What types of therapy does the therapist specialize in? I use strategies from many different schools of therapy and am always seeking to learn new strategies.
- Is the therapist willing to meet with you in addition to working with your child? I find it paramount to provide children with rights to confidentiality, but I also try to have parents informed of what they can do to support their child. In the state where I practice, Pennsylvania, at the age of fourteen teens have the same rights to confidentiality as adults. If the teen is at risk to hurt himself or others, then confidentiality guidelines do not apply in deference to the specific safety issues.

Appendix 2

Further Considerations with Age-Specific Guidelines for Managing Your Child in Cyberspace

This appendix supplements Day 4, which addressed the impact of technology on children in the context of power struggles with defiant children. I discussed in Day 4 that children in recent generations have had dramatically increasing exposure to screen technologies of all kinds, with varying time estimates converging on about seven hours per day. This includes cell phones and other mobile electronic devices, video game consoles, and TV screens.

Current recommendations of the American Academy of Pediatrics (AAP) are for children less than two years of age to be discouraged from any screen media exposure. The AAP also suggests limiting the total entertainment screen time for children from age two to eighteen to less than two hours per day. This is in contrast to the estimate stated above, that children log about seven hours per day on various forms of entertainment and communication media. As pointed out by Robert Weiss and Jennifer Schneider in their book, *Closer Together, Further Apart*, the guidelines from the AAP and other organizations may change as more long-term and reliable data shows the positive and negative impact of screen technology on our children.

On pages 268–270, I will specifically address the more obvious negative impacts of excessive screen time on children. The implications of the calm, firm, and noncontrolling approach, discussed throughout this program, will be covered as they relate to children's screen time use. Finally, age-appropriate steps will be offered that parents can use to help children manage their experiences and time with screen technology devices.

The Problematic Effects of Too Much Screen Time

The healthy use of screen time by children can help them acquire extensive knowledge and engage in fun entertainment. The AAP and other expert sources, however, state several problems for children resulting from too much screen time. These include obesity, irregular sleep, behavioral problems, impaired academic performance, aggressive and violent behaviors, and less time for play. These concerns are described below.

Weight gain or obesity. The more time your child spends passively watching screens, the greater his risk is of becoming overweight. Cell phones, tablets, computers, and TVs in children's bedrooms increase this risk. The strongest screen influence for weight gain has been TV viewing, but other screen-based devices certainly contribute to weight gain as well.

Children exposed to media are influenced by unhealthy yet appealing advertisements for junk foods, which are high in sugar and high in fat. Watching TV and portable screen devices is usually a sedentary experience. These food-related advertisements are very influential, subtly and not so subtly urging children to overeat. Compounding this issue is that these commercials show models with seemingly perfect bodies who can negatively influence some children to make unfavorable self-comparisons.

I have counseled anxious and sad children who gained weight and fell prey to such negative self-comparisons. While remaining calm, firm, and noncontrolling, parents can encourage and guide screen-absorbed children toward alternative interests such as sports and nondigital hobbies. Doing this encourages children to avoid their temptation for further screen immersion and to counter and stop their weight gain through fun exercise, and it likely also boosts their negative self-image.

Irregular sleep. The more screen time children participate in, the more likely they will have trouble falling asleep or develop an irregular sleep schedule. Children with one or more electronic devices in their bedroom appear to get significantly less sleep. This is because they stay up late using their devices, they feel overstimulated in doing so, and the actual light on the screens interferes with their sleep cycle.

I am aware of children who report receiving multiple text and instant messages overnight that make vibrating, pinging, or other noises that consequently disrupt their sleep. Older children can get caught up in crisis-laden, relationship-associated instant-message drama that further adds to loss of sleep. This, in turn, can lead to fatigue and increased snacking, usually on unhealthy foods. For these reasons, it is especially important for parents to manage screen use in children's bedrooms as discussed below.

Impaired academic performance. Neurotransmitters such as dopamine drive seeking behavior for children. The stimulation from TV programs, video games, and social media interactions are a reward for seeking, which then pushes children to desire more digital stimulation. This dopamine dance drives the problematic, coercive cycle that takes a toll on school performance.

Elementary students who have TVs in their bedrooms tend to perform worse on tests than do those who don't have TVs in their bedrooms. Older children can become internally preoccupied with their cell phones or other mobile devices, anticipating the next ping or vibration from text messages with friends.

I have seen many children who need to be focusing on homework and book reports get easily distracted by desiring the enticing neurochemically based rewards of screen communications. These electronic intrusions can take the form of e-mails, text messages, instant messages, or even exploring Google. This gets in the way of them focusing on and meeting schoolwork and homework demands. Overabsorption in screens also interferes with children's ability to appropriately plan for and commit their time to extended projects. Parents must stay mindful of children's academic efforts potentially being sideswiped by screen time.

Attention problems. Research suggests that elementary students who spend more than two hours a day watching TV or using a computer are more likely to have attention problems. Exposure to video games is also linked to an increased risk of focusing problems in children at home as well as at school.

Many parents get frustrated when their children become hyperfocused on video games and are concerned about its impact on their attention. Walter, a client of mine who was the father of two young teenagers, shared the following observation: "It amazes me how my kids can focus on video games to the exclusion of everything else around them. It is like these games become part of them and they forget the real world even exists." This common sentiment speaks to parents' needing to be mindful of their children's attention and focus when considering their screen time habits.

Aggressive behaviors/violence. There is research showing that too much exposure to aggression and fighting through video games, TV, and other forms of media, can desensitize children to violence. It has been suggested that children watching excessive amounts of TV at age four are linked with bullying at ages six through eleven. As a result of video game immersion, children might learn to accept violent behavior as a normal way to solve problems.

Children can certainly enjoy video games that are fun and thrilling. Those games with violent themes and content such as war and murder, however, can make children more aggressive and less sympathetic toward other people, according to some research studies. There is also reasonable speculation that children playing these games may be more likely to do something violent to themselves. Parents need to stay aware of what types of games their children are playing and ensure that their children remain aware of fantasy versus reality.

Less time for play. Excessive screen time leaves children with less opportunity for active, creative play. Many parents struggle seeing their children not engaging in outdoor or other fun activities with friends because they spend too much time isolated on their screen devices. This leaves children missing out on expressing themselves through play and other forms of healthy recreation. The more that parents encourage active interests with their children, such as taking walks, gardening, hiking, throwing a Frisbee, or practicing sports, the more children will be influenced to take part in these enjoyable forms of leisure.

Media Images Abound but Parents Are Still the Main Show

Electronic media is ubiquitous and children have wonderful learning opportunities to gain from it. Realizing the value of the Internet and digital media sources in general, despite the negative impacts described above, it is important that we don't demonize it. It is imperative, however, that parents help children find the "sweet spot" of a healthy quality and appropriate amount of screen time for their children to engage in.

You did not grow up amid the fiercely accelerating pace of the multiple types of continually evolving digital media streams competing for your attention that now face your child. The emotional connection between you and your child is what will be your best leverage to help guide her. The extent to which she feels connected and safe to share her feelings and concerns with you goes a long way in helping you guide your child and thwart negative digital influences. The calm, firm, noncontrolling approach gives your voice a sustained, hearable frequency to be heard by your child as she faces the whitewash-like effect created by the digital noise and blurs all around her.

You as a parent really do play a valuable role in helping your child learn to self-regulate the extent of screen use in his life and how to make good choices with it. I have seen many distraught parents concerned about their children who struggle when excessive screen time impinges on, or all together usurps, other valuable activities that they could engage in. Helping your child in an emotionally safe manner to steer through this media maze is more possible than you may think.

You will find value in using the calm, firm, and noncontrolling approach for encouraging and coaching your child to have moderation in screen time usage. This nonthreatening approach gives you leverage to help your child choose wisely amid the myriad of highly appealing, ongoing digital media choices that surround him. Being calm, firm, and noncontrolling allows you to have a guiding influence while bypassing emotional outbursts.

Calm, Firm, and Noncontrolling Keeps You Seen and Heard

I have seen over and over in my counseling practice the valuable role that tuned in, calm, firm, noncontrolling parents play in helping their children navigate the waves of digital communication images coming at them. Remember that the noncontrolling part of this antidefiance formula does not mean you have a lack of parental influence. In fact, being noncontrolling keeps your child tuned in to you versus tuning you out! Your soothing presence is a welcome respite for your child, who is coping with all the competing stimuli pulling his attention in different directions.

One example I saw in my practice involved a mother who helped her daughter veer away from a precarious social media–fueled situation. Celine and Maggie, her thirteen-year-old daughter, had seen me about Maggie's defiance and her choices of wearing provocative outfits to school and in the community. Maggie, while disclosing some emotionally charged, appearance-based insecurities, had shared with Celine some of the underlying reasons for her troubling choices of apparel. These included her angst over being moderately overweight and sadness over seeing herself being left out of peer's party postings on social media.

Celine, who was previously quite emotionally reactive, become notably more empathetic with Maggie. This influenced Maggie, in turn, to begin to tone down her promiscuous image. This mother and daughter became more emotionally connected, which increased their ability to trust each other in the situation described below.

A girl with whom Maggie had a past toxic jealous rivalry over a male peer had threatened her via instant messaging with a "beat down." Maggie, having her own impulsive tendencies, was fortunately able to feel emotionally safe enough to pause and confide about this upsetting situation with her mother. Some phone calls to school officials and involvement of the other girl's parents helped prevent the occurrence of a possible precarious event.

Just that same week, however, a teen male in a neighboring community was unfortunately lured by social media into a similar type of physical altercation. Instant messaging incited a crowd of teens to appear for a filmed fight and one child suffered injuries. While the injuries apparently did not turn out to be long-standing in nature, they were nonetheless physically and emotionally disruptive to him. Social media no doubt escalated the conflict between these youths, and parents were not in the loop.

Don't Let the Challenges Knock You Off Course

Despite the encouraging example presented on page 271 between Celine and Maggie, many parents in my practice express a sense of resignation about their screen time enforcement capabilities. This is because parents feel feeble in attempting to get their kids to truly limit screen time—especially for sustained periods. When it comes to teenagers, encouraging them to cut back on technology is even more difficult. This is discussed in depth by Danah Boyd in her book, *It's Complicated: The Social Lives of Networked Teens.*

Parents I work with find that being calm, firm, and noncontrolling has a powerful influence on their children when it comes to managing screen time. This is because children's excessive use of technology breeds strong emotional attachment to it. In the words of a client of mine, Daryl, age twelve, "When my parents come at me to stop playing my video games it makes me want to rebel and keep playing. But when they are not in my face and just ask in a calm way, or remind me calmly if I forget, then I say okay and stop playing."

Daryl's account makes it sound easy for parents to calmly manage their children's screen usage. But parents, like their children, are not perfect in managing their children's screen time. Guiding children to self-regulate and make good decisions about their screen time use and choices is loaded with obstacles as described below.

A Closer Look at the Challenges for Managing Screen Use

Studies have shown many parents either have no screen time rules or those that do have a hard time remembering what they are and enforcing them. As suggested above, managing children's screen time is easier said than done, especially with defiant children who have a proneness to high emotional reactivity. Let's take a look at some of the reasons why it is difficult for parents to monitor and successfully set limits on screen time use for their children. On pages 273–277 are some of the typical challenges that parents face on the screen time battle front. I have provided solutions for each challenge discussed.

Parents modeling excessive screen use. Children who see their parents preoccupied with digital devices of all kinds will go all in, too. In the words of Miranda, a mother who I worked with, "Dr. Jeff I know it is monkey see, monkey do with me, my kids, and my cell phone. I have to find a way to not get so sucked in by my phone, because I keep giving them the message that these distractions are okay."

Solution: The best logical solution for parents engaging in and modeling too much screen time is to cut back on their own use. I realize that this may be challenging, especially for those who rely on their cell phones and other mobile devices for work responsibilities or other pressing communication needs. That said, modeling self-awareness can help your cause.

I have discussed throughout this book your crucial role as a coach to guide and set a calm, firm, noncontrolling example for your child. The modeling dynamic that comes with you as your child's emotional coach will help him gravitate toward your demonstrated behaviors. If he sees you reading a book, he is more likely to read. If you want your child to become digitally leaner, then you need to taper down your use, too.

If you get sucked too far into digital space, encouraging your child to call you out, in a polite manner, is one way to come back. Another step you can take is to call yourself out. For example, a father I worked with named Larry said to his nine- and eleven-year-old children, "Guys, I am trying to be less preoccupied with my cell phone and be off it more. If you continue to see me using it too much, please let me know." In this example, Larry successfully managed his "weakness" to model and coached personal accountability to his children.

Parents feeling worn down by their child's resistance and manipulation. I repeatedly see well-intended parents who have a hard time being able to stick to their guns amid their child's persistent demands and sneaky manipulations to reacquire their preferred electronic media sources. Carla, the mother of eleven-year-old Owen, stated, "Dr. Jeff, I just can't keep reminding Owen that he has to get off his video games." She went on to say, "I even now avoid trying to get him off his video games because he has figured out how to get back on them when I am not paying attention. I really don't have the patience for dealing with it anymore."

Solution: If you are feeling discouraged and worn down by your child's entrenched, persistent, and seemingly relentless pattern of digital screen use, reassure yourself that you are not alone. Seek the support of your spouse, intimate partner, friends, or a therapist to stay empowered to set and maintain screen time boundaries. Let your child know that you need his help in cooperating to prevent you from doling out consequences. If you do give consequences, do so in a calm, firm, noncontrolling manner (see Day 6 Discipline Without Desperation).

Parents encouraging children to use electronic devises to occupy themselves. Fast-food and family-style restaurants are settings where children rampantly get distracted and lost in table-size portions of digital distractions. For some, it's a menu in one hand and a portable screen device in the other. Others start amusing themselves with portable digital screens right after closing their menus.

I also need look no further than my own office waiting room to see electronic babysitters. That's where I frequently have observed parents overly relying on electronic devices to help their kids ward off boredom or keep them amused when the parents speak with me. When families come to see me, there are often multiple electronic devices being used at the same time!

While your child may seem peaceably amused and occupied by his mobile screen device, it is imperative that he also learns to sit and "just be with himself." Interestingly, fourteen-year-old Carlos, one of my adolescent clients, shared with me his opinion on the matter. He asserted that his parents were too permissive and encouraged him to "play with electronic stuff." Carlos said to me, "Dude, my friends' parents make them put their phones away, but my parents tell me to play games on mine when I am bored. I'm not gonna refuse that!"

Reasons for parents falling prey to being overly permissive with their children's screen device use may be that they don't, or have lost touch with being able to, talk with and listen to their children. I have also seen parents who "take on" their child's feelings of boredom and cave in to their twisted sense of guilt that their children are suffering from monotony. Holding this belief, parents sway from setting boundaries, erroneously believing that screen devices are the best way to placate their children. This reinforces the screen overuse habit.

Solution: Stay mindful of your influence to help your child learn how to be content without desperately depending on screen devices. With younger children, keep scrap books, story books, *I Spy*–type books, maze books, age-appropriate board games, and non-screen-based toys like Play-Doh and Legos available to them.

For preteens and teens, ask them open-ended questions such as what school subjects they like best, what they would love to do on a Saturday if they had their choice, their hobbies, their web and social media interests, their music and art interests, and what they feel best about or worry about most in their lives. For many great questions to ask children of all ages, try out *The Kids' Book of Questions*, by Gregory Stock.

Give journal books or scrap books to older kids to express themselves as well. If your child wants to play games or use entertainment-based apps within reasonable time parameters, take opportunities to ask them about their games and try to make these screen entertainment activities experiences for connecting with them rather than letting them become disconnected from you.

Parents targeting time limitations and not considering location limitations. It may be easier to enforce children limiting the use of their screen devices when you make it more about location choices than just trying to keep track of time. The AAP recommends that parents establish "screen-free" zones at home by making sure there are no TVs, computers, or video games in children's bedrooms, and by turning off the TV during dinner. This is not always easy to do but it is doable.

Solution: If the TV is turned on—even if it's just in the background—it's likely to draw your child's attention. If you're not actively watching a show, turn off the TV. Keep portable devices, TVs, and computers out of your children's bedrooms or at least keep tabs on their use. Children who have TVs and screen devices in their bedrooms watch more TV and videos than children who don't. Monitor your child's screen time and the Web sites she is visiting by keeping computers in a common area in your house. I had one family in my practice that placed a basket at the bottom of the stairs for the children, as well as the parents. The parents and children had agreed to deposit their cell phones in the basket before heading off to bed.

Don't eat in front of the TV. Allowing your child to eat or snack in front of the TV increases his or her screen time. The habit also encourages mindless munching, which can lead to weight gain as described earlier.

Set school-day rules. Most children have limited free time during the school week. Don't let your child spend all of it in front of a screen. Be careful not to excessively use screen time as a reward for finishing homework and chores. It is best to rely on your influence from your calm, firm, noncontrolling voice than to defer to the sounds of video games to motivate your child.

A thirteen-year-old client of mine shared that he did not mind his parents limiting him having his smartphone in his room. He readily acknowledged that his cooperation resulted from his parents nonreactive approach, which helped him to not feel threatened. By bypassing this child's emotional reactivity, he was able to see that he became too distracted when literally left to his own devices. In building further mutual respect and cooperation, this child's parents allowed him to have screen device access in the family den for time periods that he and his parents agreed were reasonable.

Parents buying in to the "I can't right now" myth. When children and parents discuss video game usage in my office, I often hear children utter pleas such as, "Mom, if you would just let me finish that one level then I would cooperate." Too often, one level leads to another level, and so on. Billy, age fourteen, shared with me, "I think that my parents are clueless about how long a level will actually take, so I manipulate them by saying the level is not over, but it usually is, and then I want to get to the next level."

Solution: Work to reassure your child that his compliance with reasonable screen time boundaries will help ensure that he continues to have the privilege (remind him this is a privilege and not a right) to play. Try to give gentle reminders of how much time you had both agreed on and be willing to give a prompt (e.g., "Ava, please remember that your time will be up in five minutes as we agreed.").

Empathize that you realize that pausing the game or shutting it down may feel abrupt or jarring to him—after all, these games are highly engaging and stimulating. Reinforce your child with praise when she does cooperate even if initially this is not as immediate as you may desire. The more you start to "catch" your child showing self-control, the more she will likely gain it.

Parents believing that electronic interaction makes up for lack of face-to-face friendships. While not as common as some of the other reasons above, some parents may support their children, particularly those who are shy, socially disenfranchised, or highly introverted, having additional screen time. These parents believe that their children's discomfort with face-to-face interactions can be offset by screen time experiences.

One teen I worked with was recently upset about seeing social media postings of pictures of a party to which he was excluded. Being left out or having a deficit of "likes" from others can feel devastating for some children. I also have seen some parents hesitant to set boundaries on video game use because they feel it is a vital interactive experience for their child.

It may be the case that instant messaging between socially challenged, distressed adolescents and their peers may provide them a sense of support and emotional relief. Abdul, a fifteen-year-old client who was introverted, shared with me, "I'm not nervous to say things when I do instant messaging. It's really empowering!" At the same time, parents need to make sure that a child's digital diet does not replace real-life social interaction.

Solution: If your child is reluctant to try new things or meet new people, expose him to new experiences gradually. When he takes social risks, let him know you admire his efforts: "I saw you talk to those kids when we were waiting on line at the store yesterday. I know that can be difficult, and

I'm proud of you." When others call her shy in front of her (and they will), reframe it lightly, saying things like "I know you like to take things in and size up new situations." When your child ends up enjoying things he had anticipated that he wouldn't like or was initially scared of, point that out to him. Eventually, he'll learn to self-regulate feelings of wariness.

What you do not want to do is label your child as "shy." She will start to experience her nervousness as a fixed trait rather than as an emotion she can learn to control. She likely knows that "shy" is usually a criticism in our society. For more on the negative impact of parent-perceived labels on children see my book, *Liking the Child You Love*.

Setting Age-Appropriate Screen Time Boundaries

There is a huge discrepancy between findings that, in reality, children are viewing screens seven and a half hours per day and the AAP and other expert recommendations for them to engage entertainment media for no more than one or two hours per day. It is also the case that a substantial percentage of children (an estimated 40 percent of toddlers have used a smartphone or other mobile device) are allowed by their parents to exceed the AAP's screen use guidelines. It is best for parents to find a sane balance between being a responsible screen time and location boundary-setting parent and being realistic and as nonrestrictive as possible in the process.

Age-Appropriate Guidelines for Screen Use

It's important for kids to spend time on outdoor play, reading, hobbies, and using their imaginations in free play. To help kids make wise media choices, parents should monitor their "media diet." Parents can make use of established ratings systems for shows, movies, and games to avoid inappropriate content, such as violence, explicit sexual content, or glorified tobacco and alcohol use.

Dr. Kimberly Young, mentioned in Day 4, is an international expert on the impact of technology on children. She developed recommendations that are consistent with AAP guidelines and are specifically for parents to use in managing their children's use of technology. It is important to remain aware that these valuable guidelines, especially when applied with defiant children, need to be done so in a calm, firm, noncontrolling manner. While as a parent you can strive to follow these guiding principles, realize that using your calm, firm, and noncontrolling style will help make you successful in implementing and sustaining them. Age-appropriate suggested guidelines are described on pages 278–282.

Birth to Two Years Old: Avoid Any Use

The AAP discourages media use for children under two years of age. This includes smartphones, computers, TVs, and any other digital devices. While it is not clear the extent to which this advice is based on reliable studies, I know some parents who respect this advice but find it hard to adhere to.

One young mother I spoke with said the following about the AAP screen time guidelines: "I can hear what they are suggesting, but that just does not work for me. I can't worry that if my older child is playing on his mobile device and my infant daughter peers over at him this will mess her up her brain. And I can't go to another person's house insisting that the television must be off. I'm not going to worry that if we go to a restaurant with a television, I'm somehow 'damaging' my child."

The rationale for the AAP position is that any screen time impairs social communication, development, and a child's attachment to the parent or other family members. If children at this age are completely disconnected from technology, they have time to develop relationships with others and can, through play, develop other needed sensory-motor skills. It is safe to say that for children at this age, media consumption will be easier to enforce than with older children.

Three to Six Years Old: One Hour a Day

According to Dr. Young, children ages three to six years can be introduced to technology under careful parental supervision. Interestingly, research has shown that about one in four parents of children two to five years old report average daily entertainment screen time of three or more hours for their young children. Among these parents, 35 percent say they have not considered limiting total screen time each day, 24 percent say they have not set screen-free times for the whole family, and 19 percent say they have not set screen-free days for their children.

As discussed above, parents too often may give children a tablet or smartphone to occupy themselves. During these young ages, this is a crucial time in children's development for them to learn pro-social behavior and social behavior. It is important to keep them involved in activities outside of the computer and avoid multiplatform portable devices (e.g., phones, iPads, tablets, laptops).

Dr. Young's recommendations for ages three to six years for appropriate media activities are:

1. Uses an electronic reader for story time.
2. Sorts shapes and finds hidden objects on mobile apps.

3. Uses screen technology in the form of child-friendly electronic media that educate and teach numbers, letters, and vowel sounds.
4. Parents make sure child still physically plays, reads books, and engages other children.

Six to Nine Years Old: Supervised Use

For the age range of six to nine years, Dr. Young suggests that children need to balance technology with social and physical behavior. For this age group, if used consistent with the AAP guidelines, children can be allotted up to two hours of screen time per day under close parental supervision. At this age, since children have passed the physical milestones of mastery of running and kicking, and bending over without falling, screen use may include video games that the entire family can play that involve physical movement.

Appropriate activities for this age are:

1. Uses the Internet under supervision (create tech-free time to talk each day!).
2. Plays active video games with the family.
3. Takes time to create a new definition of "screen time."
4. Stays active in school clubs, sports, peers, and outside activities.

Nine to Twelve Years Old: Responsible Use

Children who are ages nine to twelve are still recommended to have no more than two hours of screen time a day, including family video game time. Dr. Young recommends that parents do not allow access to tech devices in private areas of the home such as the child's bedroom. This targeting of location boundaries was discussed earlier. Dr. Young also suggests that children at this age have no access to online gaming (especially any role-playing games).

At this age, children need to be mentally and physically stimulated through reading, taking nature walks, riding bikes, getting involved in school and sports activities, making friends at school, and spending time with family. Try to establish family time with no technology (e.g., no screens at dinner or in the car).

Dr. Young recommends that if these time boundaries are broken, that parents remove all screen devices for twenty-four hours (or longer) and lock all technology up at night. I suggest that any actions that parents take to limit use or take devices away be done consistent with the calm, firm, and noncontrolling approach. For example, a parent may say, "I know this game is important to you. I am taking it away for the night because you are having a hard time staying reasonable in the amount of time we agreed upon. I am hoping you can let me know you understand why I am doing this so I can feel good about giving it back tomorrow morning."

Appropriate activities for children ages nine to twelve years old are:

1. Uses the Internet under supervision (create tech-free time to talk each day).
2. Has independence with technology, social media with strict time limitations and rules for use.
3. Parents monitor computer homework and limit/remove all devices when screen time rules are broken.
4. Parents make sure child completes chores and stays involved in school activities.

Twelve to Eighteen Years Old: Independence

While it seems to be the case for all age groups, parents tend to be even more liberal about screen time with teens. By the middle school years, children tend to have their own portable electronic device or smartphone. A teen client of mine, Randy, age sixteen, shared that the two-hour screen time limit "is just nuts" and that "kids won't follow this." He said, "I know teenagers will just find a way to get around parents setting these crazy time limits."

Complicating matters, teens see many of their friends with unlimited screen device access. They are already resistant to rigid rules. Knowing that parents considerably vary in the management of all kinds of house rules for teens, many very determined ones are unabashed when it comes to lobbying for all the freedoms they can acquire—including related to screen devices.

One fourteen-year-old client of mine, Lester, shared what seemed to represent common practice for this age group. He touted to me how he is allowed to use his smartphone and laptop in his room. Lester further shared that he, and most friends he knows, spend at least four hours daily on the Internet doing homework, watching YouTube, going on Wikipedia, doing social media, and playing video games.

Parents will range in how open they are to their teens' unrestricted screen use. Simply setting limits won't go over well, especially with older teens, who need to have rules that make sense to them. The more that parents are calm, firm, and noncontrolling, the easier time they will have in gaining cooperation with their teens who are ravenous for independence.

Being calm, firm, and noncontrolling will remove the static noise of any potential power struggle. At this age, teenagers desire their own social media accounts and the freedom to have autonomy when using them along with any other screen use. The calm, firm, noncontrolling approach helps soften the blow for parents who check their teens' text messaging or other forms of electronic communications. I suggest, where possible, giving your teen space and avoiding being intrusive in their world. Otherwise, you will likely erode any trust you are trying to establish or reestablish.

Dr. Young suggests having teens keep a log of their technology time if the parents allow their teens' screen use to be unrestricted. This is a good idea and may work for some parents and children, but I have not seen many parents and children able to implement and sustain this strategy. By staying with your calm, firm, and noncontrolling voice, however, you can help your child, even at this age, make better choices about their activities online.

Conveying the message that you are wanting your child to feel good about himself will penetrate your teen's defensive psyche better than the almost guaranteed to backfire "You will do as I say" script. Keep your cool when discussing with your teen if he is playing video games all afternoon or doing homework. Empathize about the demands your child likely faces amid the competing interests and demands of, for example, using social media or researching a paper for school.

Like food addiction, online use is about making healthy choices. When parents rigidly restrict children from eating certain foods, they usually rebel at a later time and overconsume these foods. Balanced screen and media nutrition means that as an independent teenager the technology is used responsibly. By staying emotionally connected to your child you will be more able to stay aware of what she is connecting to in cyberspace.

Follow agreed upon reasonable expectations for responsible technology use with your teen. Stay calm, firm, and noncontrolling when deciding on, and implementing, discipline for poor media choices and overconsumption. If you temporarily suspend an allowance or restrict your child from driving for a day or a week, let him know you still emotionally support him and don't want to continue to be in a position of taking privileges away.

There is an old quote from Lucille Ball, "If you want something done, ask a busy person to do it." Bearing this in mind, encourage your teen to feel productive. Make sure that he pulls his weight by doing daily chores around the house (e.g., doing the dishes, cutting the lawn, shoveling snow, or taking out garbage).

I can't stress enough how valuable it is for teens at age sixteen and older to hold a part-time job. Working helps teenagers maintain structure in their day to avoid boredom and idol time that contributes to screen overuse and addiction. Earning their own money also helps them have "skin in the game" for their own digital devices. This helps them develop a work ethic. The busier teens are, the less time they will have to play with or use all their digital devices. Let's face it, your teen getting reprimanded by a boss for too often glancing at his mobile device may help him realize more than ever just how sweet life is at home!

Appropriate activities for teens are:

1. Has independence with technology but is open and accountable when discussing technology use and the use is consistent with agreeable limits.
2. Parents know teen's online friends—invite them to dinner and talk about how they are.
3. Completes chores and stays involved with school activities and friends.
4. Parents encourage teen to develop a time structure, maintain his own personal financial management, and develop a strong work ethic. Used appropriately, there are very helpful apps that can help teens achieve success in these realms.

Appendix 3

Guide to Handling Defiant Students

I f you are a parent, I encourage you to share this section with your child's teacher or school administrators as a way to advocate for your defiant child. Although you are your child's best advocate, remember not to "irritate." Please also be open to feedback from educators who may have additional ideas and recommendations for your child.

If you are an educator who is willing to try to use the following strategies, you will likely find that defiant students will become more manageable. I have found that the way teachers behave toward defiant students has a tremendous influence on their behavior. The key is to stay calm in the face of a defiant student's attempts to be disruptive and gain control. The strategies and information that follow will give you the necessary tools to attain this sense of calm and confidence and will provide you with two huge benefits:

- Your student(s) will become less defiant because you are taking away the satisfaction they received by watching you react in anger.
- You will have more instructional time available that used to be consumed by epic power struggles.

Understanding Student Defiance

It's imperative for you to realize that defiant students lack the skills to solve problems and to express themselves in a constructive manner. Defiant students, who tend to be emotionally immature, may not feel comfortable telling you that they don't like a class assignment, have forgotten their study materials for the third time this week, or do not know how to do the math problem that they have been asked to solve on the board. When faced with too many emotional stressors or feelings of inadequacy, these children speak through disruptive and defiant behaviors.

A student refusing to solve a math problem on the board may really be saying, "I don't want to look stupid in front of my friends, who will see me mess up." Maybe this is a case where you decide to skip over this student and instead meet with her individually to give her some extra help on the math problem. Staying calm and helping yourself and your defiant student save face will help you manage the emotional immaturity that leads to her defiance.

In the spirit of being understanding, stay mindful of special circumstances that certain children face that can influence them to appear defiant at school. Rolando had difficulty in his seventh grade Social Studies class. He refused to make any form of eye contact with his teacher and would completely ignore her when he was called to the board. Rolando's ostensible defiance resulted in disciplinary actions.

Once the learning support teacher, however, spoke with Rolando, she realized that he was turning off his hearing aids to avoid being called on in class. Rolando, in feeling understood by the learning support teacher, become very tearful and expressed feelings of shame for getting in trouble. Once he acknowledged his underlying anxiety and discussed this with his teacher and the learning support teacher, Rolando began to increase his class participation.

Don't Take a Student's Defiance Personally

Remember, you are the outlet for, not the cause of, this student's defiance—unless you are shouting, arguing, or attempting to handle him with sarcasm. Therefore, don't take the defiance personally. Rather, say, "John, what's the matter? That doesn't sound like you," or "What's making you so upset?" By using this approach, even if it doesn't reflect your feelings, you are helping rather than confronting, and you can maintain both your dignity and your professional position. In addition, you emphatically convey to all students that the defiance is the problem, not you.

Connect by Listening and Encouraging

Most defiant students feel powerless and ineffective at school. They act out by disrupting others as a result of feeling inadequate in the classroom.

I have coached many teachers at in-service training sessions on the power of listening in order to reduce defiance in students. Listening is powerful because it demonstrates to the student that you hear where she is coming from. I am not saying that you have to give in to the student's point of view if it is unreasonable. A student telling you that homework should be outlawed is not going to win your agreement. The main goal here is to let the student know that you fully comprehend her viewpoint. What you could say is that you realize that homework feels challenging and even at times overwhelming. Defiant students tend to view teachers who practice active listening as being supportive, respectful, and caring individuals.

Here are some statements you can use when paraphrasing student comments:

"You feel this is unfair because I did not give you enough notice."
"So, as you see it, the test is too hard because . . . "
"You think this lesson is pointless because . . . "

By reflecting your student's feelings as demonstrated in the above examples, you can encourage the child, when she is ready, to change her perspective about what she is learning. One way to do this is by stating, "So let's discuss how you will use this information/skill in your life."

Develop a Relationship

Cultivating a positive, trusting relationship with a student allows you to be proactive in reducing the likelihood of your student's defiant behavior. Get to know the student beyond his surface behaviors. Speak to him privately and be caring. You may want to give him magazine articles or Web site links on topics you know will interest him. Take a couple of minutes each day to engage the student. Smile more and criticize less. It may take some time, but such acts will demonstrate your empathy and caring—and are likely to have a cumulative, powerful, and positive impact on the student.

Once you have built more rapport, tell the student exactly what it is that is causing problems as far as you are concerned. Be sure you listen to the student as well. In the process, insist upon one rule—that you both be respectful. Always listen to this student. Let her talk. Don't interrupt her.

Be Calm, Firm, and Noncontrolling

The best way to manage defiant students is to remain calm. You won't get involved in a power struggle if you know how to avoid one. A defiant student will get a green light from you to continue his negative behaviors when he sees you react by doing any of the following:

- Becoming visibly angry
- Raising your voice
- Attempting to intimidate him
- Interrupting him

Praise When You Can

Most teachers I have spoken to have acknowledged that they could connect more positively with defiant students by appropriately praising them.
Many teachers are fooled by a defiant child's antics into believing that the
child is impervious to praise. This is just not the case. Your praise is powerful. It communicates approval and positive regard. It's an abundantly available natural resource that is greatly underutilized. Be careful that you have
not seen your student in an all-or-nothing way. I have seen that teachers
do tend to praise their regular students for good behavior, but they tend to
overlook opportunities to praise defiant students when they are behaving
well. Defiant students may not immediately respond to praise because of
their long history of negative interactions with the adults in their lives, but
when paired with other incentives (such as the type of reward system described below), the positive impact of praise will eventually increase.

When praising a defiant child:

- Give the praise as a soon as possible after the desired behavior has
  been demonstrated.
- Be specific and sincere about the praiseworthy aspects of the student's
  accomplishments.
- Comment on effort and ability, implying that similar successes can be
  expected in the future.
- Remind the student that you believe in him and that he is important.

Be Like Columbo

I used to enjoy the TV show *Columbo*. The main character, a detective
named Columbo, would question criminal suspects in a bewildered way. In
the spirit of Columbo, be calm and inquisitive. I suggest asking the defiant
student questions such as "What's bothering you?" or "You seem kind of
upset." This reaction may not agree with your feelings, but it will produce
the best results. Follow this response with "What happened to make you
so upset?" or "Is there anything I can do to help you?" If the student re-
plies, "Yes, leave me alone," don't lose your composure. Rather, continue
using the Columbo-like, detached stance, and the problem has a chance for
a solution rather than a guarantee of an unfortunate scene.

Delay Now, Don't Pay Later

It is often helpful not to react right away. For example, if a student says,
"I am not doing this," don't react right away. After a pause, look at her in

surprise and say, "I'm confused about what you are saying." This response gives the defiant student a chance to save face and change unacceptable behavior into a more compliant response without your reprimanding her. If your situation with the defiant student has already deteriorated to the point where you could not use this approach in front of other students, then do it privately. This problem should never be handled past this point publicly. Sometimes you can only try to quiet the student by saying, "Let's not talk about it here. Let's touch base later when you can tell me everything that's on your mind." Above all, reach an agreement with the student on how you will treat each other. Check out the example below to see how one innovative teacher helped a student emotionally de-escalate and thwarted her defiant behavior.

Hilary was arguing with her mom about going on a field trip. Hilary was adamant about not going and refused to tell her mother why. The teacher, who was informed of the situation by Hilary's mom, gave Hilary a piece of paper and a pen and encouraged her to write down her thoughts. Taking the time to get some of her feelings on paper allowed Hilary to express that she didn't want to go on the trip because she may have had to wear a bathing suit. Hilary's outside psychologist became involved and followed up with the teacher and it was agreed that Hilary would help the teacher with academic duties during the time the other students swam.

Ending Power Struggles

Teachers are only human. Some students are very skilled at dragging teachers into arguments that turn into power struggles. To disengage from potential power struggles, you can:

- *Take a few deep breaths.* For example, a teacher I worked with as a client told me that she dealt with defiant students in challenging situations by taking a deeper-than-normal breath and releasing it slowly. She said that doing this also bought her time to plan an appropriate response, rather than reacting immediately to the student's behavior.
- *Fake it till you make it.* William James, considered by many the father of psychology, famously said, "Act as if what you do makes a difference. It does." I want you to apply this to the management of your defiant student. If you act calm and contained, you will appear that way. I'm not saying that you should be smiling inside if a defiant student throws a book through the window. What I am saying is that if you do your best to act calm, firm, and noncontrolling, you will be that way.
- *Use "I" instead of "you" statements.* Beginning what you say with "I" instead of "you" can help get you out of a power struggle. "You"

statements tend to incite more negative feelings ("You should have been prepared for this test."), than "I" thoughts ("I don't understand why this is so hard for you."). That is because "you" statements imply to the listener that he or she is "wrong" and you are "right." "You" statements feel accusatory. "I" statements can reduce the potential that a teacher's criticism will lead to a confrontation with a student. I remember conducting a teacher in-service program on effective communication strategies. I asked teachers to pair off for an exercise and a teacher turned to me and said, "This is not productive, I'm not doing this." I calmly, firmly, and in a noncontrolling manner told him that I felt disappointed with his decision. The teacher then agreed to do the exercise. He later privately told me he was going through a divorce and that he was an emotional mess. He thanked me for my way of not reacting to him at the time. I thanked myself for using an "I" statement. These skills really do work!

- *Don't "go there" with ultimatums.* When a potential confrontation looms, you can let a student save face by phrasing your request in a way that lets the student preserve her self-image even as she complies. For example, a teacher who says to a student, "Sara, open your notebook now and pay attention, or I will send you to the office!" backs the student into a corner. The student ends up feeling threatened and likely won't comply because she does not want to "lose." Instead use a face-saving alternative: "Sara, I am asking you to please take out your book and pay attention. I really want you to do well on the test tomorrow."

    In another scenario, a teacher on hall duty sees Raymond standing at his locker when there should be no students at lockers. The teacher confronts an obviously agitated Raymond, saying, "Raymond, how many times have I told you not to be by your locker without a pass? Can't you understand anything? Get out of the hall before I send you to the principal's office!" In this scenario, Raymond may comply and leave, or he may respond to the teacher by acting defensive after what he takes as a personal attack. Raymond's defense may be some form of insubordination, including but not limited to inappropriate language aimed at the teacher or worse. "Don't tell me what to do!" or "Mind your own f—ing business" are examples of the kinds of responses that an agitated student might make when confronted by the teacher in this sudden power struggle.

    In this same scenario, the teacher could have used my calm, firm and noncontrolling approach to accomplish the same goal of getting Raymond to go to class and not loiter by the lockers. This interaction could have been:

"Raymond, can I talk to you for a second?" At this point the teacher speaks to Raymond quietly and says, "Raymond, can you do me a favor? I'm supposed to be making sure that the hallways are clear during class time. Can you help me out? Where are you supposed to be?" Raymond's response will be much different when he sees that the teacher is asking Raymond for help and not just scolding him. In both exchanges, the teacher has the same goal. In the second response, the teacher has a much greater chance of achieving the goal while at the same time not engendering a power struggle that would lead to discipline.

- *Stay calm, firm, and noncontrolling.* A teacher's angry response can escalate student misbehavior, resulting in a power struggle that spirals out of control. When you feel provoked, take several seconds to collect your thoughts and to think through an appropriate, professional response before you take action.

A COMPARISON OF CONTROLLING AND NONCONTROLLING TEACHER STYLES

The following table encapsulates the essence of how teachers can most effectively work with defiant students. The left side shows a controlling teacher statement, which can provoke defiance. The right side shows the calm, firm, noncontrolling approach that will reduce defiance in students.

Controlling Teacher Interaction	Calm, Firm, Noncontrolling Teacher Interaction
"Shawna, you are just out to fool around and ruin this class for the other students."	"I realize that you're laughing a lot and in a goofy mood. But I really need everyone to focus because we have a lot of new material to cover. That's why I need you to do your best to get focused. Thanks."
"If you don't sit down, Marleen, I won't help you get caught up on this assignment."	"Please sit down so I can help you with the work you missed so you're ready for today's assignment."
"Jeremy, either you get that book out now or I will send you to the office!"	"Jeremy, I'd like you to please take out your book so we can get started. I want to see you keep up with your work so you don't get cut from the football team. I know the team really needs you."

continues

continued

Controlling Teacher Interaction	Calm, Firm, Noncontrolling Teacher Interaction
"Rhonda, if you keep getting behind on your labs, you will flunk science."	"I'm confused about why your labs are getting turned in late. I see how interested you are in doing the experiments in class, and I want you to get good grades on them. Let's talk more about what is getting in the way of your completing the write-ups."
"That's it, Eric. You call out again and I'm sending you to the office."	"Eric, I appreciate your enthusiasm. I think it will help both of us if we can talk after class about how you can participate without interrupting. I would appreciate your helping me figure this out."
"Tim, you are going to sit back there by yourself if you keep bothering everyone around you."	"Tim, I want to see good behavior from you in this class. I know you can make good choices. I'd like to talk to you after lunch about how we can make things work better."

- *Change the logistics.* If you find yourself being drawn into a toxic exchange with the defiant student (e.g., raising your voice, reprimanding the student), immediately use strategies to disengage yourself (e.g., by moving away from the student and repeating your request in a neutral tone of voice).
- *Do not use social pressure.* It's a mistake to use social pressure (e.g., reprimands, attempting to stare down students, standing watch over them) or physical force to make a confrontational student comply with a request. The student will usually resist and a power struggle will result. In particular, adults should not lay hands on a student to force compliance. The student will almost certainly view this act as a serious physical threat and respond in kind. It's also against the law in many places for teachers to touch students—even in a benign way.
- *Use humor to defuse a confrontation.* By responding with humor (not sarcasm) to a defiant student, the teacher signals to that student in a face-saving manner that her behavior is about to be defused and handled. The student can join the teacher in laughing off the event and can return to participation in class activities. I suggest that you never use humor in a sarcastic or teasing manner, as defiant students are very sensitive and are likely to feel disrespected and become more defiant as a result. You may also find it helpful to have a private follow-up meeting to talk about the incident and to ensure that the student understands your concerns about her confrontational behavior.

- *Be aware that less is more.* It is best that you speak less with defiant students. Short teacher responses give the defiant student less control over the interaction and can also prevent you from inadvertently "rewarding" misbehaving students with lots of negative adult attention.
- *Don't put demands on students when they are upset.* Defiant students will be much more likely to become confrontational if you approach them with a demand to perform a task at a time when they are already frustrated or upset. When possible, give agitated students a little breathing room to collect themselves and calm down before you give them commands.
- *Let the student know that you understand what he is feeling.* If you see a student slamming his books down on his desk and muttering to himself after returning from a class, you might say, "James, you seem angry. Can you tell me what is wrong?" Once you "name" a powerful emotion such as anger, you and the student can then talk about it, figure out what may have triggered it, and jointly find solutions that will mitigate it.
- *Ask if isolation would help.* But don't force it on the student prior to talking about it. Such "surprises" will only make her more defiant. Make the student a part of any plan to change her behavior. If you don't, you'll become the enemy.
- *Pick battles wisely.* If a student comment is merely mildly annoying, ignore it. If the negative comment is serious enough to require your response (e.g., an insult or challenge to authority), briefly state in a neutral manner why the student's remark was inappropriate, and impose a preselected consequence. Then move on.

More Strategies to Manage Defiance at School

If you feel ineffective or lack support in managing your defiant student, the following may also be helpful.

- Arm yourself with as much information as is available about the student.
- Meet with the guidance counselor to discuss the student's overall school experience.
- Seek out the teachers who had the student during the past year to get some information about their experiences in dealing with her (for grades 6–12, request a team meeting).
- These teachers may share some successful teaching techniques that worked for them in dealing with the student.
- Meet with the principal or assistant principal to discuss the student and see what the administrator recommends.

- If there is a child study team in place, the teacher should refer the student to this committee for consideration.
- If the student has an IEP, call a meeting with the involved members of the child's study team to get updated recommendations for a new approach.
- If there is a mentoring program in place, discuss the child with the student's mentor to get some advice.

Sources

The following list contains sources I used in writing this book. Please note that several of these sources are Web sites that were active at the time of this writing. Web sites can change or expire on the Internet, so some of those listed below may no longer be active at the time you are reading this book.

Alone Together: Why We Expect More from Technology and Less from Each Other. Sherry Turkle. New York: Basic Books, 2012.

"Anxiety Disorders in Children and Adolescents (Fact Sheet)." National Institute of Health, National Institute of Mental Health. Accessed January 29, 2015, www.nimh.nih.gov/health/publications/anxiety-disorders-in-children-and-adolescents/index.shtml.

Aristotle quote: www.quotationspage.com/quote/20946.html.

"Attention Deficit Hyperactivity Disorder." National Institute of Health, National Institute of Mental Health. Accessed January 29, 2015, www.nimh.nih.gov/health/publications/attention-deficit-hyperactivity-disorder/index.shtml.

"Bipolar Disorder in Children and Adolescents." National Institute of Health, National Institute of Mental Health. NIH Publication No. 12–6380. Revised 2012. Accessed January 29, 2014, www.nimh.nih.gov/health/publications/bipolar-disorder-in-children-and-adolescents/index.shtml.

"Children with Oppositional Defiant Disorder." American Academy of Child and Adolescent Psychiatry. Facts for Families No. 72, March 2011; reviewed July, 2013. Accessed January 29, 2015, www.aacap.org/AACAP/Families_and_Youth/Facts_for_Families/Facts_for_Families_Pages/Children_With_Oppositional_Defiant_Disorder_72.aspx.

Closer Together, Farther Apart: The Effect of Technology and the Internet on Parenting, Work, and Relationships. Robert Weiss and Jennifer P. Schneider. Carefree, AZ: Gentle Path Press, 2014.

"Confessions of a Depressed Comic." Kevin Breel. TED talk, 2013. Accessed January 29, 2015, www.ted.com/talks/kevin_breel_confessions_of_a_depressed_comic?language=en.

"Depression in Children: Causes, Treatment of Children with Depression." Natasha Tracy. Healthy Place. Last updated January 14, 2014. Accessed January 29, 2015, www.healthyplace.com/depression/children/depression -in-children-causes-treatment-of-child-depression/.

Desk Reference to the Diagnostic Criteria from DSM-5. American Psychiatric Association. APA, 2013.

"Homework Tips for Parents," U.S. Department of Education, Office of In-tergovernmental and Interagency Affairs, Educational Partnerships and Family Involvement Unit. Washington, DC, 2003. Accessed January 29, 2015, www2.ed.gov/parents/academic/involve/homework/index.html.

"Key Differences Between Section 504 and IDEA." Pat Howey. 2012. www .wrightslaw.com/howey/504.idea.htm. See also www.wrightslaw.com for further information on educational law.

LD OnLine. From WETA, Washington, DC, in association with The Coor-dinated Campaign for Learning Disabilities. www.ldonline.org.

"Learning Disabilities Information Page." National Institute of Health, Na-tional Institute of Neurological Disorders and Stroke. Last updated Feb-ruary 14, 2014. Accessed January 19, 2015, www.ninds.nih.gov/disorders /learningdisabilities/learningdisabilities.htm.

Liking The Child You Love: Build a Better Relationship with Your Kids—Even When They're Driving You Crazy. Jeffrey Bernstein. New York: Da Capo, 2014.

"Meta-Emotion, Children's Emotional Intelligence, and Buffering Children from Marital Conflict." John Gottman. In *Emotion, Social Relationships, and Health.* Edited by Carol D. Ryff and Burton H. Singer (New York: Oxford University Press, 2001), 23–40.

"Oppositional Defiant Disorder." Mayo Clinic. Accessed January 29, 2015, www.mayoclinic.org/diseases-conditions/oppositional-defiant-disorder /basics/causes/con-20024559.

"Oppositional Defiant Disorder." WebMD. Accessed January 29, 2014. www.webmd.com/mental-health/oppositional-defiant-disorder.

"Principles of Adolescent Substance Use Disorder Treatment: A Research-Based Guide." National Institute of Health, National Institute on Drug Abuse. Last updated January 2014. Accessed January 29, 2015, www .drugabuse.gov/publications/principles-adolescent-substance-use -disorder-treatment-research-based-guide.

Raising an Emotionally Intelligent Child: The Heart of Parenting. John Gott-man, Joan Declaire, and Daniel Goleman. New York: Simon & Schus-ter, 1998.

Self-Compassion: The Proven Power of Being Kind to Yourself. Kristen Neff. New York: William Morrow, 2011.

"Social Phobia Among Children." National Institute of Mental Health. Accessed February 15, 2015, www.nimh.nih.gov/health/statistics/prevalence/social-phobia-among-children.shtml.

"Tourette Syndrome Fact Sheet." National Institute of Health, National Institute of Neurological Disorders and Stroke. Last updated April 16, 2014. Accessed January 29, 2015, www.ninds.nih.gov/disorders/tourette/detail_tourette.htm.

"What Is Autism Spectrum Disorder?" National Institute of Health, National Institute of Mental Health. Accessed January 29, 2015, www.nimh.nih.gov/health/topics/autism-spectrum-disorders-asd/index.shtml.

"What Parents Can Do About Technology Addiction at Home, Parenting Guidelines Rules for Every Age." Center for Internet Addiction Recovery. June, 2014. www.netaddiction.com/wp-content/uploads/2014/06/Screen-Smart-Guidelines.pdf.

Writing Your Way to Happiness. Sara Parker-Pope. *New York Times*. January 19, 2015. Accessed February 16, 2015, well.blogs.nytimes.com/2015/01/19/writing-your-way-to-happiness/?mwrsm=Email&_r=0.

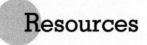# Resources

The following list contains sources I used in writing this book. Please note that several of these sources are Web sites that were active at the time of this writing. Web sites can change or expire on the Internet, so not all below may be active at the time you are reading this book.

ADHD

Children and Adults with Attention-Deficit/ Hyperactivity Disorder (CHADD)
8181 Professional Place,
Suite 150
Landover, MD 20785
Tel: 301-306-7070
Toll-free: 800-233-4050
www.chadd.org

A.D.D. WareHouse
300 Northwest 70th Avenue,
Suite 102
Plantation, FL 33317
Toll-free: 800-233-9273
www.addwarehouse.com
www.helpforadd.com
    This Web site will enable you to subscribe to Dr. David Rabiner's free e-mail newsletter called "Attention Research Update." This e-mail newsletter helps parents, professionals, and educators stay informed about important new research on ADHD.

Anxiety/Depression

Anxiety and Depression Association of America
11900 Parklawn Drive, Suite 100
Rockville, MD 20852
Tel: 301-231-9350
www.adaa.org

Depression

Depression and Bipolar Support Alliance
730 North Franklin Street,
Suite 501
Chicago, IL 60610
Toll-free: 800-826-3632
www.dbsalliance.org/

Depression and Related Affective Disorders Association
Meyer 3-18
1600 North Wolfe Street
Baltimore, MD 21287-7381
Tel: 410-955-4647
www.drada.org/

Depression and Bipolar Support Alliance (DBSA)
ATTN: Balanced Mind
Parent Network
730 N. Franklin Street
Suite 501
Chicago, IL 60654
Tel: 312-642-0049
info@thebalancedmind.org

Drugs and Alcohol

National Institute of Drug Abuse (NIDA)
National Institute on Drug Abuse
  Office of Science Policy and
Communications, Public Information and Liaison Branch

6001 Executive Boulevard
Room 5213, MSC 9561
Bethesda, Maryland 20892-9561
Tel: 301-443-1124
www.drugabuse.gov

Substance Abuse and Mental Health Services Administration
U.S. Department of Health and Human Services
200 Independence Avenue, S.W.
Washington, DC 20201
Tel: 202-619-0257
Toll-free: 877-696-6775
www.samhsa.gov

Internet Issues

Center for Internet Addiction
  The Center for Internet Addiction was founded by Dr. Kimberly Young in 1995. It provides treatment for Internet Addiction.
www.netaddiction.com/

Enough Is Enough:
Internet Safety 101
746 Walker Road, Suite 116
Great Falls, VA 22066
www.internetsafety101.org/
abouteie.htm

Learning Disabilities

International Dyslexia Association
8600 LaSalle Road
Chester Building, Suite 382
Baltimore, MD 21286-2044
Tel: 410-296-0232
Toll-free: 800-ABCD123
www.interdys.org

Learning Disabilities Association of America
4156 Library Road, Suite 1
Pittsburgh, PA 15234-1349
Tel: 412-341-1515
info@ldaamerica.org
www.ldaamerica.org

LD OnLine
  A service of WETA, Washington, DC, in association with The Coordinated Campaign for Learning Disabilities
www.ldonline.org

National Center for Learning Disabilities
32 Laight Street, Second Floor
New York, NY 10013
www.ncld.org

SchwabLearning.org
  Schwab Learning is a nonprofit organization, dedicated to providing reliable, parent-friendly information from experts and parents.

School Rights

Council of Parent Attorneys and Advocates (COPAA)

P.O. Box 6767
Towson, MD 21285
Tel: 443-451-5270
www.copaa.net

COPAA is a nonprofit advocacy group of attorneys, nonattorney educational advocates, and parents who are dedicated to securing quality educational services for children with disabilities.

Tourette's Syndrome

The Tourette's Syndrome Association

42–40 Bell Boulevard
Bayside, NY 11361
Tel: 718-224-2999
www.tsa-usa.org

Wrightslaw

Parents, educators, advocates, and attorneys visit Wrightslaw .com for accurate, reliable information about special education law and advocacy for children with disabilities. Wrightslaw includes thousands of articles, cases, and free resources about dozens of special education topics.
www.Wrightslaw.com

Organizations with General Child and Teen Mental Health Information

American Psychological Association

750 First Street, NE
Washington, DC 20002-4242
Tel: 800-374-2721
www.apa.org/

American Psychiatric Association

1000 Wilson Boulevard, Suite 1825
Arlington, VA 22209-3901
Tel: 703-907-7300
www.apa.org

Focus Adolescent Services

Focus Adolescent Services is an Internet clearinghouse of information and resources on teen and family issues to help and support families with troubled and at-risk teens.
Tel: 443-358-4691
www.focusas.com/index.html

Federation of Families for Children's Mental Health

The National Federation of Families for Children's Mental Health is a national family-run organization linking more than 120 chapters and state organizations focused on the issues of children and youth with emotional, behavioral, or mental health needs and their families.
1021 Prince Street
Alexandria VA 22314-2971
Tel: 703-684-7710
www.ffcmh.org

National Institute of Mental Health (NIMH)

Public Information and Communications Branch
6001 Executive Boulevard
Room 8184, MSC 9663
Bethesda, MD 20892-9663
Toll-free: 866-615-6464
www.nimh.nih.gov

Recommended Articles and Books on
Child, Teen, and Parenting Issues

10 Days to a Less Distracted Child. Jeffrey Bernstein. New York: Da Capo, 2007.

10% Happier: How I Tamed the Voice in My Head, Reduced Stress Without Losing My Edge, and Found Self-Help That Actually Works—At True Story. Dan Harris. New York: It Books, 2014.

"Age-Based Guidelines for Kids' Internet Use, Microsoft Safety and Security Center." Microsoft. 2014. Accessed January 29, 2015, www.microsoft .com/security/family-safety/childsafety-age.aspx.

Alone Together, Why We Expect More from Technology and Less from Each Other. Sherry Turkle. New York: Basic Books, 2012.

American Psychological Association. "American Psychological Association Survey Shows Teen Stress Rivals That of Adults." February 11, 2014. Accessed January 29, 2015, www.apa.org/news/press/releases/2014/02 /teen-stress.aspx.

"Cell Phones, Dopamine, and Development: Barbara Jennings at TEDxABQ." TED talk, October 2, 2013. http://tedxtalks.ted.com/video/Cell-Phones -Dopamine-and-Development.

Children Learn What They Live. Dorothy Law Nolte. New York: Workman Publishing, 1998.

Choices and Consequences: What to Do When a Teenager Uses Alcohol/Drugs. Dick Schaefer. Center City, MN: Hazelden, 1987.

Clinical Practice of Cognitive Therapy with Children and Adolescents. Robert D. Friedberg and Jessica M. McClure. New York: Guilford Publications, 2002.

Closer Together, Farther Apart: The Effect of Technology and the Internet on Parenting, Work, and Relationships. Robert Weiss and Jennifer P. Schneider. Carefree, AZ: Gentle Path Press, 2014.

"Confessions of a Depressed Comic." Kevin Breel. TED Talk, 2013. www .ted.com/talks/kevin_breel_confessions_of_a_depressed_comic.

Driven to Distraction (Revised): Recognizing and Coping with Attention Deficit Disorder from Childhood Through Adulthood. Edward M. Hallowell and John Ratey. Carmichael, CA: Touchstone, 2011.

Emotional Intelligence: 10th Anniversary Edition. Daniel Goleman. New York: Bantam, 2005.

The Explosive Child: A New Approach for Understanding and Parenting Easily Frustrated, Chronically Inflexible Children. Ross W. Greene. New York: Harper Paperbacks, 2014.

"Extreme Gamers Spend Two Full Days per Week Playing Video Games." NPD Group. May 27, 2010. Accessed January 29, 2015, www.npd.com /press/releases/press_100527b.html.

Focus: The Hidden Driver of Excellence. Daniel Goleman. New York: Harper, 2013.

For Parents and Teenagers: Dissolving the Barrier Between You and Your Teen. William Glasser. New York: HarperCollins, 2003.

From Emotions to Advocacy: The Special Education Survival Guide, 2nd Edition. Pam Wright and Pete Wright. Hatfield, VA: Harbor House Law Press, 2005.

"Generation M2: Media in the Lives of 8- to 18-Year-Olds." Menlo Park: The Henry J Kaiser Family Foundation, 2010.

"Helping Teenagers with Stress." American Academy of Child and Adolescent Psychiatry. Facts for Families No. 66. Last updated February 2013. Accessed January 29, 2015, www.aacap.org/aacap/Families_and_Youth /Facts_for_Families/Facts_for_Families_Pages/Helping_Teenagers _With_Stress_66.aspx.

"How to Limit Screen Time." Mayo Clinic. Accessed January 29, 2015, www .mayoclinic.org/healthy-living/childrens-health/in-depth/children-and -tv/art-20047952?pg=2.

"How Texting and IMing Helps Introverted Teens." Maia Szalavitz. *Time*. August 30, 2012. www.healthland.time.com/2012/08/30/how-texting -and-iming-helps-introverted-teens/.

How to Talk So Kids Will Listen & Listen So Kids Will Talk. Adele Faber and Elaine Mazlish. New York: Scribner, 2012.

It's Complicated: The Social Lives of Networked Teens. Danah Boyd. New Haven, CT: Yale University Press, 2014.

Liking the Child You Love. Jeffrey Bernstein. Boston: Da Capo Press, 2009.

"Media Use by Children Younger Than 2 Years." Council on Communications and Media. *Pediatrics* 128, no. 5 (2011): 1040–1045.

"Oppositional Defiant Disorder." Mayo Clinic. Accessed January 29, 2015, www.mayoclinic.org/diseases-conditions/oppositional-defiant-disorder /basics/definition/con-20024559.

Overcoming Dyslexia: A New and Complete Science-Based Program for Reading Problems at Any Level. Sally Shaywitz. New York: Knopf, 2005.

"Pediatricians: No More Than 2 Hours Screen Time Daily for Kids." Tia Ghose. *Scientific American*, October 28, 2013. Accessed January 29, 2015, www.scientificamerican.com/article/pediatricians-no-more-than-2 -hour-screen-time-kids.

"Predicting Internet Risks: A Longitudinal Panel Study of Gratification-Sought, Internet Addiction Symptoms, and Social Media Among Children and Adolescents." Louis Leung. *Health Psychology and Behavioral Medicine: An Open Access Journal* 2, no. 1 (2014).

Raising an Emotionally Intelligent Child: The Heart of Parenting. John Gottman. New York: Simon & Schuster, 1998.

Self-Compassion: The Proven Power of Being Kind to Yourself. Kristin Neff. New York: William Morrow, 2011.

Taking Your Child to a Therapist

Kids Health for Parents. www.kidshealth.org/parent/positive/family/finding therapist.html.

The Kids' Book of Questions: Revised for the New Century. Gregory Stock. New York: Workman Publishing, 2004.

"The Teen Years Explained." John's Hopkins Bloomberg School of Public Health. 2014. www.jhsph.edu/research/centers-and-institutes/center-for -adolescent-health/_includes/Teen_Stress_Standalone.pdf.

"What Parents Can Do About Internet Addiction at Home, Parenting Guidelines: Rules for Every Age." Kimberly S. Young. 2014.

"Why Parents Worry About Technology, but Struggle to Limit Its Use." Jeffrey S. Dill. March 3, 2014. Accessed January 29, 2015, www.family-studies .org/why-parents-worry-about-technology-but-struggle-to-limit-its-use/.

Your Defiant Child: Eight Steps to Better Behavior. Russell A. Barkley and Christine M. Benton. New York: Guilford Publications, 2013.

"Youth Internet Use: Risks and Opportunities." Shu-Sha Angie Guan and Kaveri Subrahmanyam. *Current Opinion in Psychiatry* 22, no. 4 (2009), 351–356.

"Zero to Eight: Children's Media Use in America 2013." Common Sense Research Study. 2013.

Acknowledgments

There are so many people who have made this book possible. I first want to thank all of the parents, children, and families who have come to me for professional help over the years. What I have learned from you as you shared your pains and joys has been immensely valuable to me. It is the struggles, determination, and victories of all of you that have helped me offer this book to the masses.

I have a support system that has been nothing short of incredible. This includes my mother and father, Evelyn and Lou, who have always been there for me in every way I could ever ask. Thank you to my colleague and partner, Dr. Marina Makous, for your encouragement, support, and insightful suggestions in my writing of this second edition. To cousins Judith, Bryan, Lillian, Ben, Adam, Marie, Asher, Rachel, and on the other side of the world, Leah, Sandra, and Judie, a big thank-you for your support over the years.

Ralph, you're just an amazing guy, a childhood friend, and the brother I never had. Tony, what a bonus you are both my friend and my colleague. Ed, thanks for your impeccable timing to show up at a time when I really needed support and friendship and for continuing to be there for me.

Thanks to all of the school personnel who have given their time and insights on how my clients have fared at school. Thanks to all of you from other professions, including those physicians and attorneys who have also shared valuable insights and collaborated with me over the years to help so many children and families.

A special thanks to Kimberly Young, PsyD., for consulting with me on technology/screen overuse and addiction issues.

Thanks also to my editor, Dan Ambrosio, and his assistant, Claire Ivette, at Perseus Books. Dan and Claire, your supportive, down-to-earth style, and solid professionalism made it a pleasure to work with both of you. Thanks as well to my copy editor, Deborah Heimann, and to my project editor, Amber Morris, at Perseus Books, for all your efforts in overseeing the finalizing and production of this book.

Index